The New York Times

MORE EASY CROSSWORD PUZZLES

Edited by Will Shortz

St. Martin's Paperbacks

THE NEW YORK TIMES MORE EASY CROSSWORD PUZZLES

Copyright © 2003 by The New York Times Company.

All of the puzzles that appear in this work were originally published in the *New York Times* daily editions, from April 6, 1998, to June 29, 1999. Copyright © 1998, 1999 by The New York Times Company. Reprinted by permission.

Cover photograph © Stefano Scata/Getty Images.

ISBN: 0-312-99429-X
EAN: 80312-99429-7

Printed in the United States of America

St. Martin's Paperbacks edition / November 2003

St. Martin's Paperbacks are published by St. Martin's Press, 175 Fifth Avenue, New York, NY 10010.

10 9 8 7 6 5 4 3

The New York Times

MORE EASY CROSSWORD PUZZLES

ACROSS

1 Gun sound
5 Gather
10 Orioles' division, with "the"
14 Pulitzer writer James
15 Powerful camera lens
16 Early Peruvian
17 1988 Costner/Sarandon film
19 Strain at a ___
20 One in a wriggly field?
21 "I cannot tell ___"
22 Component of natural gas
24 Conks out
25 R.B.I. or E.R.A.
26 Shocked
29 Pool users
33 Unlike flat beer
34 Unnamed ones
35 Daredevil Knievel
36 Ripped
37 Baseball player news
38 Grandmother
39 Catch sight of
40 First-rate
41 NBC morning show
42 Test anew
44 Porridges
45 Christmas carol
46 Rhymer
47 Plumber's tools
50 Isinglass
51 Toledo cheer
54 Either end of a magnet
55 1984 Redford film
58 Lotion ingredient
59 Platform part, perhaps
60 Cincinnati nine
61 Entre ___ (confidentially)
62 Brewer's need
63 Protuberance

DOWN

1 George Herman Ruth, familiarly
2 Malaria symptom
3 Little Dickens girl
4 It keeps hair in place
5 Charm
6 "61 in '61" slugger Roger
7 Throb
8 Mrs., in Madrid
9 Occasional
10 1988 Cusack film
11 The "I" of "The King and I"
12 Scrutinize
13 London art gallery
18 "She loves me, she loves me not" flower
23 ___-o'-shanter
24 1958 Hunter/Verdon film
25 Stockholm resident
26 Subsequently
27 Barnyard honker
28 Heavenly strings
29 1953 western hero
30 Circumvent
31 Of the kidneys

Puzzle 1 by Kenneth Witte

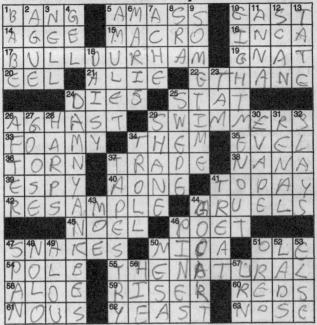

32 Does in
34 One way to fish
37 Wall hanging that tells a story
41 Pick up the tab
43 Broadway's "Five Guys Named ___"
44 Junior's jalopy?
46 Yearns (for)
47 Bridge
48 ___ contendere
49 Baseball's Matty or Moises

50 Tableland
51 Cookie favorite
52 29-Down player
53 Otherwise
56 Shake a leg
57 Ornamental vase

ACROSS

1 Andy's pal
5 Decent-sized diamond
10 Latin I word
14 Term of endearment
15 Kitchen appliance brand
16 Shed
17 LIGHTS!
20 Chop down
21 Actress McClurg
22 DNA structure
23 Carolina college
24 Bradley, the G.I.'s General
26 Composer Gustav
29 Moot
33 Red as ___
34 ___ Cove, L.I.
35 Cotton gin maker Whitney
36 CAMERA!
40 Troupes for the troops: Abbr.
41 Appearance
42 Bisect
43 Traitorous
46 Joke that causes a belly laugh
47 Franchise
48 "Stop waiting around!"
49 Heart pitapat
52 Animation frames
53 Average guy
56 ACTION!
60 French cleric
61 Fishing craft
62 One conquered by Pizarro
63 Unfairly deprives (of)
64 Playful animal
65 Big bovines

DOWN

1 1970's hitmakers from Sweden
2 "Manifesto" writer
3 Bassoon's cousin
4 The Bering, e.g.
5 Where Duncan was done in
6 Forcefully
7 Widemouthed Martha
8 "What else?"
9 ___ chi ch'uan
10 Unit named for a French physicist
11 "___ Flanders"
12 Jai ___
13 Crossing for Charon
18 Computer order
19 Spawning fish
23 Ht.
24 Indian, e.g.
25 "Death in Venice" author
26 Conductor Kurt
27 Mistreat
28 "Great blue" bird
29 French avenue
30 Board
31 "As ___ and breathe!"
32 Fall drink
34 Dance move

Puzzle 2 by Randy Sowell

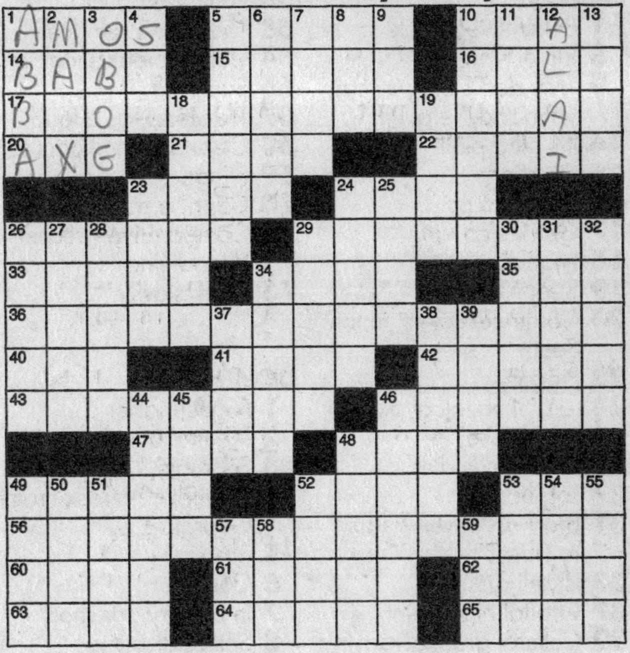

37 "___ my wit's end"
38 ___ longue
39 Bridge seat
44 Calls forth
45 Asian expanse
46 Woods, e.g., or one who uses woods
48 11-Down's creator
49 Stowe lift
50 Tracks traveler
51 L.B.J. in-law
52 Serial abbr.
53 Foredoom to failure
54 Fairy tale opener
55 Actor Richard
57 Earth-friendly prefix
58 Used a 38-Down
59 Carnival site

ACROSS

1 Borscht vegetable
5 Rip-off
9 "My dad's bigger than your dad," e.g.
14 It's all a plot!
15 Stockings
16 Raring to go
17 Gator's cousin
18 Highway
19 Sports facility
20 Cornmeal cakes, in the South
23 Piggery
24 ___ Simbel (Egyptian temple site)
25 Aardvark's diet
27 Log home
31 Brad of "Seven Years in Tibet"
33 Israeli airline
37 Orbital high point
39 Cultural grant giver, for short
40 Tick off
41 1965 Simon & Garfunkel hit, with "The"
44 Folk's Guthrie
45 Stage signal
46 One-dimensional
47 Suffix with hip or hoop
48 Another, south of the border
50 Goodman, the King of Swing
51 They may be pricked
53 Man-to-be
55 Poultry product
58 They often run deep
64 Coffee break snack
66 Bump off
67 Transport, as a load
68 Clear the chalkboard
69 Fringe
70 Capri, e.g.
71 Comparatively recent
72 Woodwind
73 Cook slowly

DOWN

1 Fugue master
2 Neutral hue
3 February 14 figure
4 "Ramblin' Wreck From Georgia ___"
5 Bush
6 Confine
7 In a hurry, for short
8 Settles disputes
9 ___ of burden
10 Boat equipment
11 Improves, as cheese
12 Telegraphed
13 Lazy Susan
21 Like windows
22 Involve
26 Unruffled
27 Spanish homes
28 To the left, to a sailor
29 Ball in the game pétanque
30 Pay no heed to
32 Deduce
34 Flax fabric

Puzzle 3 by Gregory E. Paul

35 ___ Highway (route from Dawson Creek)
36 Suspicious
38 Accompany to a party
42 New kid in town
43 Qaddafi's land
49 Accommodate
52 September bloom
54 Had title to
55 First place
56 "Earth in the Balance" author Al
57 Chew (on)

59 Comstock, for one
60 "Now hear ___!"
61 Atlantic Coast states, with "the"
62 Be king over
63 Bunch
65 Deplete, with "up"

ACROSS

1 White House's ___ Room
5 Crafts
10 Pronto
14 Close
15 Society's 400
16 Talkative bird
17 Data
18 Alaska native
19 Yemen neighbor
20 Actress's sports award?
23 Gymnastics equipment
24 50's-60's pop vocalist Barry
25 Deep-space mission
28 Up to now
30 Kind of phone
33 I am, to Caesar
34 With anticipation
37 Celebrities may put them on
38 Where a TV lawyer keeps clues?
41 Cunning
42 Transylvania's locale: Var.
43 Bat wood
44 Famous Hart
45 Crow
49 Stocking shade
51 Champagne designation
53 "___ said to the . . ." (joke line)
54 Old musical producer's annual contest?
59 Reagan Secretary of State
61 Pavlov and Lendl
62 ___ piece (Safire column)
63 Like a certain sax
64 Brown tone
65 Hawaii's state bird
66 Essence
67 Ore analysis
68 &&&

DOWN

1 Mystery
2 Virgil hero
3 Two-point score
4 1982 Disney movie
5 Fort ___, Md.
6 Poe's middle name
7 Chicken ___
8 Place for small scissors
9 6-3, 4-6, 7-6, e.g.
10 French romance
11 Formal meetings
12 Anecdotal collection
13 Greek piper
21 Place of worship
22 One NCO
26 Dueler with Hamilton
27 Spa in Germany
29 Weird: Var.
30 Studies into the wee hours
31 Movie lioness

32 City on the Rhône and Saône
35 Greek sandwich
36 Birds now raised on farms
37 Its slogan was once "Cleans like a white tornado"
38 Stance
39 Museum features
40 One of the family
41 ___ Four (Beatles)
44 Actor Gibson

46 Links championship
47 Downscale
48 Marks over n's
50 Leg-of-mutton sleeve
51 Actress Braga from Brazil
52 School assignment
55 "Mona ___"
56 The "Y" of Y.S.L.
57 Will Smith songs
58 ___ fide
59 Hardly a beauty
60 "Aladdin" prince

ACROSS

1 Bird in a cornfield
5 Critters in litters
9 High-born
14 "Star Wars" princess
15 Leave out
16 N.B.A.'s Shaquille
17 Wriggling
18 Utility in Monopoly
20 Get even for
22 Tiger Beat reader
23 Tetley product
24 Gave new hands
26 A tractor pulls it
28 Tennis's Monica
30 Rise and shine
34 Grouch's look
37 Goal attempt
39 Italian bread
40 "Yipes!"
41 Pilot's command
42 Nincompoop
43 ". . . and ___ the twain shall meet"
44 Diatribe
45 Cast pearls before ___
46 BBQer's need
48 Home planet
50 Broad valley
52 Big-billed bird
56 Reverse of NNW
59 TV's Letterman
61 Vichyssoise ingredient
62 Fictional candy maker
65 Flour factory
66 Michael Jackson boast, in a 1987 hit
67 Ukraine's capital
68 Smell ___ (be wary)
69 Dolphins' home
70 Barely beat, with "out"
71 Barely beat, with "out"

DOWN

1 Exonerate
2 Christopher of "Superman"
3 Like smooth-running machines
4 1992 movie flop (Not!)
5 Joint Chiefs chairman during Desert Storm
6 Actress Thurman
7 Big East team
8 Exorbitant
9 "Calm down!"
10 Lennon's widow
11 Former Miss America host Parks
12 Place for a cabin
13 "Born Free" lioness
19 Do tell
21 Scotsman
25 Electrical unit named for an inventor
27 "Leaves of Grass" poet
29 1953 western
31 New Zealand bird
32 Ireland
33 "Tiny" Archibald
34 Ballad
35 One-named singer/ actress

Puzzle 5 by John D. Leavy

36 "You're the ___ Care For" (1930 hit)
38 Ready to draw
41 Like some undergrad studies
45 Normandy battle site
47 Celebrated bride of 1981
49 Lay down fresh tar
51 Bring to mind
53 Capital near Alexandria
54 Rand McNally book

55 Nick of "North Dallas Forty"
56 Sidestroke, e.g.
57 California's ___ Valley
58 Napoleon's home, briefly
60 Oklahoma city
63 On the ___ (fleeing)
64 Beer party staple

ACROSS

1 Top Tatar
5 N.Y.C. gallery
9 Bygone A.M.C. car
14 Junction
15 Pop music's Clapton or Carmen
16 Allan-____
17 Hoary
20 Obliterates
21 "Hurry up!"
22 Scruff
23 Happy hour day, usually: Abbr.
24 "Piano," literally
26 Any doctrine
27 Eyepieces, in jargon
31 Opposite of pencil in
33 Settlement of 1624
36 Swarm
37 Give it ____ (attempt to do)
38 Wine connoisseur's concern
42 Extra life
47 Garbo, who vanted to be let alone
49 Beat the admission fee
50 Rage
51 Where Tulsa is: Abbr.
54 MSNBC competitor
55 Beats by a nose
57 Mama Cass of the Mamas and the Papas
59 Erratic move
62 Thoroughbred-breeding country
65 Sacrifice site
66 Yard pest
67 Diva Moffo
68 Steel plow maker
69 Copies
70 "Shoo!"

DOWN

1 The "K" of James K. Polk
2 19th ____ (golf clubhouse)
3 Throws in
4 Teachers' org.
5 Autobiographies
6 City near Provo
7 Pesky arachnids
8 Cause for a blessing
9 Audio systems, for short
10 Mideast's Gulf of ____
11 Channel port
12 Pass, as time
13 Shorten again, as a skirt
18 "Get outta here!"
19 Famine-stricken
23 Burn a steak on purpose?
25 ____-la-la
27 Neighbor of Que.
28 Middle grade
29 Hockey's Krupp
30 Astronomer's sighting
32 "The Joy Luck Club" writer
34 Big head
35 Propels a dinghy

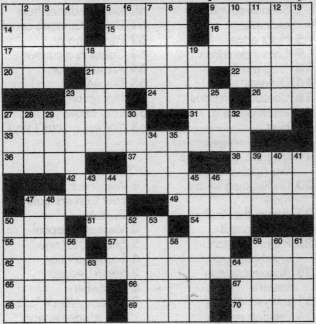

39 Apt. feature, in the classifieds
40 "What ___, chopped liver?"
41 Stimpy's TV partner
43 Ear: Prefix
44 Autumn toiler
45 Concert extenders
46 Al ___ (not too soft)
47 Car's front
48 Good name
50 ___ company (running with troublemakers)

52 Andean animal
53 Journalist Stewart
56 Burn the surface of
58 Vacation spot, perhaps
59 Brass component
60 New Rochelle college
61 Pesky flier
63 Coll. senior's test
64 Kind of station

ACROSS

1 Send overnight, for example
5 Hat's edge
9 Chin indentation
14 "___ girl!"
15 Deftness
16 Consumer Reports employee, e.g.
17 Hurt
18 Garage sale warning
19 Little ___ (part of the Big Apple)
20 Undergoing severe trials
23 Any of the Antilles
24 Scouting unit
25 Pharmaceutical watchdog grp.
28 Announces with fanfare
31 Lawyer: Abbr.
34 Fencing move
36 "___ dare to eat a peach?": Eliot
37 Estate division
38 Sick
42 Abound
43 Triple jump feature
44 High schoolers
45 Slalom curve
46 "25 words or less" event
49 H.S.T.'s successor
50 The "F" in F.Y.I.
51 With 7-Down, statement at a do-or-die moment

53 Ceaselessly
60 Remove dishes from
61 DeWitt Clinton's canal
62 Persia, today
63 Cooks in a caldron
64 Ancient Briton
65 Diligence
66 Pick up on
67 Easy throw
68 "What ___ can I say?"

DOWN

1 Awestruck
2 Four Corners state
3 Swizzle
4 Vietnam's capital
5 Snoopy, for one
6 Bacon serving
7 See 51-Across
8 Intertwine
9 Woody Allen's "___ and Misdemeanors"
10 Mr. Chips's class in "Goodbye, Mr. Chips"
11 Abbr. at the end of a list
12 Collapsed
13 Sample
21 Wedding worker
22 Jockey Arcaro
25 "Peter and the Wolf" bird
26 Desert features
27 Peruvian peaks
29 Skillful
30 Depressed
31 Hankered (for)

32 The way things are going
33 To the point
35 Turquoise or topaz
37 Broke bread
39 Rose feature
40 Sweetie
41 Room at the top
46 English Lit, e.g.
47 High standards
48 Bed covers
50 Mares' young
52 Bread serving

53 Burn balm
54 Bridle strap
55 Part of U.S.D.A.: Abbr.
56 Tom, Dick and Harry, e.g.
57 Mouth-to-mouth
58 Mercury and Saturn, for instance
59 On bended ___
60 "60 Minutes" network

ACROSS

1 Vatican City, to Rome, e.g.
8 "That's disgusting!"
11 "___ you kidding?"
14 Not as robust
15 Sib for a sis
16 Dellums or Howard
17 Discussed
19 Something to chew
20 Prefix with liter
21 Yucatán "yay!"
22 "Elder" or "Younger" Roman
23 Juliette Gordon Low, notably
27 Treaty of Nanking port
28 The Sierras, e.g.: Abbr.
29 Good buddies on the road
30 Part of a dehumidifier
31 Forbidden fruit
33 ___ Pointe, Mich.
34 Theme of this puzzle, seen seven times in the grid
36 Numbered gas rating
39 Wacko
40 Easy mark
43 French port
44 Opposite of 'tain't
45 18-wheeler
46 From Ho Chi Minh City
50 Buttonlike?
51 "___ the fields we go . . ."

52 Reached terra firma
53 W.W. II zone
54 Astonished
58 "Smoking or ___?"
59 Real cold
60 Dunk
61 Nav. rank
62 "Turn right"
63 Purse items

DOWN

1 Newt
2 Second Amendment lobby, for short
3 Where witches brew
4 Probable
5 Smart ___ (wisecrackers)
6 Of Hindu scripture
7 Victorian, for one
8 Heavy steel holders
9 Dish for Oliver Twist
10 Very popular
11 Skee-Ball and Pac-Man centers
12 Hollowing tools
13 Add one's support to
18 Lapel adornment
22 Henry ___ Lodge
23 Interstice
24 "Hallelujah, ___ Bum" (1928 hit)
25 Prefix with science
26 Tan colors
31 Beethoven's "Choral" Symphony, with "the"

Puzzle 8 by Manny Nosowsky

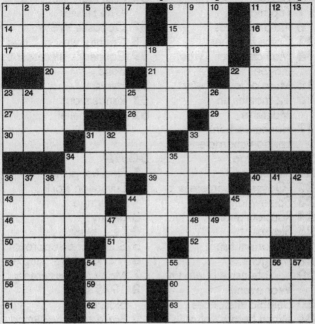

32 "Intimations of Immortality," e.g.
33 Understood
34 Too big a hurry
35 Burst of wind
36 Bluer than blue
37 Caesar salad topper
38 Old Germans
40 Transparent, modern-style
41 Some radios
42 Cobbler
44 Color fabric

45 Hits, old-style
47 Alto or tenor
48 Grammy winner Judd
49 Grads
54 Rug on the noggin
55 Cambridge sch.
56 WNW's reverse
57 ___ Moines

ACROSS

1 Top monk
6 Indian princes
11 Come together
14 Mail deliverer's woe, maybe
15 Muse of love poetry
16 12 months, in Monterrey
17 Hanna-Barbera cartoon character
20 Encourage
21 Massages
22 "Odyssey" sorceress
23 Somewhat:Suffix
24 Roosters' mates
25 Slaves
26 Aquarium fish
28 Disfigure
29 ___ offensive (Vietnam War event)
30 Delphic utterances
34 Word before "of nails" or "of roses"
35 Agent noted for Oscar night bashes
37 School transportation
38 Son of Agamemnon
39 Needlefish
40 "___ Poetica"
41 Film units
45 Think highly of
47 Bettor's card game
50 ___ gratias (thanks to God)
51 Brief affair
52 Vogue competitor
53 Helsinki native
54 Paul Newman's role in "The Hustler"
57 Opposite WSW
58 Country west of Chad
59 Connery's successor as Bond
60 Hwys.
61 Rendezvous
62 Group belief

DOWN

1 Find not guilty
2 European stock exchange
3 Brainy
4 "___ bitten . . ."
5 Sound of disapproval
6 "Nick at Nite" staple
7 Many Mideasterners
8 1975 shark blockbuster
9 Banking convenience, for short
10 Game with a goalkeeper
11 Strangler
12 Passed, as laws
13 Bottommost
18 Rap's Dr. ___
19 Old Dodger great Hodges
24 Mata ___
25 Attacks
27 Sculls
28 ___ Diner, on "Alice"
31 Ere
32 Middles: Abbr.

Puzzle 9 by Hugh Davis

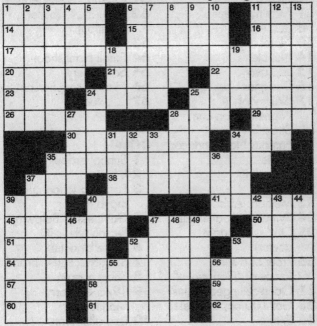

33 Burning substance
34 Corner of a diamond
35 Conjectures
36 Worst possible test score
37 South Dakota geographical feature
39 Electrician on a film set
40 Silver-colored
42 Inventor of Menlo Park
43 Poe's "rare and radiant maiden"
44 Shakespearean verse

46 Abbr. on a bank statement
47 Tsetses and gnats
48 Wide-eyed
49 Game official
52 Nervously irritable
53 Sheet of ice
55 Agency head: Abbr.
56 Ambulance crew member, for short

ACROSS

1 May honorees
6 ___ A to Z
10 Notability
14 Nimble
15 ___ avis
16 Designer Cassini
17 Blakley of "A Nightmare on Elm Street"
18 Famous New York cop Eddie
19 Preceding
20 Buckle
23 Method: Abbr.
24 Sympathetic attention
25 OB/___ (certain doctor)
26 Front of a semi
29 James of "Gunsmoke"
31 Open-ceilinged rooms
33 Got 100 on, as a test
36 Expire
37 Pre-book book
38 Buckle
41 Prom queen props
42 Wonderland drink
43 Betting ratio
44 Photographer Adams
45 Window shade, e.g.
47 "Norma ___"
48 Tell a whopper
50 Part of a balance
51 Everything
54 Buckle
57 ___-in-the-bone (deeply ingrained)
60 Intravenous infusions

61 Obtain, as vengeance
62 "You ___?" (butler's question)
63 Pith
64 Small plant shoot
65 Sailor's cry
66 Model Macpherson
67 ___ voce

DOWN

1 School grades
2 It hurts
3 Part of a school grade, maybe
4 Guinness or Baldwin
5 Person who's it
6 Carte blanche
7 Spaghetti sauce brand
8 Shaggy apes
9 1975 #1 Barry Manilow hit
10 Late afternoon
11 Mountain near Zurich
12 N.Y.C. opera house, with "the"
13 Self
21 "The Blues Brothers" director John
22 Put into practice
26 Throng
27 Was laid up
28 Cotillions
29 Idolize
30 Fistfight
32 Group of Girl Scouts, e.g.
33 Essence of roses

Puzzle 10 by Stephanie Spadaccini

34 Canton's country
35 Rub out
37 Underwater experiment site
39 When repeated, a Washington city
40 Spouse
45 Do a shoemaker's job
46 Word of qualification
49 Not quite grammatical answer to "Who's there?"
51 Detached

52 Legal
53 Loosen one's hold
54 Stressed out
55 Russia's ___ Mountains
56 World's fair, for short
57 Bikini top
58 "Hooray!"
59 Musician Brian

ACROSS

1 Opening for a coin
5 Baby buggy
9 Sell illegally, as tickets
14 Learn's partner
15 Hard to come by
16 No-no
17 Church response
18 Auction caution
19 More than plump
20 Kirstie Alley sitcom
23 Parks who wouldn't sit still for injustice
24 Ignited
25 Slangy turndown
28 On the same family tree
31 Once around the track
34 Drawings that deceive
36 Gun grp.
37 Ten: Prefix
38 New England resort
42 Very top
43 China's Chou En-___
44 "When pigs fly!"
45 ___ Moines
46 Kind of greens
49 Suffix with legal
50 Foe of the Luftwaffe: Abbr.
51 Carrot or turnip, e.g.
53 Andrew Wyeth painting
61 Sunday supper
62 Credit's opposite
63 ___ de force
64 Halo wearer
65 New York Indian
66 The "A" of Thomas A. Edison
67 Fliers in V's
68 Skyrocket
69 In case

DOWN

1 Eastern European
2 Margarita fruit
3 Walkie-talkie word
4 Pavarotti, e.g.
5 Tout
6 Mischievous one
7 "Tosca" tune
8 Clutter
9 Unemotional
10 ___ Cove ("Murder, She Wrote" setting)
11 Beame and Burrows
12 Misplace
13 Gwendolyn Brooks, e.g.
21 What's up at Rand McNally?
22 Fresh from the shower
25 Bedouin
26 Quickly
27 Bathes in sunlight
29 Smithy's device
30 Prefix with lateral or lingual
31 Bid adieu
32 Realtors' units
33 Priest
35 Hwy.
37 Recolor
39 Skyward

Puzzle 11 by Gregory E. Paul

40 Mule on the 65-Across Canal
41 Provide with a permanent fund
46 Windsor, for one
47 Mecca's land
48 Scorecard lineup
50 Moves skyward
52 All-out
53 Rugged rock
54 Sharpen
55 Mania
56 One day in March

57 Detective Wolfe
58 Part to play
59 Brand at the bottom?
60 "Oh, fudge!"

ACROSS

1 "Candida" playwright
5 Sings like Tormé
10 Extensive
14 Entire: Prefix
15 "La Campagne de Rome" artist
16 Aware of
17 Utah city
18 Stop on ___ (halt abruptly)
19 They can be Horatian
20 Slot machines
23 40 winks
24 Scooby-___ (cartoon dog)
25 Authorized
28 Carrier to Oslo
31 Cavaradossi's love, in opera
35 Sale items, for short
36 I.R.S. visits
38 Globe
39 Chris Evert specialty
42 ___ Bravo
43 They're in a stable environment
44 Baseball's Mel and others
45 The blahs
47 Born
48 Wall climbers
49 Org. that called 60's strikes
51 Niger-to-Libya dir.
52 Picnic event
61 Works in the garden

62 Race tracks
63 Wall Street optimist
64 Language written in Persian-Arabic letters
65 Engendered
66 Pitcher Hershiser
67 ["You don't mean . . . !"]
68 Generous helpings
69 Orangeish vegetables

DOWN

1 "Begone!"
2 Honker
3 Toward one side of a ship
4 Effeminate
5 Little rascal
6 Secret language
7 Saharan
8 Taj Mahal, e.g.
9 Lieu
10 Kind of doll
11 "The King ___"
12 Copy editor's marking
13 Chuck
21 One who blabs
22 "___ fast!" ("Hey!")
25 Unit of petrol
26 Professor Corey
27 Sing softly
28 Khartoum's land
29 Fred's light-footed sister
30 Move laterally
32 Conductor who studied under Bartók

Puzzle 12 by Elizabeth C. Gorski

33 Big olive oil exporter
34 Great depression
36 Farm worker?
37 Boob tubes
40 "All kidding ___ . . ."
41 Beau
46 Exhausts
48 Neither Rep. nor Dem.
50 Unkempt ones
51 Homes on high
52 Hoodlum
53 Wedding dance
54 Scarlet and crimson

55 Stuntmeister Knievel
56 Baby talk
57 Goo unit
58 New Ageish glow
59 Skelton's
     Kadiddlehopper
60 Additions

ACROSS

1 Has speech difficulties
6 On ___ (like much freelance work)
10 Opera star
14 Brilliant success
15 Bathroom flooring
16 Japanese sashes
17 Diner offering
20 Hire
21 Partygoer
22 Shakespearean king
24 Historic periods
25 Walter Cronkite's network
28 Plant part
30 Amount eaten
34 The triple of a triple play
36 Org. overseeing fairness in hiring
38 Specified
39 Restaurant offering
42 Week or rear follower
43 Min. components
44 Author ___ Stanley Gardner
45 Emblems on Indian poles
47 Bucks' mates
49 Initials in fashion
50 In ___ land (dreaming)
52 "Three men in ___"
54 Living
58 Apache souvenirs
62 Lawn party offering
64 Sale caveat
65 Swallow
66 Emulate Cicero
67 Used E-mail
68 Verbally joust (with)
69 Continue a subscription

DOWN

1 ___-majesté
2 Computer signpost
3 False coin
4 Like John Paul II
5 Old Wells Fargo vehicles
6 Regular: Abbr.
7 Tower locale
8 Exhilarate
9 Prefix with -fugal
10 Like New York City, to Albany
11 Footnote abbr.
12 Bad habit, so to speak
13 Arthur ___ Stadium (U.S.T.A. facility)
18 Tidy up
19 Actress/singer Durbin
23 Marsh plants
25 Kitchen cleanser
26 It's good in Guadalajara
27 German city
29 Bike that zips in and out of traffic
31 Writer Cleveland ___
32 Starting points in shipbuilding
33 1950's Ford flop
35 Hardest and strongest

37 Drink with a marshmallow
40 Spanish fleet
41 Pesky African insect
46 Broken arm holders
48 Aid and comfort
51 Ending words in a price
53 Wilkes-___, Pa.
54 They were once "The most trusted name in television"
55 Facility

56 Injure, as a knee
57 ___ monster
59 Not having much fat
60 Cracker topping
61 Eurasian duck
63 Life-saving skill, for short

ACROSS

1 Bay of Naples isle
6 Custard base
9 Hamburger, e.g.
14 Marriage
15 Word for a superior
16 Nebraska's biggest city
17 Pipe parts
18 Sports Illustrated's 1974 Sportsman of the Year
19 Not so strict
20 "Impossible" achievement
23 Poly-___ (college major)
24 Faux pas
25 Language name suffix
28 Excise
30 Strikingly unusual things
35 March Madness org.
37 Offshore apparatus
39 Prohibitions for Junior
40 "Impossible" discovery
44 Reach in amount
45 Parisian article
46 Toy on a string
47 Not always
50 Furry TV alien
52 Beachgoer's goal
53 Andy's boy, in 60's TV
55 One of ___ own
57 "Impossible" activity!
65 Angler of morays
66 Holm of "Chariots of Fire"
67 More than some
68 Kind of acid
69 English ___
70 Goosebump-raising
71 Inner connection?
72 "Don't Bring Me Down" rock grp.
73 Not neatniks

DOWN

1 Zodiacal delineation
2 Get the pot going
3 Dock
4 Frolics
5 Bug
6 Birthright seller, in Genesis
7 Poisonous desert dwellers, for short
8 Radiator front
9 Sportsman's mount
10 Amo, amas, ___
11 Curbside call
12 Lt. Kojak
13 Kitten's plaything
21 Pageant topper
22 Variety
25 Prefix with structure
26 Reconnoiterer
27 Visit again and again
29 Top of a clock dial
31 Was in, as a class
32 Eskimo
33 Terra ___
34 Visibly frightened
36 Voting "no"
38 African antelope

Puzzle 14 by William S. Cotter

41 It's another day
42 Out ___ limb
43 One who has life to look forward to?
48 Smog-battling org.
49 Pretty as a picture, e.g.
51 "Killing Me Softly" pop group, with "the"
54 Quick communication
56 "Boléro" composer
57 They may be strained in young families
58 Do-___ (cabbage)

59 Actress Lena
60 Biological trait carrier
61 Enjoying, in slang
62 ___ Beach, Fla.
63 Tot's place
64 Whiskies

ACROSS

1 Essence
5 Fable finale
10 ___ facto
14 London district
15 Fruit container
16 See 47-Across
17 1944 Oscar-winning song by Bing Crosby
20 Jobs to do
21 Radiant
22 Inflation-fighting W.W. II org.
23 Vote of support
24 Actor Gibson
25 Years and years
27 Oats for horses, say
29 Hotel capacity
30 Commence
33 Pie ___ mode
34 Start of a counting-out rhyme
35 Like some Jewish delis
36 Berlin's home: Abbr.
37 Court divider
38 Like 10-watt bulbs
39 Friend in France
40 Not give up an argument
42 Spy's writing
43 Litter member
44 Japanese camera
45 Middle ears?
46 Church niche
47 With 16-Across, depressed
48 Doc bloc
49 Wield

50 Sure-footed work animal
52 Send, as money
54 Send elsewhere
57 1951 hit with music by former Veep Dawes
60 Christmastime
61 Go fishing
62 Tiptop
63 Soviet news agency
64 They're counted at meetings
65 See 45-Down

DOWN

1 "Hey there!"
2 Hawkeye State
3 1937 Benny Goodman hit
4 Reacted like a taxi driver?
5 Sprint rival
6 Embellish
7 Tattered
8 The Marshall Islands, e.g.
9 Jay who has Monday night "Headlines"
10 Conditions
11 1960 song from "Bye Bye Birdie"
12 Polaroid
13 Gumbo plant
18 Fed. property overseer
19 Stunning
26 Extra-play periods, for short

Puzzle 15 by William Canine

27 Dickens thief
28 1983 Nicholas Gage book
29 Red vegetable
31 Tale-spinning Uncle
32 Rubbish
34 Tangle up
35 Youngsters
38 Fight (with)
41 Charged particle
42 ___ and goings
45 With 65-Across, a Spanish highway

46 Sour brew
49 ___-Raphaelite
50 "It ___ pretty!"
51 Portico
53 Verve
55 Austen heroine
56 Stagger
58 Smith and Gore
59 "For ___ a jolly . . ."

ACROSS

1 Moby-Dick chaser
5 Hobble
9 Alternative if things don't work out
14 Vincent Lopez's theme song
15 Met highlight
16 Refuges
17 TV turner
18 Bridge, in Bretagne
19 Vowel sound
20 Modern times, to Auden
23 Paris airport
24 Stop ___ dime
25 Nudge, as the memory
28 Copperhead's weapon
30 Snub, in a way
32 One of the Mrs. Sinatras
33 The 1890's, historically
37 Performing ___
39 Acquire
40 Individuals
41 Sherlockian times
46 Scottish refusal
47 Chameleonlike creature
48 Confrere
50 Acquire, slangily
51 Explosive letters
53 Flabbergast
54 The 1980's, to yuppies
59 "East of Eden" director
62 Part of N.B.
63 Christiania, now
64 Brewer Samuel
65 Kind of proportions
66 ___-mutton
67 Sioux dwelling
68 Smaller cousin of 67-Across
69 Expensive

DOWN

1 "Put Your Head on My Shoulder" singer
2 ___ Kong
3 Tissue softener
4 Coarse dimwit
5 One of the Canary Islands
6 Often-missed humor
7 Impudent girl
8 Lanai
9 Stamps
10 Gossamer
11 Cigar leaving
12 Novel
13 Jamboree grp.
21 "Pennies ___ Heaven"
22 Home of Phillips University
25 Actress Barnes or Kerns
26 Severe test
27 Skein formers
28 Ill-tempered woman
29 Devours
31 Cpl., e.g.
32 Like Mann's mountain
34 "That's awful!"
35 Dog doc

Puzzle 16 by Jonathan Schmalzbach

36 Summer on the Riviera
38 70's terrorist org.
42 Like some gazes
43 The Daltons, for example
44 Take back
45 Greenish-blue
49 Countless
52 Ism
53 Take effect
54 Broadway musical with the song "We Need a Little Christmas"

55 "Huh-uh"
56 "Things are becoming clear"
57 Masha and Irina's sister, in Chekhov
58 Queen of Jordan
59 Krazy _____
60 Fruity quaff
61 Last sound some bugs hear

ACROSS

1 Total
4 Castle protector
8 Sipper's aid
13 "___ tu" (Verdi aria)
14 Open, as a gate
16 Rapid-fire
17 Beavers' project
18 Former Bangkok-based grp.
19 Yens
20 Question of understanding, to a Spanish count?
23 Undemanding, as a job
24 Recede
25 "___ girl watcher" (1968 song lyric)
28 Actor Morales
29 Plant again
32 Boast
33 "The Old Wives' Tale" dramatist George
35 "Ars Poetica" poet
37 What a doctor prescribes, to a Spanish count?
40 Lacking interest
41 "Same here"
42 Harvest
43 Important element of rap lyrics
45 Where baby sleeps
49 ___ Lanka
50 Coffee alternative
51 Alan Ladd western

52 Minute nutritional components, to a Spanish count?
56 House V.I.P. Dick
59 Cease-fire
60 Cause for a Band-Aid
61 Perjurers
62 Swashbuckling Flynn
63 Word repeated in "takes ___ to know ___"
64 Slight contamination
65 Mailed
66 Bloodshot

DOWN

1 Tempt
2 Planet beyond Saturn
3 Brunch drink
4 Like cooked oatmeal
5 Prime draft classification
6 Blind as ___
7 Jacques of French cinema
8 Edible pigeon
9 Swirl
10 Trucker's truck
11 Serve that zings
12 Divs. of months
15 He was asked "Wherefore art thou?"
21 Creates quickly
22 "Charlotte's Web" author
25 Shah's land, once
26 Anti-attacker spray
27 "___ before beauty"
29 "Foul!" caller

Puzzle 17 by Evie Eysenburg

30 Shade provider
31 Rundown
32 Sweet roll
34 Long, long time
36 World Series mo.
37 Stags and does
38 Town east of Santa Barbara
39 Barely lit
40 P.S.A.T. takers
44 Swiftness
46 Ill will
47 What musical instruments should be

48 Defeated
50 Rendezvous
51 Relative of the salmon
52 Graceful aquatic bird
53 Goes astray
54 Tempt
55 Supply-and-demand subj.
56 Not the main route: Abbr.
57 Narrow inlet
58 ___ tai

ACROSS

1 Won't-keep-you-up-at-night beverage
6 Improvisation
11 Hon
14 Beethoven dedicatee
15 The supreme Supreme
16 Similie's center
17 Not discreet
19 Rendezvoused
20 Mekong River land
21 English university city
23 Fixes securely
27 Morsel
29 Whole
30 Kind of microscope
33 Plucked instruments
34 Put (down), as money
35 Power serve, perhaps
36 London "stops"
37 Rounded the edges of
38 Catcher's catcher
39 Advice giver Landers
40 Fragrant trees
41 French legislature
42 Portions
44 Word before Highness
45 Not in port
46 Broke off (from)
47 Poem
49 Portion
50 Video maker, for short
51 Hardly generous
58 Numbered rd.
59 Up ___ (stuck)
60 Maine university town
61 Frowning

62 Puts in an overhead compartment, say
63 Three trios

DOWN

1 Dover's state: Abbr.
2 "Do Ya" group, for short
3 A.F.L.-___
4 Dummkopf
5 They're put out at times
6 "See ya!"
7 Ballroom dance maneuvers
8 Napkin's place
9 Like Bach's Violin Sonata No. 3
10 Casino affliction
11 Not too smart
12 Preowned
13 Chocolate factory sights
18 Highway division
22 C.P.R. expert
23 "You guys . . ."
24 "Tennis, ___?"
25 Bullied
26 Father's Day favorites
27 This puzzle has 78
28 Tear apart
30 Some fashion magazines
31 Gas rating
32 Snared
34 One of Columbus's ships
37 Rare-coin rating

38 French mother
40 Madrid money
41 Arrondissement, in Paris
43 Holyoke and Sinai, e.g.: Abbr.
44 Slave
46 Fills up
47 Some RCA products
48 "I could ___ horse!"
49 Piano mover's cry
52 Blue chip giant
53 Miracle-___ (garden brand)

54 Sold-out inits.
55 Heavy weight
56 Atlanta-to-Raleigh dir.
57 Part of an E-mail address

ACROSS

1 Feudal workers
6 Italian money
10 Con artist's art
14 Characteristic
15 Scent
16 Barbershop emblem
17 Indy 500 competitor
18 Suckling spot
19 Landed (on)
20 First step for a would-be groom vis-à-vis his intended's father
23 Director Craven
24 Mauna ___
25 Arrow's path
26 New Deal org.
29 Kind of talk the would-be bride had with mom
32 Commedia dell'___
35 A.F.L.'s partner
36 ___ into holy matrimony
37 Sets of pews
38 Namely
41 "___ pin and pick it up . . ."
42 Bullwinkle, e.g.
44 Opposite of WSW
45 Coffee servers
46 How the would-be groom proposed
50 Actor Fernando
51 Wedding ___
52 Letters on a Cardinal's cap
53 Shoot the breeze

56 What the bride's father did vis-à-vis the reception
60 "Neato!"
62 Director Kazan
63 Kind of lily
64 Dull sound
65 Notes after do
66 Ebb and neap, e.g.
67 Peeved
68 British gun
69 What italics do

DOWN

1 Scarecrow stuffing
2 Wipe out
3 Pool ball sorters
4 Where 1-Across slaved
5 Golf shot
6 Ladies' man
7 ___ fixe
8 Greet with loud laughter
9 Prefix with -pod or -scope
10 Bridge unit
11 It's thrown on bad ideas
12 He K.O.'d Foreman 10/30/74
13 Bumped into
21 Take countermeasures
22 Be in pain
27 Groom carefully
28 Gillette razors
29 "Siddhartha" writer

30 Hauled
31 Follow as a result
32 Knight's garb
33 TV news exec Arledge
34 Common board size
39 Tough job for a dry cleaner
40 Tithe amount
43 Within: Prefix
47 Library gadgets
48 Shoelace hole
49 Votes into office
53 Funny lady Radner

54 Funny man Woody
55 Great time, or great noise
57 Kind of shoppe
58 Onetime phone call cost
59 Get-out-of-jail money
60 Pennies: Abbr.
61 "Well, what's this?!"

ACROSS

1 Chair part
5 Stuff
9 Blackmore heroine Lorna
14 Salon focus
15 Capital of Latvia
16 Writer Sinclair
17 Meat inspection inits.
18 Journey for Caesar
19 5 to 1, say
20 Best Picture of 1987
23 Der ___ (Adenauer)
24 Malt kiln
25 Neighbor of Chile: Abbr.
28 Woodlands
30 Actress Novak
33 "Vive ___!" (old French cry)
35 Truman's nuclear agcy.
36 Grandma, affectionately
37 Opera by Glinka
41 Others
42 Furrow
43 Nutso
44 Encountered
45 Educator Mary McLeod ___
48 Fifth quarters, so to speak: Abbr.
49 Rip
50 Pres. Reagan and others
52 Popular dish often served with rice

58 Shoot at, as tin cans
59 Excellent
60 Getting ___ years
61 Mooch
62 The "brains" of 58-Down
63 "___ girl!"
64 Saccharine
65 Pianist Myra
66 Missing

DOWN

1 Closed
2 Eye swatter?
3 White House staffer
4 Cheery song syllables
5 "The Count of Monte ___"
6 Singing cowboy Tex
7 Pulitzer writer James
8 Squirrellike monkey
9 Compulsion by force
10 Some 60's paintings
11 Germany's ___ von Bismarck
12 Roulette bet
13 Rock's Brian
21 1966 movie or song hit
22 Quilt part
25 Car protector
26 U.S. Grant opponent
27 Mill fodder
29 Astronauts' returning point
30 Musical toy
31 Unfitting

Puzzle 20 by Arthur S. Verdesca

32 "The Bells of St. ___"
34 Frequently
36 Sgt., e.g.
38 Carnival oddity
39 Community service program
40 "Maria ___" (1941 hit song)
45 St. Thomas who was murdered in a cathedral
46 Seventh planet
47 Surprisingly

49 Slight color
51 Toast
52 Lobster pincer
53 Cover up
54 Slangy denial
55 Engrossed by
56 Pesky insects
57 Pesky insect
58 Modern office staples, for short

ACROSS

1 Sound astonished
5 "Hound Dog" man
10 Chicken bite
14 "Tell ___ My Heart" (1987 hit)
15 Nickels and dimes
16 Author Hunter
17 One who runs a jail?
19 Fiddler while Rome burned
20 Alpha's opposite
21 ___ school (doctor's training)
22 Chronic nag
23 Twisty curve
24 Broach, as a subject
27 Toe woe
28 Direct path
32 Gas pump rating
35 Adds to the mixture
36 Undecided
37 Something to believe
39 "___ kleine Nachtmusik"
40 Overfrequently
42 TV's Greene and Michaels
44 Seasoned vets
45 Pianist Myra
46 First in time
48 Long time
51 Hardly any
54 Chicken ___ king
55 Waned
57 Walk the waiting room
58 Sautéing, jail-style?
60 Partner of "done with"
61 Poke fun at
62 Singer Adams
63 Kennedy and Turner
64 Viper
65 Views

DOWN

1 Army figure
2 Parts of molecules
3 Hogs' homes
4 Ping-___
5 Environmentalist's prefix
6 One at the bottom of the totem pole
7 Grew like ivy
8 Worse than awful, foodwise
9 Kazakhstan, once: Abbr.
10 Jail cells?
11 Always
12 Give a hoot
13 Have memorized
18 Hawk's grabber
22 British submachine gun
25 ___Set (kid's builder)
26 Pokes fun at
27 Jail keys?
29 "The doctor ___"
30 Prime time hour
31 Chemical endings
32 Director Preminger
33 Groovy
34 Tramped (on)
35 London's Big ___

Puzzle 21 by Nancy Salomon

1	2	3	4		5	6	7	8	9		10	11	12	13
14					15						16			
17				18							19			
20						21				22				
23				24	25				26					
			27					28				29	30	31
32	33	34					35							
36					37	38					39			
40				41					42	43				
44						45								
			46				47				48	49	50	
51	52	53			54				55	56				
57				58				59						
60				61						62				
63				64						65				

38 Put back on the agenda
41 "Animal House" grp.
43 Blender maker
45 Final transport
47 Story of Achilles
48 Put up with
49 Magical wish granter
50 Noses (out)
51 TV commercial
52 Bat's home
53 Scored 100 on
56 Tournament passes

58 Train terminal: Abbr.
59 Not agin

ACROSS

1 Carpenter's gadget
6 XXXI times V
9 Hardly spine-tingling
13 Express again
14 China's Chou En-___
15 Capital NW of Twin Falls
16 With 58-Across, a classic line associated with 47-Across
19 Ethel Waters's "___ Blue?"
20 Concert equipment
21 Apprehensively
22 Oscar-winning actor in 47-Across
26 Hope is here: Abbr.
27 Automne preceder
28 "Indubitably"
31 Coeur d'___, Idaho
34 "Your Erroneous Zones" author Wayne
35 I.B.M., e.g.
36 Kind of wagon
38 Section of Queens, N.Y.
40 Yard tool
41 Like ___ out of hell
43 Church cries
44 Wks. and wks.
45 Baby blossom
46 "We ___ the World"
47 Oscar-winning film
53 Inflationary path
56 Inlet
57 Lyric poem
58 See 16-Across

62 Seal fur trader
63 Boeing 737, e.g.
64 Window parts
65 Pioneer's heading
66 Hit show sign
67 Confuse

DOWN

1 "Iliad" king
2 Auxiliary proposition
3 Name on many planes
4 Steamed
5 "Ciao!"
6 What clematis plants do
7 Slippery one
8 Rome's Appia or Veneto
9 Like some B'way performances
10 Biography
11 On the main
12 München mister
15 Link
17 Bit of yarn
18 Frisco gridders
23 Arm of a knight-in-arms
24 Snack that's bitten or licked
25 Corroded
28 Time long past
29 Leprechauns' land
30 Get-well spots
31 Out of whack
32 Limerick maker
33 Lodge fellows

34 Fix a computer program
35 Doomsday cause, maybe
37 Old phone company sobriquet
39 Skater Lipinski
42 Embellisher
46 Many miles away
47 Rainbow ___
48 ___ monde (society)
49 "Same here"
50 Keep after
51 Eponym for failure
52 Dodger Hall-of-Famer
53 "Pygmalion" writer
54 Soccer superstar
55 Boardwalk refreshments
59 Spinners' spinners?
60 Pollution stds. setter
61 Tattoos, currently

ACROSS

1 Mah-jongg piece
5 "Saved by the ___!"
9 Het up
14 Declare
15 "Garfield" dog
16 Confused struggle
17 Small skirt
18 Chew like a beaver
19 Perfect
20 North Dakota tourist attraction
23 Building annex
24 Attack
25 Campus military org.
27 "Auf wiedersehen" wisher
31 Gymnast Korbut
34 Indian prince
38 Facility
39 British pound, informally
40 To the left side of a ship
41 Fleur-de-___
42 Good ol' boy's nickname
43 Comedian Danny of "The Court Jester"
44 Run pledges through the gantlet, say
45 Positive replies
46 Isle of exile for Napoleon
47 English cathedral city
49 ___-friendly
51 Neighborhood
56 Show ___ (Hollywood and such)
58 Fatty bulges
62 Seeped
64 "I smell ___!"
65 Nonglass parts of glasses
66 Martin or McQueen
67 Position
68 Woodwind
69 Person who gives a hoot
70 Miffed, with "off"
71 Neighbor of Wis.

DOWN

1 Home of the Buccaneers
2 Wall-climbing plants
3 Horne and Olin
4 Writer Jong
5 Stupefy
6 Poet ___ St. Vincent Millay
7 Tall-tale teller
8 Bawdy
9 Certain acid
10 Homer Simpson's neighbor
11 Singing groups
12 Not imaginary
13 Cry
21 Pieces of ___
22 Sea eagle
26 Brimless hat
28 Kick back
29 Indian corn
30 Good thing to have
32 Barbed remark

33 Nabokov heroine and others
34 Gather leaves
35 "Be ___!" ("Help me out!")
36 Prankster's item
37 Zones
42 Poet who originated the phrase "truth is stranger than fiction"
44 Submarine
48 Thrilled to death
50 Church V.I.P.

52 Modern multimedia tool
53 Accused's need
54 Wretched car
55 City on the Ruhr
56 Popular pear
57 Infinitesimal amount
59 Infinite
60 Lake that feeds Niagara Falls
61 Abhor
63 Apple picker

ACROSS

1 Automobile pioneer
5 Baby's affliction
10 Sailing maneuver
14 Pub missile
15 "Is that ___?" ("Really?")
16 Precollege, briefly
17 Military attire
19 Iranian money
20 Reggae relative
21 Yarn maker
22 Troutlike fish
23 Plants with small, fragrant flowers
27 Kind of lantern
29 Playwright O'Casey
30 Masters and Jonson, e.g.
31 Pellet propeller
35 Jerk
36 ___ the good
38 Sportscaster Berman
39 One of the Virgin Islands
42 On the ___ (not working)
44 Sign
45 Go along with
47 Leafy dish
51 Willow twig
52 One of the "back 40"
53 Motorists' org.
56 "Scat, cat!"
57 Breakfast side dish
60 Computer list
61 Cow of note
62 Anniversary, e.g.
63 Kiln
64 Check writer
65 Potato features

DOWN

1 Lotto info
2 Escapade
3 Most marvelous
4 Ave. crossers
5 Mountain retreats
6 Recently
7 Actress San Giacomo
8 Diamonds, to a yegg
9 Pennies: Abbr.
10 End points
11 1979 sci-fi classic
12 Classroom supply
13 Glasgow garb
18 Turns sharply
22 Fight, but not for real
24 It borders four Great Lakes: Abbr.
25 "___ me?"
26 Pianist Peter
27 Calculating types
28 Welcomer
31 Capp and Capone
32 Takes to the air
33 Riga native
34 Auto maker Ferrari
36 New World abbr.
37 Get, as a job
40 Finish putting
41 Bridge expert Sharif
42 Less restrained
43 Cartoon canine

Puzzle 24 by Rich Norris

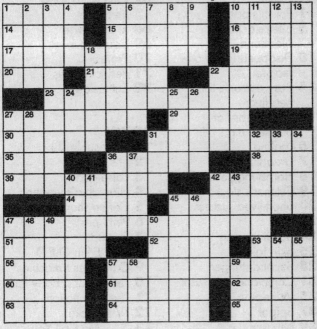

45 Comic strip redhead
46 Big name in baby food
47 Kramer of "Seinfeld"
48 Actor Milo
49 Club members since 1917
50 Given to gabbing
54 What's required to be "in"

55 "___ Death" (Grieg work)
57 Wise
58 It goes before carte, but not horse
59 Keats creation

ACROSS

1 Polish's partner
5 Silents actress Normand
10 Disappearing phone feature
14 Busy person's list heading
15 "The Barber of Seville," e.g.
16 Loafing
17 Dreadful end
18 Hornswoggle
19 Butcher's stock
20 Short-lived success
23 Skull
24 Building wing
25 Skirt fold
28 Second-stringer
31 Command to Bowser
35 Windpipe, e.g.
37 Spigot
39 Not worth a ___
40 Backstabber
44 6-3, in tennis
45 Letter before "cue"
46 Forewarns
47 Crumble, as support
50 Any planet
52 Analyze
53 "Independence Day" invaders
55 Farm fraction
57 Old fogy
63 Trendy
64 Die down
65 Sombrero feature
67 One of six for a hexagon
68 x, mathwise
69 Liquid rock
70 Profess
71 Perfect places
72 Enthusiasm

DOWN

1 The usual: Abbr.
2 [It's gone!]
3 False god
4 Hiawatha's weapon
5 Coffee shop order
6 Plant pests
7 Existed
8 The "E" in Q.E.D.
9 Carpenter's machine
10 Feature of a baby face
11 The very notion
12 TV's Thicke
13 "___ Me Call You Sweetheart"
21 Caterpillar hairs
22 North Pole toymaker
25 Old hat
26 The Titanic, e.g.
27 Muse of poetry
29 Out-and-out
30 Old-fashioned "Phooey!"
32 Russian royals
33 ___ Rica
34 Impudent girl
36 Kennel sound
38 Black-eyed ___

Puzzle 25 by Gregory E. Paul

41 Prefix with colonial
42 Blinding light
43 Look like
48 Salt, e.g.
49 And so on, for short
51 Close securely, with "down"
54 Rollerblade
56 Deep Blue's game
57 Switchblade
58 Ocean motion
59 Footnote abbr.
60 Christen

61 Russia's _____ Mountains
62 Beverly Sills, e.g.
63 Civil War letters
66 Million _____ March

ACROSS

1 Arctic dweller
5 Cuneiform stroke
10 "Pronto!"
14 Treaty signer
15 About the line of rotation
16 200-meter, e.g.
17 Onetime feminine ideal
20 Big chunk of a drug company's budget
21 Golf's ___ Cup
22 Same old, same old
23 Release money
25 Strait of Dover port
29 Novelty singing feature
33 Modern surveillance tool
34 Actress Winslet
35 Certain theater, for short
36 1941 Lillian Hellman play
40 Barely make, with "out"
41 Wine sediment
42 Big name in stationery
43 Insane
46 Incenses
47 Filly, e.g.
48 "What's more . . ."
49 ___ Park, N.J.
52 Sun circler
57 Anthony Burgess thriller, with "A"
60 Et ___
61 Foreign
62 Nonplus
63 Emperor in "Quo Vadis?"
64 Primed
65 After-dinner drink

DOWN

1 Cowardly Lion portrayer
2 Cream ingredient
3 "Not only that . . ."
4 Combustible pile
5 Bewhiskered creature
6 On the money
7 Menu offering
8 Xenon, for one
9 Pixie
10 Having a diamond-shaped pattern
11 50's-60's Mideast king
12 A lot of lot
13 Equal
18 Showy
19 Showy flower
23 Spa
24 On the sheltered side
25 Sounded crowlike
26 Suffering from insomnia
27 Subsequently
28 N.C. State's athletic org.
29 Doomed
30 Stale
31 Drift
32 Uncaps
34 Prepare to be knighted

Puzzle 26 by Arthur S. Verdesca

37 Gymnast Korbut
38 Provide
39 Witch
44 1955 merger
45 Out-of-the-way place
46 "Friends, Romans, countrymen" orator
48 Begged
49 Shoemaker Thom
50 Lui's partner
51 Film ___
52 Song for Carmen
53 Hoof smoother

54 Aware of
55 Helicopter pioneer Sikorsky
56 Educ. or H.U.D., e.g.
58 Gulf ___
59 Ring cheer

ACROSS

1 Presidential caucus state
5 Relax
9 "The ___ Ranger"
13 Some of it is junk
14 Go ___ detail
15 Rescued
16 French 101 infinitive
17 Croaker
18 Revise
19 1986 Newman/Cruise movie
22 Site of a ship's controls
23 Debtor's note
24 One-named comedian with a talk show
28 Chaos
32 Like a stadium crowd
33 Stewpot
35 ___ Grande
36 Cynical foreign policy
40 Earnings on a bank acct.
41 Lemon and lime drinks
42 Commie
43 Sites of lashes
46 Pressure
47 "Are you a man ___ mouse?"
48 Landlocked African country
50 "Fiddler" refrain
58 Up and about
59 TV's talking horse
60 Comfort
61 Fred's dancing partner
62 Not yours

63 Cake finisher
64 Carol
65 Picnic invaders
66 Library byword

DOWN

1 "___ a man with seven wives"
2 Sworn word
3 Telegram
4 Actor Guinness
5 Ransacked
6 Register, as for a course
7 Tempest
8 Like some restaurant orders
9 Hope/Crosby co-star Dorothy
10 Kiln
11 State bird of Hawaii
12 Whirlpool
15 Pago Pago's land
20 John who wrote "Butterfield 8"
21 Last
24 "Sexy" lady of Beatles song
25 Certain humor
26 Actor Nick
27 ___ Harbour, Fla.
28 Swiss heights
29 Construction site sight
30 Rubes
31 They're used in walking the dog
33 Bettor's stat

34 Golf position
37 Traffic tool
38 Kind of nerve
39 Russian space station
44 Massachusetts city
45 "Goodnight" girl of song
46 Playground equipment
48 California county
49 "___ You Glad You're You?" (1945 hit)
50 Persia, today
51 Pooch's name

52 "Gotcha"
53 Austen heroine
54 Legatee
55 Riot spray
56 Sailing
57 Uncool sort

ACROSS

1 Front-line chow, once
5 Observer
10 Neighbor of Libya
14 Ear part
15 Fall color
16 In vigorous health
17 Scores on a serve
18 1996 film for which Geoffrey Rush won Best Actor
19 Chester Arthur's middle name
20 Start of a thought by Oscar Wilde
23 Neither's partner
24 Good Housekeeping award
25 Diddley and Derek
28 From the jungle
31 Brew vessels
35 Conductor Klemperer
37 Cozy corner
39 Iron bar
40 Part 2 of the thought
43 New Testament king
44 Flute part
45 Part of Q.E.D.
46 "Gunsmoke" star
48 Back-to-school mo.
50 Peter, Paul and Mary: Abbr.
51 Sleep phenomena
53 Flight
55 End of the thought
63 Up to it
64 Followed a coxswain's orders
65 Kind of miss
66 Safe deposit box item, perhaps
67 Witch
68 Great-great-grandson of Augustus
69 When the French fry?
70 Carved
71 Annexes

DOWN

1 Wooden piece
2 Little of Verdi?
3 Genesis brother
4 A quark and an antiquark
5 90's fashion accessory
6 ___ Rios, Jamaica
7 Waiflike
8 Birds at sea
9 Brand of peanut butter cup
10 Dare
11 Fair share, maybe
12 Jai ___
13 Game rooms
21 "I'll never do it again," e.g.
22 Dine at home
25 South African politico
26 Multiple-choice answer
27 Unsmiling
29 Clark's interest
30 Do's and ___
32 Stravinsky et al.
33 Yogurt type
34 R.B.I.'s and such

36 Wind player's purchases
38 Locale for a spanking
41 Ford flub
42 Blew inward
47 Buss
49 Scot's topper
52 Entrap
54 Food from heaven
55 Stow, as cargo
56 Sarcastic response
57 ___ Bailey
58 Increase

59 Québec's Lévesque
60 "___ I say more?"
61 Joker, e.g.
62 Love's inspiration

ACROSS

1 More than dislike
6 Big name in computer games
10 Fish from Dover
14 Be loud, as a radio
15 Cawer
16 Let ___ a secret
17 Write without a single mistake
20 Cosmonauts, by definition
21 Perfume essence
22 Phone no. at the office
23 Letters starting naval carrier names
25 With 28-Down, a university in Dixie
26 Cass Elliot was one of them
30 Watering holes
31 Kimono sashes
32 1961 Best Actor Maximilian
34 British rule in colonial India
37 Not play it safe
40 Ave. crossers
41 Nal, e.g., chemically
42 Poems of praise
43 Look surreptitiously
44 Search
45 Prefix with cycle
48 6-pt. scores
49 Sigma follower
51 Spotted pony
53 Sunrise and sunset locales
58 O.K.
61 Sea eagle
62 First number in season records
63 French pupil
64 High schooler
65 Like custards
66 Called one's bluff

DOWN

1 Shortened form, in shortened form
2 ___ cheese dressing
3 Dutch artist Frans
4 Mined metals
5 Knots again
6 Bloodhound's trail
7 Goofs
8 Opposition for Dems.
9 Wonderment
10 Refine, as flour
11 "And ___ grow on"
12 Hometown-related
13 ___ nous
18 I.R.S.'s share
19 Grapple (with), colloquially
23 Overturn
24 Soothing ointment
26 Swabs
27 Adjoin
28 See 25-Across
29 Baseball wood
30 Valentino title role, with "the"
32 Covered the foot
33 Yields

Puzzle 29 by Bill Ballard

34 Went on horseback
35 King Kong and others
36 It's said with a poke in the ribs
38 First-rate
39 Cardinals great Brock
44 In sets of 24 sheets
45 Come-from-behind victory
46 Saltpeter: Brit.
47 Silly
49 She said "I 'spect I growed"

50 Dadaism founder
52 Govt. agents
53 Be suspended
54 French novelist Émile
55 "Roger, ___ and out!"
56 Central church area
57 Winter toy
59 Be indebted to
60 Not worth a ___

ACROSS

1 Legally impedes
7 May school event, often
11 Like 1, 3 or 7
14 Filled with the old school spirit
15 The last Mrs. Chaplin
16 By way of
17 ST
20 Spreading tree
21 Legal offense
22 Main bloodline
23 Hair division
24 Pharmaceutical-approving org.
25 TU
33 Cut dramatically
34 Not quite closed
35 Life force, in Eastern philosophy
36 Luke's mentor, in "Star Wars"
37 Bombastic
39 Bunny's tail
40 When repeated, a dance
41 Bulging earthenware vessel
42 Legal setting
43 UV
47 Toward the tiller
48 Meadow murmurs
49 Jellied dish
52 Young seal
54 Sign of success
57 VW
60 Little ___, 60's singer
61 Disney's "___ of the South"
62 Runoff point
63 Actress Susan
64 Tarzan's home
65 Canine covering

DOWN

1 Highlands tongue
2 Political comic Mort
3 Relative of Geo. and Robt.
4 Hart Trophy winner, 1970-72
5 1987 Wimbledon winner
6 Steinhauer of the L.P.G.A.
7 Sonnet, e.g.
8 Teased mercilessly
9 Switch settings
10 El toro's opponent
11 Completed
12 Weight loss plan
13 Spreadsheet numbers
18 Silents star Naldi
19 Speckled horse
23 Leaning Tower's city
24 Come apart at the seams
25 Course in which to study Freud
26 Wahine's welcome
27 Kind of beacon
28 Like Fran Drescher's voice
29 What to wear when one goes beddy-bye

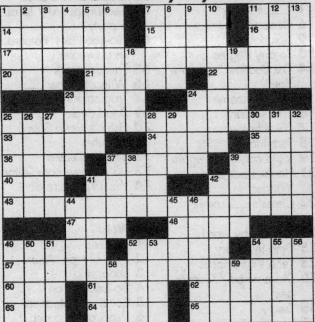

30 Come to pass
31 "Star Trek" lieutenant
32 ___-gritty
37 Overabundance
38 The whole enchilada
39 Drunkards
41 Thrown away
42 Johnny Appleseed's real surname
44 Seriously wound
45 "Yeah, sure!"
46 Aplenty
49 Like some cheddar cheese

50 P.G.A. golfer Ballesteros
51 Talk in church
52 Go downhill
53 Bigger than the both of us
54 Fat-free, as milk
55 Russo of "In the Line of Fire"
56 Hurler Hershiser
58 Neither's partner
59 Gardner of "The Barefoot Contessa"

ACROSS

1 "___ Marner"
6 Plopped (down)
9 Luxurious
13 To any degree
14 The Beatles' "___ Love You"
15 French income
16 Prickly plants
17 "Gotcha!"
18 Terminator
19 Train car/Strips again
21 Hooks back up / Winder
23 Chess's ___ Lopez opening
24 Early baby word
25 Time in history
28 Tennis's Sampras
30 Did a no-no / Comics pest
35 Treaty
37 Some paintings
39 Ace plus one
40 Above
41 What each word of six or more letters in this puzzle does
43 Kind of talk
44 Bo of "10"
46 60's singer Sands
47 Pencil filler
48 Writer Hubbard / Grow threefold
50 Sicilian peak
52 Blvds.
53 Profess
55 Opposite of a ques.
57 Security guard / ID at a party
61 No-goodnik / Patches, as a sweater
65 Thunderstruck
66 Without further ___
68 Tropical fruit
69 Dead duck
70 Fish off Nova Scotia
71 Vicinities
72 Squid defenses
73 US Airways competitor
74 West Yorkshire city

DOWN

1 Pouches
2 Type of type: Abbr.
3 Shoestring
4 Do tailoring on
5 Boo-boo / Students
6 Work out in a ring
7 Shade of blond
8 Pageant crown
9 Carson's successor
10 Loosen
11 Dance bit
12 For the woman
15 Newly placed / Telephoner
20 ___ newt (witch's ingredient)
22 Sullivan and Harris
24 Bring to the door / Hugely unpopular
25 Lyric poem
26 "Boléro" composer

Puzzle 31 by Mary E. Brindamour

27 Sour
29 Scrabble piece
31 Simon or Diamond
32 Art subjects
33 Brilliance
34 Scout's good works
36 Genealogy display
38 Roasting rod
42 French legislature
45 "Seinfeld" guy /
   Comment
49 Southern power
   provider: Abbr.

51 "20 Questions"
   category / Layer
54 Put into effect
56 Entangle
57 1958 musical
58 "Mr. X"
59 Desert Storm vehicle
60 She sheep
61 Fizzy drink
62 On bended ___
63 "Holy moly!"
64 Supreme Diana
67 ___ Jones

ACROSS
1 Artist Chagall
5 Words to live by
10 Kind of liquor
14 Coloratura's piece
15 Units to be subdivided
16 ___ vera
17 Water source
18 Financial wherewithal
19 Storm
20 Supermarket tabloid subject #1
23 Fifty-fifty
24 Hosp. procedure
25 Like marble
28 Like Charlie Chan
33 Research facility: Abbr.
34 Policy position
35 Gardner of "Show Boat"
36 Supermarket tabloid subject #2
40 Coach Parseghian
41 Exudes
42 "Stat!"
43 Romeo
45 Cars that are in the shop a lot
47 Hate grp.
48 Donaldson and others
49 Supermarket tabloid subject #3
56 Appear ahead
57 It starts with Genesis
58 Mideast carrier
60 Tulip planting
61 Sans company

62 Rhody, in an old song
63 Concerning
64 More green
65 Lockbox document

DOWN
1 Gullet
2 Geometrician's figuring
3 Brook
4 Hot, in Jalisco
5 "Out, ___ spot!": Lady Macbeth
6 Continental divide?
7 Snag
8 Darn
9 Not checking to make sure
10 1990's Fox sitcom
11 Jai ___
12 Nike's swoosh, for one
13 Popular youth magazine
21 Woman in a garden
22 Words to live by
25 Goldsmith's "The ___ of Wakefield"
26 Start of a new año
27 Faith of five million Americans
28 Playful animal
29 Beams
30 Renaissance Italian poet
31 Birdlike
32 Reindeer herders
34 Judge, with "up"

Puzzle 32 by Hugh Davis

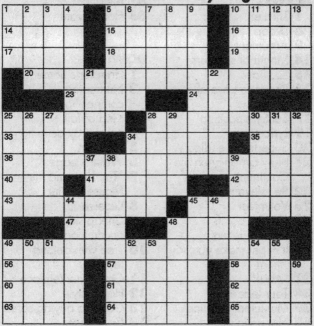

37 Knocks on the noggin
38 Elton John or Mick Jagger
39 Three-time Masters champ
44 Like some arms
45 Soap (up)
46 Record label inits.
48 Classic 1953 western
49 Isle of exile
50 Reed and Costello
51 Electric unit
52 Seat of Allen County, Kan.

53 Sprout
54 Collagist's need
55 Sensible
59 Inc., abroad

ACROSS

1 Thicket
6 Droop
9 Arguments
14 Month of showers
15 ___-haw
16 Return to base after a fly ball
17 Sentry's position
19 Lyric poem
20 Superlative ending
21 New currency on the Continent
22 Be relevant to
23 Volunteer
25 Central points
29 Genetic letters
30 It might make you say "Aha!"
31 "Aha!"
34 Tour leader
39 Municipal building
42 Nonnational
43 Surf's sound
44 Sorts
45 Lamb's mother
47 Plug's place
49 Quarterback option
55 Bee house
56 Site of Napoleon's first exile
57 Rink surface
60 Lacquer part
61 V.I.P. protector
63 Minotaur's island
64 French article
65 Goaded, with "on"
66 Kind of seal
67 Neighbor of Isr.
68 Flamboyant

DOWN

1 Hamster's home
2 Numbered composition
3 Kind of fall
4 Knight, by definition
5 Firstborn
6 Water's edge
7 "The Lion and the Mouse" writer
8 Receive
9 Cheap ship accommodations
10 Tree with oblong leaves
11 Greek marketplace
12 House style
13 Go on a buying spree
18 Contributes
22 "___ appétit!"
24 Norse love goddess
25 Isinglass
26 Movie star
27 Prefix with god
28 Word said before "time" and "place"
32 Fathered
33 D.D.E.'s command in W.W. II
35 Company part
36 "___ be a cold day . . ."
37 Astronaut Slayton
38 Once, once

40 Like some income on a 1040
41 Stills and Nash partner
46 Twisted
48 Practices
49 You can't take it seriously
50 "The Barber of Seville," e.g.
51 Stair part
52 Actor Ralph of "The Waltons"
53 Flashy flower

54 Birch relative
57 "Othello" villain
58 Airplane staff
59 Small whirlpool
61 Tour transportation
62 "That's horrid!"

ACROSS

1 Lady with a title
6 Mirth
10 Evil
13 Carefree song syllables
14 Transport for Huck Finn
15 A large part of Mongolia
16 Stock secretarial ploy #1
19 Catch ___ (start to get)
20 Decorative window shape
21 Artist Max
22 It's baked in a square
24 Strike callers
26 Genteel affair
29 Juices
31 Crones
35 Skylit rooms
37 "Yes, ___!"
38 Command to Dobbin
39 Stock secretarial ploy #2
43 Bingo-like game
44 Pi follower
45 Cockeyed
46 Sharp rebuff
47 It lets off steam
50 Many a Little League coach
51 Seamstress Betsy
53 "___ kleine Nachtmusik"
55 Village smith, e.g.
58 Pantomimist Jacques
60 Meadows
64 Stock secretarial ploy #3
67 Lighten (up)
68 Queen before George I
69 Jaunty
70 Commotion
71 Stink
72 Left one's seat

DOWN

1 Roman emperor in A.D. 69
2 Birdhouse bird
3 Magazine publisher Condé ___
4 "Cats" poet
5 Wasn't colorfast
6 Act servile
7 Turner, the 40's Sweater Girl
8 Offensive smells
9 Beach time in Bordeaux
10 Rhine city
11 Basics
12 Many a New Year's resolution
15 " 'S Wonderful" composer
17 Pepsi, e.g.
18 Business solicitor, for short
23 "___ Mommy Kissing Santa Claus"
25 Dramatist Connelly
26 Duties

Puzzle 34 by Robert Dillman

27 A Barrymore
28 Gladiator's locale
30 "___ the Sheriff" (1974 hit)
32 Leading
33 Slangy word of intention
34 Full, at last
36 Liquid in synthetic rubber manufacture
40 Nettles
41 What witnesses take
42 Mortgage, e.g.
48 Pet restraint

49 CVI halved
52 Cortez's quest
54 Box ___ (tree)
55 Where Dwight Gooden once pitched
56 Principal
57 ___ buco (Italian dish)
59 79 for gold, e.g.: Abbr.
61 Architect Saarinen
62 Inquires
63 Kind of terrier
65 Chinese ideal
66 Health facility

ACROSS

1 "Pow!"
5 Italian sports cars
10 Places for rent: Abbr.
14 Be sore
15 Tennis star Agassi
16 Fox or turkey follower
17 "No way!"
19 Architect Saarinen
20 Busybody
21 Lid decoration?
23 B.&O. and Reading, e.g.: Abbr.
24 Mas' partners
26 The March King
27 "No way!"
31 Bus stations
34 Sneaky scheme
35 Money for old age, for short
36 ___ Stanley Gardner
37 Put in rollers
38 Hosiery problem
39 Woody's ex-mate
40 ___ de vivre
42 Churchill flashed them during W.W. II
44 "No way!"
47 Common sprain spot
48 Gene material, in brief
49 Baby bear
52 One who can see what you're saying
55 Classic Alan Ladd western
57 Jacob's twin
58 "No way!"
60 French seas
61 "No man is an island" poet John
62 Drubbing
63 Clockmaker Thomas
64 Speechify
65 Teachers' favorites

DOWN

1 Nymph chaser
2 Yellowish brown
3 Spots for goatees
4 Clark of The Daily Planet
5 Airline watchdog grp.
6 Eat
7 "An apple ___ . . ."
8 Auditions (for)
9 Light detectors
10 "Relax, private!"
11 Before
12 Matador's threat
13 Put in the overhead rack
18 Finito
22 More than large
25 Complete jerk
27 Slangy coffee
28 Less constrained
29 Teheran's nation
30 Places for prices
31 Moore of "G.I. Jane"
32 Land of the leprechauns
33 Share (in)
37 Delivery entrance, often
38 Bro's counterpart

Puzzle 35 by Nancy Salomon

40 Diner music player, informally
41 Home of Disney World
42 Florist's vehicle
43 Break into smithereens
45 Surge
46 Roving, as a knight
49 It needs a good paddling
50 In its original form, as a movie
51 Red vegetables
52 Moon vehicles

53 Psychiatrist's reply
54 Sicilian spouter
56 Angel's instrument
59 Dee's predecessor

ACROSS

1 Swiss peaks
5 Sea that's really a lake
9 Morley of CBS
14 Tip seller
15 Paying passenger
16 Florida city
17 Poe writing
18 Washington suburb
20 Mythical strongman
22 Family girl
23 A few coins, in slang
26 Tempe sch.
29 Cool, once
30 Mil. address
31 Botanist Mendel
33 Perfumes
36 Like higher-priced beef
37 You can't enjoy this if
   you've lost your
   marbles
42 Ages and ages
43 Dorm room staple
44 Crackpot
47 Was first
48 Ring org.
51 Martians and such
52 Detective with a large
   family
56 Check (out)
57 Sturm und ___
58 Dog restraint
63 Choir voice
64 Poisoned, for instance
65 Wee, in brief
66 Ardor
67 All tuckered out
68 Female V.I.P.
69 Humorist Bombeck

DOWN

1 Glue (to)
2 Detest
3 Pilot's maneuver
4 Kind of cleaning
5 Steelers' org.
6 Stadium cheer
7 Venue for 48-Across
8 "Deathtrap"
   playwright
9 World Cup game
10 Pine (for)
11 Org. that keeps an eye
   on pilots
12 Golfer Ernie
13 Actress ___ Dawn
   Chong
19 Safecracker
21 Bowler's feat
24 Naval noncoms
25 Realtors' sales
26 Pulitzer winner James
27 Catch the wind under
   one's wings
28 Cemetery sights
32 Nevada county or its
   seat
33 Years, to Caesar
34 Do something
35 Beach souvenir
37 Arrived
38 Greenhouse effect?
39 Physics particles
40 ". . . ___ saw Elba"
41 Gave up

Puzzle 36 by Janet R. Bender

45 One way to identify a foreigner

46 Fudge ingredient: Abbr.

48 Capt. Ahab or his ship

49 Big name in paperback publishing

50 Neighbor of Zambia

53 Plant pest

54 Gaucho's rope

55 Mania

56 Trapper's offering

58 Modern records

59 Turning point?

60 Keats's "___ to Psyche"

61 Political subject

62 "Bill ___, The Science Guy"

ACROSS

1 "Spare" items at a barbecue
5 Popular athletic shoes
10 Bullets and such
14 Melville tale
15 Beatle with a beat
16 Many a Seattle weather forecast
17 Classic pickup line #1
20 "Six Days, Seven Nights" co-star
21 Early night, to a poet
22 Permit: Abbr.
23 Prefix with -metric
24 Heavy hammer
27 Proofreader's mark
29 Not glossy, as a photo
32 Captain Morgan's drink
33 "Norma ___"
36 Dish served under glass
38 Classic pickup line #2
41 Geometric measurement
42 What Yahoo! searches, with "the"
43 Whichever
44 ___-off coupon
46 Mets stadium
50 Directs (to)
52 Ecol. watchdog
55 The "I" in T.G.I.F.
56 Prefix with skeleton
57 Numbers usually in parentheses
60 Classic pickup line #3
63 Pitcher
64 Genesis woman and namesakes
65 Allen of "Candid Camera"
66 Smart-mouthed
67 Cove
68 Fr. holy women

DOWN

1 Kansas City team
2 "Consider it done"
3 Dribble
4 Achy
5 City where van Gogh painted
6 Broadcasting giant
7 Ruler unit
8 Poet and novelist James
9 Michigan's ___ Canals
10 Napoléon led one
11 Wisconsin Avenue, in Georgetown
12 Opposite of max.
13 Washington's bill
18 ___ Beta Kappa
19 Let go of
24 Uncompromising
25 "Peter ___" of 50's-60's TV
26 Ambulance driver, for short
28 Car on rails
30 To the left, to sailors
31 Fri. preceder

Puzzle 37 by Brendan Emmett Quigley

34 Suffered humiliation
35 ___ Park, Colo.
37 Takes a chair
38 Soave, e.g.
39 Spring woe
40 Liking
41 Flag-waving org.
45 Churn
47 Went into seclusion
48 Endless, poetically
49 Liabilities' opposites
51 Put forth, as effort
53 ___ Blue Ribbon

54 Smashing point?
57 "You said it, brother!"
58 Sincere
59 Murders, slangily
60 Cool, once
61 Wonderment
62 ___ Lilly and Company

ACROSS

1 Droops
5 Hula-Hoops, lava lamps, etc.
9 Tooth trouble
14 24-karat, goldwise
15 Settled down
16 The Sorbonne, e.g.
17 Mediterranean seaport
18 Punjabi peeress
19 Confine
20 Basketball player's credo?
23 Free of charge
24 Blockhead
25 Pindaric work
28 Starchy tuber
29 You, right now
32 Allege as fact
33 Waters
34 Sacramento's Arco ___
35 Soldier's credo?
39 Science fiction, for one
40 "Over the Rainbow" composer Harold
41 "Dragonwyck" author Seton
42 Numb, as a foot
44 Wane
47 Superman foe ___ Luthor
48 Cookout leftover?
49 Armstrong's program
51 Bodybuilder's credo?
54 Worrier's woe, it's said
57 Tickled-pink feeling
58 Quiz show sound
59 "Waterlilies" painter Claude
60 Equipment
61 Prefix with -derm or -therm
62 ___ bear
63 Talks noisily
64 Costner, in "The Untouchables"

DOWN

1 Like foam rubber
2 Display in the night sky
3 Kind of cracker
4 French lawmakers
5 Sends down to the minors
6 Actor Alda
7 Producer De Laurentiis
8 Squelch
9 Fix, as software
10 Environmental sci.
11 "Friends" co-star Courteney
12 He stung like a bee
13 Japanese bread
21 Off-color
22 "___ Town"
25 Finished
26 Say it ain't so
27 Mesozoic or Paleozoic
30 Carol syllables
31 Corruptible
32 Elvis ___ Presley
33 Taj Mahal site
34 Syrian city

Puzzle 38 by Randall J. Hartman

35 Hawaiian honker
36 Cameo stone
37 Bauxite or hematite
38 Grain gatherers
39 ___ Friday
42 Nile biter
43 Like a yak's coat
44 "Seinfeld" role
45 Duck hunters' shelters
46 Beatniks beat them
48 Central artery
50 Rhymester Nash
51 Poverty

52 Intestinal sections
53 Minimal high tide
54 "Kill the ___!" (ball park cry)
55 Mauna ___
56 MSNBC rival

ACROSS

1 Help at a heist
5 Calls to a shepherd
9 Deadly
14 Easy gait
15 Qualified
16 Functional
17 Trebek of "Jeopardy!"
18 Spot on a radar screen
19 Fancy British car, informally
20 Walt Disney's first sound cartoon
23 Aria, e.g.
24 Wriggly fish
25 TV adjunct
28 Unbeatable rival
31 Downward bend
34 Lose underpinnings
36 Time delay
37 Catherine ___, wife of Henry VIII
38 Life of the party
42 Pinnacle
43 Mystery writer Deighton
44 Lend-___ Act
45 Shade of blue
46 Late, great crooner
49 Reading room
50 One ___ time
51 Surrounds, with "in"
53 Show girl's suitor
61 Inner circle
62 "Peek-___!"
63 Puerto ___

64 Durant who co-wrote "The Story of Civilization"
65 Singer Braxton
66 List shortener
67 Greenbacks
68 In the public eye
69 Watered-down

DOWN

1 Word of regret
2 Length of fabric
3 Blunted blade
4 Lone Star State
5 Talk nonsensically
6 Flowering
7 Inter ___
8 Labor Day's mo.
9 Avenging spirits of mythology
10 Wake Island, e.g.
11 Cash drawer
12 "___ Do Is Dream of You" (1934 hit)
13 ___-majesté
21 "Waterlilies" painter
22 Consider the pros and cons of
25 Golden Nugget casino locale
26 Stew container
27 Spacious
29 Actress Verdugo
30 Biological container
31 Kind of fork
32 Come to light

Puzzle 39 by Gregory E. Paul

33 White House's ____ Room
35 1950's White House monogram
37 Ante-
39 Trojan War epic
40 Fraternity members
41 Site of Crockett's last stand
46 Blue-gray
47 Royal seat
48 Counterreply
50 Jibe

52 Woman with a temper
53 Con game
54 Hawaiian tuber
55 Score after deuce, in tennis
56 Feed bag fill
57 Cousin of a bassoon
58 Nick at ____
59 Org. with eligibility rules
60 The sunny side, in sunny side up

ACROSS

1 Leave without paying
6 Over the edge
10 Not fooled by
14 Group that has its own organ
15 "The Black Stallion" boy
16 Denunciate, with "at"
17 1958 Rosalind Russell comedy
19 As to
20 British sports cars
21 Utopias
22 Dial sounds
23 Plus
24 Like unwashed hair
25 1955 Fred Astaire/Leslie Caron musical
31 Gardens amidst the sands
32 Left, at sea
33 Photo ___
35 Abbr. on an envelope
36 Free, as knots
37 ___ Alto, Calif.
38 Mink's coat
39 Hankerings
40 Arrived
41 1981 Joan Crawford exposé starring Faye Dunaway
44 Chops (off)
45 "She loves me ___"
46 Clumps of earth
48 Take care of
51 Verse on a vase
54 Throw a tantrum
55 1963 film of a Chekhov classic with Laurence Olivier
57 Word after "Roger"
58 Wit Mort
59 Animated Fudd
60 Caution
61 "I" problems
62 Title pages?

DOWN

1 Rip-off
2 Hood
3 They're charged
4 Like a fiddle?
5 Hit 1990's NBC sitcom
6 Clue, for one
7 Money guru Greenspan
8 Precious stones
9 Woodsman's tool
10 Cal Ripken, for one
11 Female butters
12 Spare, maybe
13 Bullfight bravos
18 Whirlpool
22 Pinball foul
23 Yemeni city
24 Very nasty sort
25 It's a fact
26 Reader of heavenly signs
27 Hope of "Peyton Place"
28 Made a choice
29 Ping or zing

Puzzle 40 by Nancy Salomon

30 Challenge for a bowler
31 Bumbling one
34 Junior
36 "Exodus" author
37 Dickinson or Frost, e.g.
39 Ballpark figures
40 Moved to the music, slangily
42 Contemporary
43 Upfront money
46 Meal for the humble?
47 Volcanic flow

48 Barely catch
49 Kind of chamber
50 Building extensions
51 Treater's words
52 Changed colors
53 Pairs with drums
55 Take advantage of
56 Hearty brew

ACROSS

1 Put one's foot down
6 They sometimes accompany photos
10 Onetime Iranian chief
14 Harness racer
15 Answer an invitation
16 Mini's opposite
17 All-out response
20 Criticize, in 90's slang
21 Glimpsed
22 Messenger ___
23 Slalom curve
24 Country north of Chile
25 Tipsy
27 Rich desserts and soap operas, say
34 "Heaven forbid!"
35 Hockey legend Bobby
36 "The World According to ___"
37 Director Jean-___ Godard
38 Having hair like horses
40 Menagerie
41 Monastery titles
43 Aviation hero
44 Alex Trebek, e.g.
45 Jewelry and gold doubloons, maybe
50 Sciences' partner
51 Strived (for)
52 Scottie's bark
55 "Mamma ___!"
56 Time in history
57 Hang on the clothesline
60 Absolutely confident
64 Do as directed
65 River deposit
66 Had title to
67 Treat lavishly
68 P.M. periods
69 Dame Rebecca and others

DOWN

1 Went like the dickens
2 Curbside call
3 Fall mos.
4 Mal de ___
5 Like some stations on a car radio
6 Concoct
7 Any doctrine
8 Rescuee's cry
9 Coronado was one
10 Dallas sch.
11 Tortoise's opponent
12 Chopping tools
13 Snake's warning
18 One of two English queens
19 Gives under pressure
24 Arafat's grp.
26 Warm welcome
27 Does a round of nine
28 Swahili for "freedom"
29 Like an old empire of 24-Across
30 Hermit
31 Gillette product
32 Uneven, as leaves

Puzzle 41 by Alan Jay Weiss

33 Card markings
38 Decimal part of a logarithm
39 Pretends
42 Music with a blend of folk and calypso
44 1963 Paul Newman film
46 Writer Bombeck
47 Turns inside out
48 Suffix with million
49 Endangered animal in Florida

52 Beginning
53 Hick
54 Guitar part
57 Actress Sothern et al.
58 Skeptic's comment
59 Marge Schott's team
61 It takes in the sights
62 Final: Abbr.
63 Amazement

ACROSS

1 Web surfer's need
6 Gulf war foe
10 Moola
14 Levi's "Christ Stopped at ___"
15 In ___ (undisturbed)
16 Iris's place
17 "Eat hearty!"
18 Play opener
19 Puppies' plaints
20 Clotheshorses
23 106, to Caesar
25 Bit
26 Booby trap
27 Harsh conditions
29 See 33-Across
32 Earthy hue
33 With 29-Across, "Barbarella" star
34 ___ Na Na
37 Signal receivers
41 Soon-to-be grads: Abbr.
42 Noted lithographer
43 Finland, to the Finns
44 Rocky rival Apollo ___
46 Tar pits locale
47 Put on, as glue
50 Tinker or Evers or Chance
51 C & W channel
52 Common tabloid topics
57 Artificial bait
58 Led Zeppelin's genre
59 Grinned from ear to ear

62 "Right on!"
63 Shot, e.g.
64 Relaxed
65 Sermon passage
66 Suds
67 Colorado ski resort

DOWN

1 Club ___
2 "Shogun" apparel
3 Sopwith Camel/Fokker clashes
4 Lamb's "Essays of ___"
5 Old-time trouper
6 "Why? Because ___ so!"
7 "Little Caesar" role
8 Envelope abbr.
9 Witty remark
10 Neighbor of Suriname
11 Title role for Madonna
12 Shunned one
13 Café au lait holder
21 Owns
22 "Acid"
23 Antivampire aid
24 "The ___ of Wakefield"
28 Change from a krone
29 Ill-___ (doomed)
30 Wallet wad
31 Beatty of "Deliverance"
33 Nonsense talk
34 Rizzuto or Reese
35 Macho types
36 Like most Turks

38 "The check is in the mail," perhaps
39 Backer of Columbus
40 Long sandwich
44 Grisham title, with "The"
45 Painter Rembrandt van ___
46 Capt. Jean-___ Picard
47 Key above G
48 Old-fashioned pen
49 Heat-resistant glass
50 "My Fair Lady" director George

53 Snatch
54 A few
55 Zenith
56 Guadalquivir et al.
60 Take advantage of
61 Parker or Waterman

ACROSS

1 Moistureless
5 Feeling for the unfortunate
9 Onetime late-night host Jack
13 Provide with a new soundtrack
15 Nabisco favorite
16 Wheel rod
17 Ice cream flavor #1
20 Vulgarity
21 ___ Lee cakes
22 Neither masc. nor fem.
24 "Too many cooks spoil the broth," e.g.
28 Ice cream flavor #2
33 Model airplane wood
34 Team at Shea
35 Massachusetts' Cape ___
36 Ad-___ (improvises)
37 Mocks
39 Sewing case
40 Brew
41 Grab hold of
42 $1.09 a dozen, say
43 Ice cream flavor #3
47 Mister, in México
48 Argue (with)
49 Faddish 90's collectibles
52 Cause for a blessing?
56 Ice cream flavor #4
61 Merle Haggard's "___ From Muskogee"
62 G.M. or MG product
63 Safe investment, informally
64 Gardener's problem
65 Keep, as cargo
66 Any day now

DOWN

1 Comet's path
2 20's-30's cars
3 Someone who's looked up to
4 North Carolina school
5 Charlatan
6 Lyricist Gershwin
7 Change for a twenty
8 "Star Wars" sage
9 Independence Day event
10 Pink-slip
11 Pie ___ mode
12 Rock group with the 1994 #1 album "Monster"
14 Environmental activist Jagger
18 Book before Daniel: Abbr.
19 Shelled critters
23 Fools (with)
25 Frigid
26 Chronic complainer
27 Singer Gormé
28 Person who holds property in trust
29 Popular catalogue company
30 Buffoon
31 "Do you get it?"
32 A TD is worth 6 of these

Puzzle 43 by Brendan Emmett Quigley

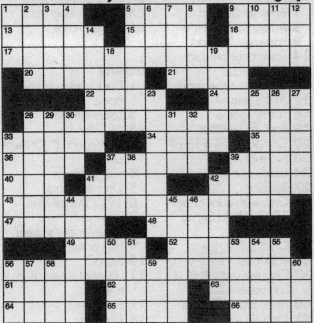

33 Down-in-the-dumps feeling, with "the"
37 Boxer's punch
38 Wanted poster abbr.
39 Directional suffix
41 Spasm of pain
42 Least tainted
44 Made a better offer than
45 "Strangers and Brothers" novelist
46 Throw a tantrum
50 Mardi ___

51 Porn
53 Sicilian spouter
54 Jerusalem's Mount ___
55 Opposite of endo-
56 Comic book punch sound
57 Make (out)
58 Item for Little Jack Horner
59 Judge Lance ___
60 Barbie's beau

ACROSS

1 Book jacket part
5 Admonition to Fido
9 Preserves, as pork
14 Lawn care product
15 Feel the ___
16 Send via cyberspace
17 At the summit of
18 "Dirty" game
19 Bad, as weather
20 Composer on a spree?
23 Nairobi native
24 Land, as a fish
27 Baubles
31 Grp. with a lot of pull?
32 1973 World Series stadium
35 Crucifix inscription
36 Hilo feast
37 Disguise oneself as a composer?
40 Mont Blanc's locale
41 Utah ski spot
42 She loved Narcissus
43 British suffix with American
44 Quadrennial candidate Harold
46 Pesto seasoning
48 Taoism founder
53 Composer's personal attendant?
57 Baby deliverer
59 Raindrop sound
60 Robin Cook novel
61 Find the value of x
62 Points (at)
63 "Redemption" author
64 Dirty political tactic
65 Wear a long face
66 Wine choice

DOWN

1 Back pocket liquor bottle
2 Loose-limbed
3 "___ for the Misbegotten" (O'Neill play)
4 Full of energy
5 On one's back
6 1982 Disney film
7 Bug-eyed
8 Cheerleader's cheer
9 Has a hunch
10 Stun
11 Ultimate satisfaction, in a way
12 Small bird
13 Like a fox
21 Polytheistic
22 Professor Corey
25 State with a panhandle
26 Seagoing: Abbr.
28 Novelist Cather
29 Flying pests
30 Puccini pieces
32 Tortilla chip topper
33 "I could eat a horse," e.g.
34 Asner and Bradley
36 Driver's need: Abbr.
37 Secretary of State under Reagan

Puzzle 44 by Gene Newman

38 Flat fixer
39 French legislature
44 More disgusted
45 Pass by
47 Caterpillar or grub
49 Come about
50 From top to bottom, informally
51 Teamsters' wheels
52 Wipe out
54 W.W. II fare
55 Award for Saatchi & Saatchi
56 Frolic
57 Snaky sound
58 Mr. Turkey

ACROSS

1 Toasted sandwiches, for short
5 Politician Alexander
10 Very funny one
14 Dublin's land
15 Habitation
16 The "I" in "The King and "I"
17 Send out
18 Suppers
19 Hoof it
20 Agitated
23 Caustic substance
24 Mrs. Kowalski, in "A Streetcar Named Desire"
25 Hall-of-Famer Yogi
27 1950's car with a horse-collar grille
30 Yak, yak, yak
33 Buffoons
36 "The Wind in the Willows" character
38 World leader who gave his name to a jacket
39 Zilch
40 Browbeat
42 Trains to the Loop
43 Bring out
45 Fodder holder
46 Lose sleep (over)
47 Harbor a grudge about
49 Frisco gridder
51 Softens, with "down"
53 Golf shoe features

57 Word repeated in "Does ___ or doesn't ___?"
59 Agitated
62 Prayer receiver, with "the"
64 Sweater size
65 Neck hair
66 Comply
67 Turn outward
68 Tommie of the 60's-70's Mets
69 Portend
70 "Walk Away ___" (1966 hit)
71 Brainy, socially inept sort

DOWN

1 Strengthens, with "up"
2 See 56-Down
3 Said too often
4 Pays, as a bill
5 Chew out
6 Have ___ in one's bonnet
7 Castle defense
8 Wing it, speechwise
9 Visited again
10 Inexperienced
11 Agitated
12 "Members ___"
13 Give's partner
21 Long in the tooth
22 Guzzled
26 I-95, e.g.: Abbr.
28 Seemingly forever
29 Rabbit fur

Puzzle 45 by Gregory E. Paul

31 Writer ___ Stanley
     Gardner
32 Reddish-brown
33 Lulu
34 Candy striper, e.g.
35 Agitated
37 Takeout lunch provider
40 Redhead's secret,
     maybe
41 Basement floor
     material
44 Corp. numero uno
46 One released from
     bondage

48 Bank employee
50 Antlered animal
52 Work like a dog
54 "If it ain't broke, don't
     fix it," e.g.
55 Radio part
56 With 2-Down, 65
     miles per hour, say
57 Hardly a neatnik
58 Tramp
60 Songbird
61 Fearsome one
63 Hair coloring

ACROSS

1 Volcano flow
5 Kind of drum or fiddle
9 Halloween disguises
14 Passing notice
15 Get sore
16 Tatum or Ryan
17 Makeup brand
19 Join forces
20 French farewell
21 March of ___
23 Nada
24 Ran first
25 Accountant's software
28 Porterhouse or T-bone
29 Many a Melville setting, with "the"
30 They may be served with a twist
33 Pork cut
37 Like some pre-Columbian culture
38 Golden attribute?
41 Filmdom's Joel or Ethan
42 Removes gently
43 Home of the Bears and the Bulls: Abbr.
46 Exhibit annoying satisfaction
47 Silky-haired dog
51 Pvt.'s boss
54 Little piggy?
55 Skater Hamilton
56 Wedding seater
58 Full of chutzpah
60 End-of-filming gala
62 See eye to eye
63 Bit of Italian bread?
64 Verne's captain
65 Exams
66 1974 Sutherland/Gould spoof
67 Broadway star Verdon

DOWN

1 The slo-o-o-ow train
2 Dwelling
3 Lively, as an imagination
4 Suit to ___
5 Grocery tote
6 Harmful precipitation
7 Screams
8 Alabama march city
9 Puddinglike dessert
10 ___ Arbor, Mich.
11 Take by force
12 Couric of "Today"
13 "George Washington ___ here"
18 Rural
22 Asner and Begley
26 Baseball's Tony or Alejandro
27 Most hearty
28 Horrid smell
30 Computer that doesn't use Windows
31 ___ dye (chemical coloring)
32 Way to go: Abbr.
34 Mrs. Lennon
35 Hosp. section
36 After-tax amount

Puzzle 46 by Nancy Salomon

38 Healthful
39 "Time ___ My Side" (Stones hit)
40 Precede, with "to"
42 Swellhead's journey?
44 Corned beef dishes
45 Co. abbr.
47 Chance for a hit
48 Smithy
49 First, second, reverse, etc.
50 Bays, in a way
51 Chronic nag

52 "___ to the Church on Time"
53 Don at the tailor's
57 Crooned
59 Put in rollers
61 Mas' mates

ACROSS

1 Money in a wallet
5 Playbill listing
9 "Pooh!"
14 Elbow-wrist connection
15 Mixed bag
16 Florida city
17 Down under toy
19 Comedian Richard
20 Finalize, with "up"
21 Prefix with cycle
22 Bears witness (to)
24 Country west of Togo
26 "___ do you do?"
27 Make the rounds in a police car
30 Haphazardly
35 Assumed name
36 Unseal
37 Russo of "Ransom," 1996
38 Barbecue entree
39 What each of the four long answers in this puzzle is
40 Dewrinkle
41 Nights before
42 Brainbusting
43 Par ___ (airmail label)
44 Oust from authority
46 Droopy-eyed
47 Engine need
48 Part of a flight
50 Russian plain, with "the"
54 Wane
55 Place for a plane

58 ___ diem (seize the day): Lat.
59 Upgrade from a tropical storm
62 Flying saucer flier
63 Diarist Frank
64 District
65 Molson's and Coors, e.g.
66 Rolling stones lack it
67 Place for a fisherman

DOWN

1 Chicago nine
2 Burn balm
3 The "white" of "White Christmas"
4 Western omelet ingredient
5 Place to break a bronco
6 Actor Delon
7 Kind of tax
8 Roman robe
9 Soda-can opener
10 Tool belt item
11 Makes bales of alfalfa
12 Zillions
13 Battles
18 Community spirit
23 Express gratitude to
24 Singing insect
25 Has hopes
27 Skinned
28 ___ and kicking
29 Dalai Lama's land
31 Borrow's opposite

Puzzle 47 by Gregory E. Paul

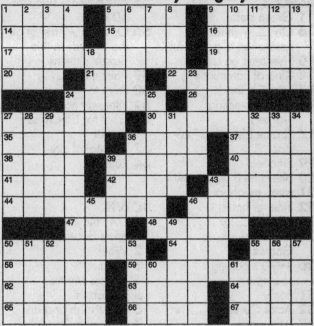

32 Mountaintop home
33 Meddle
34 Funnyman Youngman
36 Algerian port of 600,000
39 Wild Asian dog
43 Accused's excuse
45 Matures
46 Buffalo's N.H.L. team
49 Sea swallows
50 Sign of healing
51 Saga
52 New York's ___ Canal

53 Hoax
55 Madras dress
56 Spoon-playing site
57 2001, e.g.
60 Lively card game
61 Spending limit

ACROSS
1 Green stuff
6 On ___ (without assurance of payment)
10 Fivesome on a five
14 Kind of committee
15 Spanish snack
16 Org. protecting workers
17 "Some Like It Hot" co-star
19 Innocent
20 Like a hit B'way show
21 Mex. neighbor
22 Filler of holes
24 Make ___ for it
25 Mrs. Addams, to Gomez
26 1990's boxing champion
31 Fairly
32 Actor Cariou
33 Little worker
35 Worker's demand
36 Bro's kin
37 Housing unit
39 Extra-play periods: Abbr.
40 Essen exclamation
41 TV cop Chris
42 Country star who sang "Roses in the Snow"
46 "Othello" role
47 Commedia dell'___
48 Level, in taxes
51 Columnist Marilyn ___ Savant
52 Triangular sail
55 Music genre since the 50's
56 Onetime winner of all the awards in this puzzle's theme
59 Raison d'___
60 Privy to
61 Intensely hot
62 Treat for Little Miss Muffet
63 Taj Mahal city
64 Ruffled

DOWN
1 They may be left at one's doorstep
2 Whiff
3 "Curses!"
4 Actress Myrna
5 On target
6 Leave high and dry
7 Frisk, with "down"
8 Formal correspondence
9 Sea north of Iran
10 Blanket wrap
11 Writer Dinesen
12 Rizzuto or Collins
13 Protected
18 Great deal of interest
23 Blonde shade
24 Takes steps
26 Take to the soapbox
27 Earthquake
28 Friend of Job
29 One-named New Age musician

Puzzle 48 by Gilbert H. Ludwig

30 Aconcagua and environs
31 Old hand
34 Trifle
36 Darting
37 Hauls away
38 Grimm figure
40 Camus's birthplace
41 Rebound shot
43 It's a knockout
44 Jabber
45 Castro's capital
48 Suds

49 "Portnoy's Complaint" author
50 Bit of a spread
52 Minced oath
53 Start of a legal memo
54 "Cheers" bartender Woody ___
57 Rocky peak
58 Estuary

ACROSS

1 Actor Baldwin
5 Will-o'-the-wisp locale
10 Peninsula south of California
14 Watch face
15 Bone below the femur
16 Satanic
17 Prefix with -nautics
18 Top talent
19 ___ Strauss & Co.
20 Test type
23 Sacred
24 WSW's opposite
25 Cowlike
28 Disaster often not covered by insurance
33 Sports event site
34 ". . . bombs bursting ___"
35 Doctors' org.
36 Anthem
37 Possible answers for 20-Across
38 Proverbial inheritors
39 ___ nutshell
40 Fine china
41 Andrew Wyeth's "___ Pictures"
42 Come crashing down
44 Astronomical object with a large red shift
45 It's south of Eur.
46 Heaven's Gate, e.g.
47 D, often
54 Prod
55 Flu cause
56 Too

57 Good luck symbol for King Tut
58 "You ___ kidding!"
59 Animal with a mane
60 Mediocre
61 Soup onions
62 Cuts with garden shears

DOWN

1 Actor Baldwin
2 Stead
3 Viscount's superior
4 Duds
5 Paper clip alternative
6 "Free" whale of film
7 Irish Rose's guy
8 Odds and ends: Abbr.
9 Terribly weak, as an excuse
10 Dogma
11 With: Fr.
12 Jazz talk
13 ___ Baba
21 Island of the Inner Hebrides
22 ___ about (approximately)
25 Acronymic computer language name
26 Maine college town
27 Open to bribery
28 One place to hook up the jumper cables
29 Give a hoot
30 Scottish Highlanders
31 Symbol of resistance

Puzzle 49 by Matthew Lees

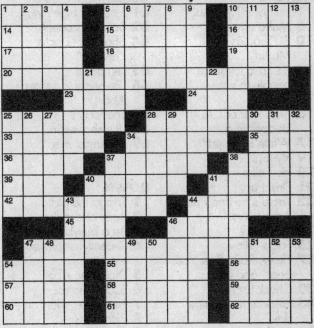

32 Capital of Senegal
34 Nigerian natives
37 "Thumbs up" signification
38 Spaghetti topper
40 Sound's partner
41 Dance done in grass skirts
43 Crow's-nest cry
44 Grand searches
46 Solid portion
47 Naughty deed
48 Acorn sources

49 Order after "aim"
50 Logic diagram
51 Hodgepodge
52 Initials on a brandy bottle
53 Incalculable amount of time
54 Tank filler

ACROSS

1 Part of P.T.A.: Abbr.
5 Make sense
10 St. Thomas or St. Martin
14 It's hard for some people to carry
15 Dough
16 N.Y. Met or L.A. Dodger, e.g.
17 White's dessert?
19 Fly high
20 Ho hello
21 Dried up
22 There's no free ride on these hwys.
23 Key task?
25 Fable fellow
27 "Row, Row, Row Your Boat" and others
30 Check for fit
33 Prepare for a rainy day
36 Bud's buddy
37 Disco spinner
38 Prop in slapstick
39 Carrey's snack food?
41 Mine find
42 Shows flexibility, in a way
44 Hit like Holyfield
45 Numero uno
46 Free-for-all
47 Western howler
49 Blender maker
51 Like Joe Average
55 From pillar to ___
57 Televises
60 Bid the bed adieu
61 ___ in a blue moon
62 Sawyer's beef?
64 Sharif of "Doctor Zhivago"
65 Leg bone
66 Life-or-death matter: Abbr.
67 The lady's
68 Like snakeskin
69 Madams' men

DOWN

1 Trip to the plate
2 Rude and sullen
3 Be a busybody
4 Recently employed worker
5 Diplomat: Abbr.
6 Bucks' mates
7 Fuss over, with "on"
8 Extremists
9 Check casher
10 Coming up
11 Pesci's sandwich?
12 Faucet failure
13 Screws up
18 Billionth: Prefix
24 Patsies
26 Stern's opposite
28 "___ won't be afraid" ("Stand by Me" lyric)
29 Flying elephant
31 They fit in locks
32 Nikita's "no"
33 Junk E-mail
34 Glorified gofer

Puzzle 50 by Nancy Salomon

35 Wilde's entree?
37 Popular pencil brand
39 Let it be, editorially
40 Newborn child, for one
43 Bothers à la baby brother
45 They may be black and blue
47 Siskel or Ebert
48 Warty-skinned critter
50 Bridge positions
52 Home of the N.B.A. Heat

53 "Lou Grant" star
54 Salacious looks
55 Christopher Robin's pal
56 Treater's words
58 Singer McEntire
59 Go yachting
63 Mary ___ of cosmetics

ACROSS

1 The "A" of N.E.A.
5 Vittles
9 Take ___ at (try)
14 Cookout in Honolulu
15 Convenience
16 Hangman's ___
17 Snapshots
18 Perfectly draftable
19 1966 movie or song
20 Judge's query to a jury
23 Army div.
24 Confucian path
25 Muhammad ___
28 Apothecary's weight
31 Sparkly rock
36 Nothin'
38 "___ Coming" (1969 hit)
40 Prom, say
41 Jury's reply to the judge
44 Irregularly edged
45 Word to a fly
46 Pioneering 70's video game
47 ___ Cranston (the Shadow, of old radio)
49 Shoemaker's tools
51 Golf ball prop
52 It lacks refinement
54 ___ Abner
56 Judge's comment to the spectators
65 Actress Adams and others
66 Live wire, so to speak
67 Nile queen, informally

68 Gladiator's battleground
69 More than a goblin
70 German philosopher
71 "Stop worrying!"
72 Prison area
73 Within: Prefix

DOWN

1 Brand for Bowser
2 Make a mess of
3 Diplomat's forte
4 Fish food?
5 Tale spinner Chaucer
6 Rajah's mate
7 Druggie
8 Admirer of Beauty
9 Tight wrapper?
10 Unassisted
11 Bean curd
12 X ___ xylophone
13 Shade of red
21 Stop
22 Dog's ID
25 Broadway backer
26 Classic 1944 mystery film
27 "Going to the dogs," e.g.
29 "Oh, woe!"
30 Baryshnikov, to friends
32 Marshal Wyatt
33 Gold bar
34 Public spat
35 Marsh plant
37 "Not only that . . ."
39 Garbage boat

42 Jazz combo instrument
43 Yelled
48 Prefix with chloride
50 Urge to attack, with "on"
53 Provide with funds
55 English philosopher
56 "The Rubáiyát" poet
57 Stamp designation
58 Hamilton's last act
59 ___ St. Vincent Millay
60 Costume for Claudius
61 Mister, in Münster

62 ___ Bator, Mongolia
63 Monthly money
64 Dog in Oz

ACROSS

1 Flashlight's projection
5 Bus. get-together
8 Adjust on the timeline
14 With 2-Down, "My People" author
15 Pacific battle site, in brief
16 Fromm and Remarque
17 Australian ranch hand
19 Lunatics
20 Pyrenees nation
21 Pretty marble
22 Showy parrot
24 Chinese food additive
27 Dali or Corot
28 Mass robe
31 Needed liniment
33 Tot's game
36 Braincases
38 Connect via phone
39 Leaping marsupial
42 Pacific island nation
43 Workout facility
44 Tax on imports
47 Certain M.I.T. grads
48 Cowboy
50 In its entirety
53 Austrian Alpine pass
58 Where 26-Down is
59 Algonquian Indian
60 Donut coatings
61 Drink on draft
62 Peru's capital
63 "Murder Must Advertise" writer Dorothy
64 Tripper's turn-on
65 Like some drinks

DOWN

1 Mexicali locale, for short
2 See 14-Across
3 Alphabetical start
4 Shark variety
5 Medicine chest door, usually
6 Having one intermission
7 Baby syllable
8 Did a framer's job
9 Sappho's Muse
10 Child's reply to a taunt
11 Highest point
12 Unnamed ones
13 Feudal worker
18 Los Angeles suburb
21 Job for Holmes
23 Laotian money
24 Baseball's Connie and others
25 Dump into a Dumpster
26 Lake Volta's country
28 Once in ___ moon
29 River through Tours
30 Year-end check, maybe
32 Our lang.
34 Relations
35 Motorists' org.
37 Where nudes may be sketched

40 Tasting like certain wood
41 Man-mouse connector
45 Certain letter-shaped tracks
46 Involuntary, as a landing
48 Pool table fabric
49 Gastric woe
50 Makes "it"
51 "Man ___ Mancha"
52 Caterer's carrier

54 "Road" picture destination
55 Colossal
56 City on seven hills
57 Prod
59 ___ Kan (pet food brand)

ACROSS
1 Shirking working
5 Wetland
10 Big dud
14 Butter substitute
15 80's-90's singer Baker
16 Not prerecorded
17 Kids' building playthings
19 Prophetic sign
20 Rat fink
21 Private instructors
23 Corrida cry
24 Deep chasm
26 Actress Lollobrigida
28 Wily
29 It gives an artist backing
33 Carson's successor
34 Not mass-produced
36 Santa ___, Calif.
37 Tolkien creatures
38 "Mamma ___!"
39 Queen's subject?
41 Tilt, as the head
42 Oregon's capital
43 Actor Vigoda
44 Excellent, in modern slang
45 "Stars and Stripes Forever" composer
47 "Ben-___"
48 ___ scampi
51 Winnie-the-Pooh's creator
55 Telly Savalas's lack
56 Small telescopes
59 First word in a fairy tale
60 "Silas Marner" novelist
61 Soviet news agency
62 Lyric poems
63 Salad bar servers
64 1988 Olympic gold-medal swimmer Kristin

DOWN
1 Oodles
2 Came down to earth
3 Greek philosopher of paradox fame
4 John Lennon's wife
5 One of the Osmonds
6 Poker player's payment
7 Brazilian city
8 Pigs' digs
9 Rash
10 Ocean debris
11 Car with a bar
12 Out's partner
13 State prisons
18 Grammy winner Fitzgerald
22 Computer operators
24 Poor woodcutter of folklore
25 "by Peter Gordon," e.g.
26 Italian salami city
27 Counting everything
28 Israeli natives
30 Neighbor of Fiji

Puzzle 53 by Peter Gordon

31 Proclamation
32 Breach of secrecy
33 Young woman
34 Gout spot
35 Giant slugger Mel
37 Phrase spoken with a wave into a TV camera
40 Longs for
41 His art is a wrap
44 Mountain lion
46 Win for the underdog
47 Ceases

48 "Git!"
49 Round of applause
50 Houston university
51 Full of excitement
52 Future attorney's exam: Abbr.
53 Hornet's home
54 Old gas brand
57 Arafat's org.
58 Yang's counterpart

ACROSS

1 Supreme Diana
5 Distiller Walker
10 Shade of blue
14 1975 Wimbledon winner
15 Solo
16 Plunks (down)
17 Summer resort off the coast of Massachusetts
19 Bring in
20 Elixirs
21 Saviors
23 Ward of "Sisters"
25 D'Amato and others
26 The "S" of R.S.V.P.
29 Elvis's home
33 "At Seventeen" singer Janis
36 Hut material
38 Two socks
39 On a single occasion
40 Scented pouches
43 Quaker's "you"
44 Mine extracts
45 Balance sheet item
46 Make soaking wet
47 Sound systems
49 60's radicals: Abbr.
50 Surgery sites, for short
52 Jugglery
54 Make king
59 Regal headwear
63 Henry ___
64 1984 Prince hit
66 Have ___ good authority
67 Cream

68 Book after II Chronicles
69 Late-night regular
70 Athletic shoe feature
71 Hard to fathom

DOWN

1 Undivided
2 Norse capital
3 Blackball
4 Common carriers
5 Pain in the neck
6 Hurting
7 Wander
8 Author Rice
9 Club ___ (resorts)
10 Blooming time
11 Funny feeling
12 Neighbor of 27-Down
13 Nile creatures
18 Old-time deliverers
22 Carrier to Stockholm
24 Current name
26 Smelling ___
27 The Oregon Trail crossed it
28 Aphrodisiac
30 Cutter
31 Many a snake
32 Recipient of annual contributions
34 Didn't dillydally
35 Hatching places
37 Spell-off
39 Sounds of surprise
41 Precise moment
42 "A Chorus Line" girl
47 Ukr., once

Puzzle 54 by Elizabeth C. Gorski

48 Means of release
51 Safari sight
53 Dog-____ (well-worn)
54 Fiendish
55 Evening, in adspeak
56 Intl. acronym since 1960
57 Not valid
58 Toledo's lake
60 Bring the house down
61 Billion follower
62 Ginger cookie
65 Org. looking after kids

ACROSS

1 Modern communication
6 Holland export
10 1944 battle site
14 Where Pago Pago is
15 "La Bohème" heroine
16 One with a lookalike
17 Interpreter of the news
19 Epidemic
20 C.I.A. predecessor
21 "___ Irae" (Latin hymn)
22 Mishandles
24 Soccer great born Edson Arantes
25 "Rob Roy" author
26 The ___ that be
29 Magic charm
32 They're worn on the day after Mardi Gras
33 Dot on a computer screen
34 Sumac whose voice covered five octaves
35 It's dipped in a dip
36 Carpentry grooves
37 Actress Adams of James Bond films
38 Suffix with mountain
39 Respected man
40 Iranian language
41 Soup crackers
43 More subdued
44 Babble
45 Peace symbol
46 Victors' reward
48 Car at an auto dealership
49 ___ Paulo, Brazil
52 Stage accessory
53 Recovery
56 Prisoner's spot
57 Burden
58 Upper crust
59 Church recess
60 Beep on a beeper
61 Frighten off

DOWN

1 Exxon predecessor
2 Guidebook features
3 French friends
4 It's charged in physics
5 Fire truck equipment
6 Host
7 Dah's counterparts
8 Latin 101 word
9 Smokey Robinson's group, with "the"
10 Swaggers
11 "Make me do it"
12 Time Inc. magazine
13 Wallet stuffers
18 Rembrandts, e.g.
23 Seethe
24 Chick's sound
25 Anglo-___
26 Walks a hole in the carpet
27 Actor Milo or Michael
28 Fancy bath features
29 Neap and ebb
30 Make smile
31 Very depths
33 Check casher

Puzzle 55 by Richard Chisholm

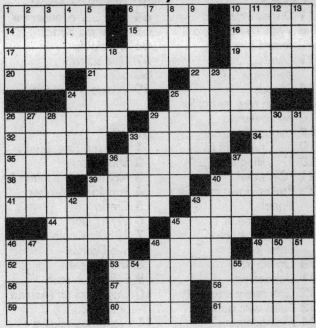

36 "Keep going!"
37 Stag attender
39 Clock face
40 Having winning odds
42 Almost a homer
43 Knocked-out state
45 Impenetrable
46 Pet protector, for short
47 Kind of school
48 The "D" of D.E.A.
49 Diamonds, e.g.
50 Chip in
51 Frankfurt's river

54 Spanish article
55 Corrida cry

ACROSS

1 Disney's deer
6 With 16-Across, a famed diarist
11 "Am ___ believe . . . ?"
14 'Hoods
15 Get a new tenant for
16 See 6-Across
17 Mighty Cardinal
19 ___ Cruces, N.M.
20 ". . . sting like ___"
21 "Oh wow!"
22 Broken-down motorist's signal
24 Nickname of 17-Across hero Babe Ruth
28 On the train
31 Unbending
32 Gets really steamed
33 Suffix with gang
34 Massachusetts' Cape ___
37 Turn loose
39 Official reproach
42 N.F.L. scores
43 Cooperate with a shooter
45 Playful animal
46 Lamb Chop's mentor
48 Had relevance to
49 Call after a hit by 17-Across
53 Minxes
54 "Cara ___" (1965 hit)
55 Diva's big moment
59 State next to Miss.
60 Title for 17-Across
64 ". . . ___ a lender be"
65 Clear the board
66 Contradict
67 Little scurrier
68 Sees socially
69 Where Minos ruled

DOWN

1 Crimson Tide, briefly
2 Show horse
3 Nothing more than
4 Popular fund-raiser
5 Credo
6 Vernacular
7 1980's sitcom with two Darryls
8 The Greatest
9 Suffix with cash
10 Opponent for Martina or Monica
11 Nonblood relative
12 Princess topper
13 Beginning
18 Common ailment
23 Hallucination cause
25 Constellation bear
26 One in the family
27 Very nasty sort
28 Border on
29 007
30 Squelches a squeak
33 Pint-sized
34 Like a button
35 After-lunch sandwich
36 Actor Bruce
38 Bit of a tiff

40 American-born Queen of Jordan
41 Runner in the raw
44 Kind of cat
46 Pacifier
47 Quite quiet
48 Bridges of Hollywood
49 The Donald's first ex
50 Eagle's gripper
51 Bright
52 Takes on
56 Get to, so to speak
57 "What's ___ for me?"

58 Onetime Time film critic James
61 Man-mouse link
62 Welcome ___
63 "ER" network

ACROSS

1 "It's a Wonderful Life" director Frank
6 Quiet valley
10 New York Shakespeare Festival founder Joseph
14 Apportion
15 Roof overhang
16 "Hair" song "____ Baby"
17 With 61-Across, what the judge said to the bigamist?
20 Japanese wrestling
21 Your and my
22 Nearly
23 Appear, with "up"
25 At rest
26 Sneeze sounds
29 Casey Jones, notably
33 When repeated, a Latin dance
34 Raison ____
36 Musical composition
37 Put on ____ (act snooty)
39 Peter or Patrick, e.g.
41 "Cut that out!"
42 Smooth and shiny
44 Catch fish, in a primitive way
46 Time in history
47 Modern-day halts to kids' fights
49 "Messiah" composer
51 "You wouldn't ____!"
52 Green flavor
53 Aussie "chick"
56 Dracula, at times
57 "Oh, nonsense!"
61 See 17-Across
64 Elderly's svgs.
65 Caspian Sea feeder
66 "Hi"
67 Defrost
68 "Auld Lang ____"
69 Baby bird

DOWN

1 Low islands
2 Baseballer Matty or Felipe
3 Prune, formerly
4 Highly ornamented style
5 Tell ____ glance
6 Outfit
7 Comic Bert
8 A Gabor
9 State east of the Sierras
10 Easy monthly ____
11 It follows "peek" in a baby's game
12 Name of 12 popes
13 Saucy
18 Hangmen's needs
19 "Dallas" matriarch Miss ____
24 16 1/2 feet
25 "Goodnight" girl of song
26 ". . . with ____ of thousands!" (Hollywood hype)
27 Texas cook-off dish

Puzzle 57 by Stephanie Spadaccini

28 Sultan's ladies
29 Excursions
30 Quiet
31 Be crazy about
32 Where Everest is
35 Nibble on
38 Most flea-bitten
40 Idyllic South Seas island
43 Aussie "bear"
45 Hit head-on
48 Neighbor of Saturn
50 Huey, Dewey or Louie, to Donald Duck

52 Soup server
53 Take some off the top
54 Tortoise's rival
55 List-ending abbr.
56 Noggin
58 "___ be a cold day in hell . . ."
59 Only
60 What 69-Across will grow up to do
62 Arid
63 Nevertheless

ACROSS

1 "Peanuts" boy
6 Exile of 1979
10 Carry on, as a campaign
14 Take for one's own
15 Shells, e.g.
16 Allege as fact
17 With one's fingers in a lake?
20 Grand larceny, e.g.
21 "___ Darlin' " (jazz standard)
22 Sugary drink
23 "Relax, private!"
26 Longed (for)
28 Adorns unnecessarily
31 Toiletries holder
33 Brouhaha
34 A.T.M. necessity
35 Wagnerian heroine
39 With one's fingers in a skyscraper?
43 Like last year's styles
44 Part of U.C.L.A.
45 KLM competitor
46 Echo, e.g.
48 An ex of Xavier
50 Bob Cousy's team, for short
53 Duds
55 "Bravo!"
56 Wax producer
58 Latino lady
62 With one's fingers in a socket?
66 Bering Sea island
67 At no time, to poets
68 Ceramists' needs
69 Element #10
70 City to which Helen was abducted
71 Kind of shooting

DOWN

1 Joke response, informally
2 ___ fixe (obsession)
3 December air
4 Send to a mainframe
5 Is miserly
6 Decline in value
7 Seagoing inits.
8 Evil repeller
9 Pueblo dweller
10 Kind of chest or paint
11 For the birds?
12 Hollow rock
13 Blew it
18 "The Science Guy" on TV
19 Ciudad Juárez neighbor
24 Similar
25 Marathoner's shirt
27 Borodin's prince
28 Meower, in Madrid
29 Matinee hero
30 Blaring
32 0's and 1's, to a programmer
34 Absolute worst, with "the"
36 One of the Simpsons
37 Cherished

38 Sinclair rival
40 Cyberspace conversation
41 Grimm youngster
42 Launderer's step
47 ___ Brothers
48 Haunted house sounds
49 Playwright Ibsen
50 "Over There" composer
51 Make jubilant
52 Slowly, on a score
54 Approximation suffix

57 "___ Too Proud to Beg" (1966 hit)
59 Look at flirtatiously
60 Tennis's Lacoste
61 Like some profs.
63 Pester for payment
64 Prefix with logical
65 Have a bawl

ACROSS

1 Pitcher
5 Egyptian vipers
9 TV's Pyle
14 Lose brilliancy
15 Shed, as skin
16 The "I" of IM
17 Nonstop round-the-clock, informally
20 Clement Moore's "right jolly old elf"
21 Watches for
22 ___ longa, vita brevis
24 Most optimistic
28 NASA's Armstrong
31 Stumped solvers' requests
34 CCLVI doubled
35 California's Fort ___
36 Crunchy sandwich
37 Raison ___
38 Start of a free call
42 Dress lines
43 "No problem!"
44 Not a particular
45 From Santiago to Buenos Aires
46 Cop's ID
48 Actual being
49 Olympian's no-no
51 Boston Red ___
53 Transcript listings
56 Fire's start
60 Boeing plane
64 Teheran resident
65 Christie's "Death on the ___"
66 Mining locale
67 Trousers
68 Sporty 60's cars
69 Kids' winter schoolday wish

DOWN

1 Newts in transition
2 Trumpet sound
3 Genesis garden
4 Avis offering
5 "Once in Love With ___"
6 Parlor seat
7 David Mamet's "Speed-the-___"
8 Jeb of Bull Run fame
9 Essences
10 Not balanced
11 VH1 rival
12 Before, once
13 Skedaddled
18 Road crew's supply
19 Spanish streams
23 Lively old dance
25 Epic film screenful
26 Temptresses
27 Do 60's clothing designs
28 Snare parts
29 Mr. Hemingway
30 Think creatively
32 "___ bin ein Berliner"
33 Was aware of
36 "___ the season . . ."
37 Letters after Daniel Moynihan's name
39 Newly formed

Puzzle 59 by Robert Dillman

40 Witch
41 Applications
46 Diagonal
47 Totaling
48 Kicks out
50 Birdlife
52 W.W. II agcy.
54 Passage out
55 Breakthrough battle in Normandy
57 Stratford's stream
58 Completely fix
59 Was in the loop

60 Not guzzle
61 Pitcher's stat
62 Vehicle with sliding doors
63 "You betcha!"

ACROSS

1 Wings
5 Rick's love in "Casablanca"
9 Carry's partner
13 One of 39-Across
14 On toast, in diner slang
15 Commedia dell'___
16 Intended
17 Illuminated sign
18 MTV's "The ___ World"
19 One of 39-Across
21 One of 39-Across
23 Shoebox marking
24 Sex researcher Hite
25 "Welcome" site
28 Europe's highest active volcano
30 Took care of
34 Labor Dept. division
36 Troubles
38 Practice piece
39 Theme of this puzzle
42 Monopoly piece
43 Jazz singer James
44 Jonathan Larson musical
45 Unwanted noise
47 Simplicity
49 Lao-___
50 Tackle box contents
52 Neighbor of Wyo.
54 One of 39-Across
57 One of 39-Across
61 Part of 36-24-36
62 Whitish
64 Ab strengthener
65 Bridge position
66 Uniform
67 What your nose knows
68 Lover of Aphrodite
69 Actress Russo
70 Info

DOWN

1 One of the Baldwins
2 Rachel's sister, in the Bible
3 "Bull Durham" character
4 Main course
5 Brainstorm
6 Bagel topper
7 Sound of a basket
8 Part of a pregame ceremony
9 One of 39-Across
10 Calculus calculation
11 Symbol on a Cowboy's helmet
12 Remained fast
13 Baseball V.I.P.'s
20 Fix a road
22 Some native New Yorkers
24 Greets the general
25 Naphthalene repels them
26 "___ in the Dark"
27 Angle symbol
29 "Good going!"
31 Comforter
32 Perfect places

33 Al ___
35 February stones
37 Mlle., in Spain
40 Untouchable Ness
41 Mr. Arafat
46 One of 39-Across
48 Town in central New Jersey
51 Jack
53 Casual comment
54 It erupted on October 27, 1986

55 When repeated, a 1997 Jim Carrey comedy
56 Church part
57 Kind of pool
58 Put away
59 Not theirs
60 Brit. legislators
63 Novelist Deighton

ACROSS

1 Castle protection
5 Watch chains
9 Moby-Dick, for one
14 Tuneful Fitzgerald
15 Nabisco cookie
16 Sponsorship
17 Coal stratum
18 True
19 Affixes in a scrapbook, say
20 Willie Mays at the Y?
23 Traffic arteries
24 Corrida cry
25 Olympic awards
28 Study of verse
32 Standing
33 Horse color
35 Slice
36 Crossword by Joe DiMaggio, e.g.?
40 Somme summer
41 TV's Nick at ___
42 NBC newsman Roger
43 She played the pretty woman in "Pretty Woman"
46 Not mono
47 Former Mideast inits.
48 Was inquisitive
50 Ken Griffey Jr. at 100?
56 Disappearing phone features
57 Final notice
58 Part of a marching band
59 Wally's pal in "Leave It to Beaver"
60 Post-Christmas event
61 Dutch cheese
62 Hippie attire
63 Ogles
64 Lairs

DOWN

1 Phoenix suburb
2 Designer Cassini
3 Jai ___
4 American larch
5 Former Supreme Court Justice Abe
6 Mountain nymph
7 Rays
8 Alone
9 Move rapidly from side to side
10 Footballer's protection
11 Chills
12 Legal claim
13 Test-track curve
21 Nick of "The Prince of Tides"
22 Opposite of everybody
25 Notorious Lansky
26 Muse with a lyre
27 Star in Cygnus
28 Leaf
29 Less welcoming
30 ___ pie (sweetheart)
31 French pen
33 Reformer Jacob
34 It's west of Que.
37 ___ nous (confidentially)
38 Citer

Puzzle 61 by Sheldon Bernardo

39 Like a first draft
44 Geometer of 300 B.C.
45 Workers' rewards
46 Ice hockey equipment
48 Cornered
49 Photog's request
50 Helper
51 Zippo
52 Sniffer
53 Classic art subject
54 Israel's Abba
55 Butts
56 Society girl

ACROSS

1 Pile
5 Alternative to plastic at a supermarket
10 Winter transport
14 Stewpot
15 Where Sun Valley is
16 Fashioned
17 Crockett or Jones
18 Static
19 Mideast bigwig
20 Lose it
21 Vessel in an alcove
22 Society's 400
23 It's a waste of time
27 Thespian
30 Lily plants
31 Vehicles with booms
33 Bread for a stew, e.g.
34 Missile berth
38 Inner city structure
41 Some sheep
42 Terhune title character
43 Cram into the hold
44 Warner Brothers' ___ J. Fudd
46 Antique shop item
47 1967 Agatha Christie thriller
52 Jeopardy
53 Nicotine's partner
54 Inventor Elias
58 Chapters in world history
59 Well-coordinated
61 Privy to
62 Malicious
63 Butter up?
64 Hardly Mr. Cool
65 New Year's Eve song word
66 Hold for later, as big news
67 Legs, to a zoot suiter

DOWN

1 Bricklayers carry them
2 Flair
3 Thomas ___ Edison
4 Corner conveniences
5 Betty Grable's photo, for one
6 Idolizes
7 Modern driller?
8 Remark requesting elucidation
9 Fish eggs
10 Food fish
11 Female vampire
12 Tweaks a manuscript
13 Rock's ___ and the Dominos
22 Serpentine curve
24 City SSW of Moscow
25 Subjects of clashes
26 Second-year students, for short
27 Yearn
28 Brag
29 Domesticated
32 Convinces of
34 Nero Wolfe's activity
35 Roman road
36 ___ Strauss & Co.
37 Hydrox rival

39 Menaces for warplanes
40 Inscribe for good
44 Slippery one
45 Commercial center in Venice
47 Olympians' blades
48 Having chutzpah
49 Bathtub part
50 Knit goods thread
51 In leaf
55 Draft classification
56 Apple spoiler
57 Winds up
59 Stomach muscles, for short
60 Toujours ___

ACROSS

1 Step
6 Canyon reply
10 Place to plop down
14 Vietnam's capital
15 Sticky stuff
16 Building additions
17 Mimicking
18 Fraternity rush period
20 French article
21 Pulitzer winner James
23 Kitchen appliances
24 Took out to dinner
26 Trophy display room
27 Young 'un
28 Note excusing tardiness
33 Access AOL, e.g.
36 "___ Misbehavin'"
37 "Blondie" kid
38 Rocky's nickname, with "the"
41 Gangster's girl
42 What unfriendly dogs do
43 Mournful poem
44 Simple folk
46 Have a debt
47 Mauna ___
48 Joining
52 More convenient
56 Even's partner
57 Neither's partner
58 Brand of cocoa
60 With 61-Down, a California city
62 Bridge-crossing fee
63 Pain in the neck?
64 They bend in prayer
65 Sunburn soother
66 Lascivious look
67 Football gains

DOWN

1 Commandment word
2 Become narrow
3 Licorice flavor
4 Charged atom
5 Tubular pasta
6 Urged (on)
7 Apple leftover
8 Farmer's tool
9 Light musical work
10 Stitched
11 Designer Cassini
12 Run away
13 Questions
19 "Citizen ___"
22 Understand
25 Many of the Marshall Islands
26 "The Divine Comedy" writer
28 Shopping aids
29 Blowgun ammunition
30 "I cannot tell ___"
31 Visibility reducer
32 Walkman maker
33 Walk falteringly
34 Siouan speaker
35 Big party
36 Activist Bryant
39 Strange
40 1998 name in the news

Puzzle 63 by Peter Gordon

45 Pub offerings
46 Lennon's mate
48 Racing great Al
49 Word with circle or city
50 Famous
51 What Astroturf replaces
52 "Cómo ___ usted?"
53 M.P.'s quarry
54 Fodder holder
55 ___ of Wight
56 Wimbledon winner, 1975

59 Rocks, to a bartender
61 See 60-Across

ACROSS

1 1977 George Burns film
6 Stays idle
10 Sentry's cry
14 Bottom of a suit
15 Blue-pencil
16 Rose's fellow
17 Bad
18 Learning method
19 "___ Lisa"
20 Backs of 45's having a sudden change in direction?
23 "Ah, me!"
24 Moon goddess
25 Operatic soprano Geraldine
28 Gush forth
30 Alfonso XIII's queen
31 Tall footwear for rappers?
36 Bank adjuncts
38 It may be lent
39 Writer Ephron
40 Trackside aid that can't be beat?
45 Buddhism sect
46 Playwright Clifford
47 Certain steak
49 Chatterbox
52 Taj Mahal site
53 Portable writing surface for an equestrian?
57 Inlet
58 Verve
59 Boring fellows

62 Singular fellow
63 Full-fledged
64 Weird
65 Hankerings
66 Skyrocket
67 Dozed

DOWN

1 Harem room
2 Chop
3 Malarkey
4 Eyepiece
5 Old Testament temptress
6 Feudal underlings
7 Hero
8 Former Yugoslav chief
9 Accelerates
10 Burr's duel victim
11 Domicile
12 Kind of cabinet
13 Josh
21 ___-mutuel
22 Albanian foe
25 Exploit
26 Against
27 Highway exit
28 Iranian royalty
29 A sweater uses it
32 Annoyance
33 Seep
34 It's just over 14-Across
35 All there
37 Plugs
41 Like Pindar's works
42 Kitchen gadgets
43 Therefore

Puzzle 64 by Diane C. Baldwin

44 Diatribes
48 Race (along)
49 Hatfield's foe
50 "Leave me ___!"
51 Starting point in decision making
52 Baseball's Doubleday
54 Hodgepodge
55 One of the Three Bears
56 Serious
60 Lulu
61 Established

ACROSS

1 Like giants
5 Colorado resort
10 Up to the task
14 Inspiration
15 Puppeteer Lewis
16 Emcee Trebek
17 1966 Beatles song
20 Journalist Pyle
21 Door sign during store hours
22 Refusals
23 Newspaper customers
26 Tire pattern
28 Not for minors
30 Begins, as work
33 Classifieds, e.g.
36 Pile
38 Close, as a windbreaker
39 1976 Harry Chapin song
43 Germless
44 Narrate
45 Road-paving stuff
46 New Jersey N.H.L.ers
48 Smacks
51 Poet T. S. ___
53 Smacked the baseball good and hard
57 Have title to
59 Hot Springs and others
61 "___ Doone" (1869 novel)
62 1950 Ethel Merman song
66 De-wrinkle
67 Occupied
68 Pottery oven
69 Jamboree shelter
70 Unable to flee
71 Home runs or r.b.i.'s, e.g.

DOWN

1 Princeton or Clemson mascot
2 Love to pieces
3 Hotelier Helmsley
4 "Well, ___!" ("Ain't you somethin'!")
5 Solid ___ rock
6 Like a wallflower
7 El ___, Tex.
8 Blow one's top
9 S.F. footballers, informally
10 "Say ___" (doctor's order)
11 Lane changer's danger
12 Comic Jay
13 Donald and Ivana, Burt and Loni, etc.
18 Monopoly acquisition
19 Reason to say "Gesundheit!"
24 German industrial locale
25 Got some shuteye
27 Working hard
29 "The Canterbury ___"
31 Big brass instrument
32 0, on a telephone: Abbr.

Puzzle 65 by N. Salomon and B. Frank

33 Multiple choice choices
34 Strike out, as text
35 Eisenhower opponent
37 Becomes tiresome
40 Follow closely
41 Join the military
42 Bear's scratcher
47 Actress Loren
49 ___ Alto, Calif.
50 Baby deliverers, in birth announcements
52 Corrupt

54 Mom's urging to a picky eater
55 ___ Gay (W.W. II plane)
56 Intimidate
57 Parting words?
58 "The Way We ___"
60 Elitist's rejection
63 Big bang maker
64 Govt. property overseer
65 Whimsical

ACROSS

1 Carried on
6 "Think Fast, Mr. ___" (1937 mystery)
10 Dour
14 Single-handedly
15 ". . . and make it snappy!"
16 Field of work
17 Poles, e.g.
18 Fingerprint or dropped handkerchief, say
19 Kimono sashes
20 Oppose
23 Some ancient writings
25 Exploit
26 Just-passing grade
27 Gone by
28 Mournful cries
31 Drudges
33 Dinner at boot camp
35 The Baltic, e.g.
36 Home on the farm
37 Wall Street fixture
42 Exclamations of regret
43 Bud's pal
44 Empty, in math
46 "Amerika" author
49 Film critic Jeffrey
51 The Greatest
52 Lofty lyric
53 Utter
55 Asian capital
57 Like some tenors
61 Mean one
62 Compote fruit
63 Fine suit material
66 Property claim

67 Island dance
68 Bequeath
69 Lavish affection (on)
70 Site of Iowa State
71 Bud Grace comic strip

DOWN

1 Is no longer
2 "Is that ___?"
3 Kicker's target
4 Accredited diplomat
5 Catch sight of
6 Jet speed measure
7 Capital near the 60th parallel
8 Ford debut of 1986
9 Makes the first bid
10 Gentle firelight
11 Psychic energy, to Freud
12 Married
13 Interlocks
21 Newsstands
22 Nasal partitions
23 Tennis's Shriver
24 Census data
29 Teeny
30 Without strict oversight
32 Boston suburb
34 Overcharge, slangily
36 Railroad switches
38 Many a climactic movie scene
39 Dove's cry
40 Protector
41 Raines of 40's-50's; film

Puzzle 66 by Arthur S. Verdesca

45 Author ___ Yutang
46 German goblin
47 Slow ballet dance
48 Animal that drives rabbits from their burrows
49 Lecture hall
50 Not demand everything one wants
54 Beginning
56 Tree cutter
58 Actor Auberjonois
59 Sound in body

60 Times to live through
64 56, to Flavius
65 Grant's opposite

ACROSS

1 Labor's partner, in a garage bill
6 Pro ___ (proportionate)
10 Some urban air
14 Big name at video arcades
15 Dutch cheese
16 No-no: Var.
17 Homeowners may take them out
20 Uttered
21 Corn units
22 Watermelon part
23 Tee precursor
24 Author Tyler
25 Found at this place
27 Good-as-new tire
29 Put down, slangily
30 Caribbean, e.g.
31 Op ___
32 Elsie's chew
33 Bank earnings: Abbr.
34 Journalists, as a group
40 "Yo!"
41 Legal thing
42 Org. that gets members reduced motel rates
43 It's found in the ground
44 Exchange I do's
45 All thumbs
49 Made good on, as a loan
51 Jai ___
52 Baked Hawaiian dish
53 Helpful ___
54 Singer Anita
55 Amount to make do with
56 "The Pastoral," formally
59 Big oil company
60 Pastrami place
61 River to the Rhône
62 Glimpsed
63 Historical spans
64 Spanish houses

DOWN

1 Overtaker on the road
2 "Relax, soldiers!"
3 Bigot
4 Walked (on)
5 Confession in a confessional
6 Send back to a lower court
7 Like a lot
8 Sailors
9 Tsp. or tbs.
10 One step
11 Milk of ___
12 Following orders
13 Gloomy guy
18 Like alcohol that's unfit for drinking
19 Some college tests, for short
24 Prefix with dynamic
25 Treehouses and such
26 Basketball's Archibald
28 W.W. II fliers: Abbr.
29 Comment made while slapping the forehead

Puzzle 67 by Elizabeth C. Gorski

32 Pennies: Abbr.
34 Comic book superhero
35 Open receiver's cry, maybe
36 Lens
37 Sunburned
38 H. H. Munro's pen name
39 Playing marble
44 "Get ___ it!"
45 Singer Morissette
46 Peaks
47 Spots for speakers

48 Spode pieces
50 Susan of "Goldengirl"
51 Writer ___ Rogers St. Johns
54 Dispatcher's word
55 "Mona ___"
56 Undergrad degrees
57 Poem of praise
58 [their mistake, not mine]

ACROSS

1 Some fathers: Abbr.
4 Winter Palace ruler
8 Big name in hotels
14 Private eye, for short
15 $75/night, e.g.
16 Microscopic creature
17 Like: Suffix
18 Picnic raiders
19 Maritime hazard in W. W. II
20 Richard Benjamin's film debut, 1969
23 Stubborn beasts
24 Hospital cry
25 Enzyme ending
26 ___-Israeli relations
27 Dangerous date for Caesar
28 Ripening agent
29 Vamoosed
31 E.M.T.'s procedure
33 & 34 1996 action film sequel
37 "Rubber Soul," "Revolver" and others
38 Only so far
40 Apple or pear
43 Disavow
44 "Leave ___ Beaver"
45 Article in Arles
46 Quake locale
48 Tempestuous spirit?
49 Cage/Shue picture of 1995
52 Clapboards, e.g.
53 Locale
54 Inits. in long distance

55 Beloved of Aphrodite
56 ___ about (approximately)
57 New: Prefix
58 Least cooked
59 Politician Gingrich
60 "Don't give up!"

DOWN

1 Marks of shame
2 Backup help
3 Academic types
4 Shore dinner entree
5 Off-the-wall
6 One who shows up
7 Saved
8 Carries
9 Permeate
10 Weaver's apparatus
11 It may land in hot water
12 Hardly brainy
13 Sadat's predecessor
21 Disastrous collapse
22 Surg. areas
27 Little devils
28 Large wardrobe
30 Navigator's need
31 Supercomputer name
32 Bad sound for a balloonist
34 Actress Joan of "Rebecca"
35 Plaintiff or defendant
36 Aardvark
38 Runs to mom about

Puzzle 68 by Jeremy Thomas Paine

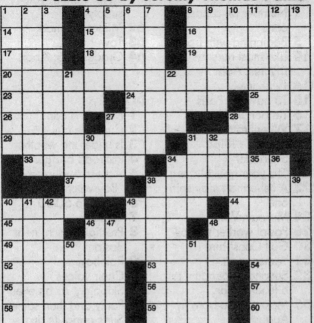

39 "Anna Karenina" author
40 Astronomical object
41 Iroquoian tribe
42 Field
43 Grooved on

46 The end
47 Dread
48 Turn aside
50 Morning glory, e.g.
51 Put away

ACROSS

1 Number on a baseball card
5 Beginning with frost
10 Like most nursery rhymes: Abbr.
14 Twosome
15 To have, in Paris
16 Timber wolf
17 Wheel rotator
18 Butcher's ship?
20 Squander
22 "To your health!," e.g.
23 A fisherman may spin one
24 Museum V.I.P.
26 Postal worker's ship?
30 Gulf Coast bird
31 Yemeni port
32 Second addendum to a letter: Abbr.
35 Most people born in August
36 Spoke wildly
38 Codger
39 Pins or penny preceder
40 Fillet of ___
41 Beta's follower
42 Manicurist's ship?
45 Summer park event
49 Boaters pull them
50 Informed (of)
51 Storm protectors
55 Highlighter's ship?
58 Pass over
59 Espies
60 Become accustomed (to)
61 Egypt's main water supply
62 Misses the mark
63 Tower of ___
64 Grades 1–6: Abbr.

DOWN

1 Meat in a can
2 Curbside call
3 Is under the weather
4 Railroad bridges
5 Actress Anderson of "Baywatch"
6 Closer to 50-50
7 Turnpike
8 Prestigious sch. near Boston
9 Rainbow
10 Choir voices
11 Skipping, as an event
12 Portly and then some
13 Sur's opposite, in México
19 Sometimes illegal auto maneuver
21 Treaty
24 Beach washer
25 Critic Rex
26 Sandwich that's been heated
27 "A Death in the Family" author
28 Multivitamin supplement
29 Get tangled
32 Magnificence
33 Fleshy fruit

Puzzle 69 by Cynthia Joy Higgins

34 Polaris, e.g.
36 Crowd sound
37 Came down
38 Crowning event
40 Show scorn
41 Braced
43 Stick (to)
44 Victory emblem
45 ___ célèbre
46 Tenant's counterpart
47 Consumerist Ralph
48 Green garnish
51 Rebuff

52 Olympic track
    champion Zatopek
53 Tick off
54 Flower holder
56 Conservative's foe:
    Abbr.
57 ___ heartbeat
    (instantly)

ACROSS

1 Skiing mecca
5 Dogs and cats, e.g.
9 Hidden room's secret opening
14 Comic Sahl
15 "Dies ___"
16 Idolize
17 Vulgarian
18 Seagoing: Abbr.
19 Have a feeling about
20 X
23 Old-time entertainer ___ Tucker
24 Morse code component
25 Quiche, e.g.
26 The Emerald Isle
28 Hairpiece
31 60's protest
34 "Time ___ My Side" (Rolling Stones hit)
35 Demonstrate
36 X
39 Music synthesizer
40 Malarial fever
41 The Phantom's instrument
42 Switch positions
43 Quaker's "you"
44 Prefix with nuptial
45 ___ Paulo, Brazil
46 Italian cheese
49 X
54 Slow mover
55 ___ Orange, N.J.
56 Hollow response
57 Pancake syrup flavor
58 Friend, to Françoise
59 Actress Perlman
60 Like some stomachs
61 Look closely
62 Burn quickly

DOWN

1 Prefix with dexterity
2 Makes off with illegally
3 TV teaser
4 Big and strong
5 Finger that curls
6 Rub out
7 Tight as a drum
8 Clockmaker Thomas
9 Die, euphemistically
10 Highly skilled
11 Forbidden thing
12 Once, once
13 Attorney F. ___ Bailey
21 Zoo beast
22 Patsy's pal on "Absolutely Fabulous"
26 In the style of: Suffix
27 Debaucher
28 Supporter of the American Revolution
29 Little bit
30 17th-century actress Nell
31 Japanese wrestling
32 Get ___ the ground floor
33 W.B.A. calls
34 "Come Back, Little Sheba" playwright
35 Naked runners

37 "Yippee!"
38 Designer Kamali
43 Writing pad
44 Baggage handler
45 "Look happy!"
46 First name in TV talk
47 Hiding spot
48 Milo or Tessie
49 Ginger cookie
50 Blabs
51 Spring
52 Renown
53 Fly like an eagle

54 Texas Mustangs, for short

ACROSS

1 Fearless
5 Nicholas I or II
9 Sears rival
14 The Buckeye State
15 Queen of Olympus
16 1960's enemy capital
17 "___ Like It Hot"
18 Completely bollix
19 Positive pole
20 "Bleak House" writer
23 C.I.A. predecessor
24 Lend a hand
25 Stick on
29 More than once around the track
31 J.F.K.'s predecessor
34 "Cheesy" Italian city
35 Germany's ___ Valley
36 Not written
37 Storyteller's embellishment
40 Win's opposite
41 Silly syllables
42 Hopping mad
43 "Aye, aye!"
44 Give up
45 Gets around
46 Halloween greeting
47 151 on a monument
48 Young ones
56 Use, as a chaise longue
57 Author Haley
58 Inventive thought
59 "Remember the ___"
60 ___-mutuel (form of betting)

61 Shooting matches?
62 Razor sharpener
63 Pitcher
64 Reply to "Are you hurt?"

DOWN

1 49-Down variety
2 Cry of anticipation
3 Peru's capital
4 Not the retiring type
5 Beat hard
6 Children's Dr.
7 Mojave-like
8 Punjabi princess
9 Military uniform
10 Like a horse or lion
11 Soon, to a poet
12 Serling and Stewart
13 Gift from Monica to Bill
21 Nearby
22 Bay of Naples isle
25 With suitability
26 Nevada skiing locale
27 Rapunzel feature
28 Rock concert necessities
29 Wood-shaping tool
30 Sounds of delight
31 Great fear
32 "The Divine Comedy" poet
33 Nobody ___ business
35 Breeder
36 Gumbo ingredient
38 Classic theater

Puzzle 71 by Elizabeth C. Gorski

39 Kind of duty
44 Like arcade games
45 Magical drink
46 Stomach soother
47 Dear, in Dijon
48 Delta deposit
49 Fall fruit
50 Stare
51 Cat's scratcher
52 Green fruit
53 Mild cheese
54 In legend, he fiddled in a fire

55 Neighbor of Alta.
56 ___Vegas

ACROSS

1 Polish border river
5 Lazy girl?
10 It's uplifting
13 Comic's missiles
14 Strangle
15 Stimpy's TV pal
16 Character created by 58-Across
18 F.D.R. measure
19 Spiral-horned sheep
20 "Ready, ___ . . . !"
21 Tiny stream
22 Employers of 58-Across
25 Greek H
26 Army cops
27 Frozen desserts
28 German spa
30 Claiborne or Smith
32 West Pointer
33 1951 film featuring 58-Across
37 Patrick of "Marat/Sade"
40 Ernie Els's org.
41 Comic DeLuise
44 Patti of opera lore
47 Under the weather
49 Caviar
51 Where 58-Across died, 1979
54 Bandy words
55 Burgle
56 Parrots, in a way
57 SST's fly over it: Abbr.
58 Memorable Big Top star born 12/9/1898

60 King of Kings
61 Drops in the letter box
62 Ciardi's "___ a Man"
63 Leandro's love
64 "I give up!"
65 So-called monster's home

DOWN

1 Surgeon's decision
2 You're working on one
3 Showed on TV again
4 Sanctuary
5 ___-fi
6 Old Polish lancer
7 Pyramid and cube
8 Like some arms
9 Society page word
10 Grilled
11 Satiated
12 Wall Street worker
16 ". . . gimble in the ___": Carroll
17 Nun's headdress
21 Decorative strip of fabric
23 "Oh, you wish!"
24 Medieval chest
29 Of a stone pillar
31 Nuke
34 "Who does he think ___!"
35 End-of-week cry
36 Xylophone tool
37 Knead
38 Converting device: Var.

Puzzle 72 by Frances Hansen

39 First name in TV talk
42 Gregg Olson and others
43 Early assembly-line cars
45 Bates of "Psycho"
46 Extremely tiny

48 Commit unalterably
50 "Duck soup"
52 Clear as ____
53 Part of a sentence, in linguistics
58 Cassowary's cousin
59 Mao ____-tung

ACROSS

1 A three-of-a-kind beats it
5 Glided
9 Stun
14 Too
15 Newsweek rival
16 Poorer, as excuses go
17 Formal dance
18 Give off
19 Trim limbs
20 Something of trivial importance
23 "My Cousin Vinny" Oscar winner Marisa
24 Televise
25 Bad ___ (German spa)
28 Alcott classic
33 Spawning fish
37 Buck's mate
38 Michelangelo statue
39 Achingly desire
41 "The Mary Tyler Moore Show" co-star
43 Make amends
44 Muhammad ___
45 To be, in Toulouse
46 Don Ho's theme song
50 Porker's pad
51 Actress Zadora
52 "The Lion King" lion
57 Windmill setting
62 Think out loud
64 ___-American relations
65 Inter ___
66 String bean's opposite
67 Oklahoma city
68 Huge
69 Test, as a garment
70 Certain NCO's
71 Gaelic

DOWN

1 Big name in brewing
2 "Remember the ___"
3 44-Across's faith
4 Esther of TV's "Good Times"
5 Part of a process
6 Prom night transport
7 Ape
8 Particular
9 Brand for Bowser
10 Stallion's mate
11 Kind of park
12 Buddhist state
13 Before, in poetry
21 Diamond ___
22 Three, in Torino
26 Poet's constraint
27 Entrap
29 Bride's words
30 High craggy hill
31 Depression-era program: Abbr.
32 River to the Seine
33 Tiffs
34 Bandleader's cry
35 Fame's opposite
36 When said three times, a liar's policy
40 Jan. follower
41 Pipe bend
42 Go out, as a flame
44 Letting up

Puzzle 73 by Randy Sowell

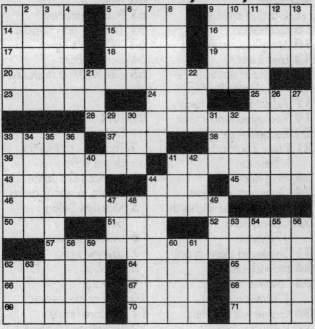

47 Wire service inits.
48 Slants
49 Opposite NNW
53 "___ at the office"
54 Back tooth
55 Ecstasy
56 ___ worse than death

58 Not ___ many words
59 Sign gas
60 Measuring standard
61 Axles
62 Many a time
63 Golfer's goal

ACROSS

1 Garden crasher
5 Gather up
10 Mary ___ cosmetics
13 Less inept
15 Futuristic slave
16 "___ Gotta Be Me"
17 Addition to the family
19 Replayed tennis shot
20 Recent hires
21 New Zealand tribesman
23 Hog heaven?
24 Ques. counterpart
25 Rolling Stone Richards
27 Colloquialism for 17-Across
31 Shattered pane piece
34 Individuals
35 "Blame It on ___" (Caine comedy)
36 Game with mallets
37 Religious law
39 "___ never fly!"
40 "Sure thing, skipper!"
41 German car
42 Disconcerted
43 Colloquialism for 17-Across
47 Fool (around)
48 Jerusalem is its cap.
49 Quiz
52 Crockett's last stand
54 Poshness
56 Square dance partner
57 Colloquialism for 17-Across
60 Adam's madam
61 Public persona
62 Ten ___ (long odds)
63 When it's light
64 Behind bars
65 Like many a mistake

DOWN

1 Desires
2 Thumbs up/thumbs down critic
3 Broncos QB John
4 Figure skater Thomas
5 Marshal Dillon's portrayer
6 Unruly crowds
7 Lawyer's org.
8 Blubber
9 Thwarts
10 Unit of frequency
11 Declare firmly
12 Himalayan legend
14 George's predecessor
18 Russo of "Get Shorty"
22 Versatile transport, for short
25 Bingo relative
26 Utopia
27 Sis's sib
28 Kind of boom
29 Aswan Dam locale
30 Narrated
31 Bickering
32 Boxer Oscar De La ___
33 "Roots" writer

Puzzle 74 by Patrick Jordan

37 Cows' mouthfuls
38 Together, in music
39 Author Fleming
41 Like some exercises
42 Drew a blank
44 ___ Perignon
45 Worked the soil
46 "Gotcha"
49 Pear variety

50 Teatime treat
51 Tensed, with "up"
52 Not young
53 Volcanic flow
54 Cutting part
55 Get an ___ effort
58 Actress Thurman
59 Broken-down
     47-Across

ACROSS

1 Long story
5 Rich kid in "Nancy"
10 Panhandles
14 Shangri-la
15 Hoopster Shaquille
16 One of the Four Corners states
17 Penny purchase, years ago
19 "Ali ___ and the Forty Thieves"
20 "A" or "an"
21 Incomprehensible, as a message
23 Parasite
24 Business bigwig
25 Miss Kett of old comics
28 Liveliness
32 Custard dessert
36 "Horrors!"
38 Rocket stage
39 Gofer
40 Jelly fruit
42 E pluribus ___
43 Throng
45 Seize with a toothpick
46 Forest growth
47 Mortarboard attachment
49 Actress Lanchester
51 Grand jury's activity
53 Pueblo site
58 Jack of "City Slickers"
61 One making a medical inquiry
63 On

64 Penny purchase, years ago
66 Fish entree
67 Treasure store
68 "This round's ___!"
69 Bridge whiz Sharif
70 Gung-ho
71 Poverty

DOWN

1 Flower part
2 Be wild about
3 "Beau ___"
4 Shenanigan
5 Paper towel unit
6 "Going ___, going . . ."
7 Meadow
8 Slow, in music
9 Opposite of youth
10 Penny purchase, years ago
11 Catchall abbr.
12 Kotter of "Welcome Back, Kotter"
13 Certain herring
18 Pain
22 ___ fever (be hot)
24 Endangered Florida creature
26 Dress (up)
27 Therefore
29 Snap-marriage locale
30 Wildebeests
31 Thanksgiving side dish
32 Almanac tidbit
33 Money in Milano

Puzzle 75 by Fred Piscop

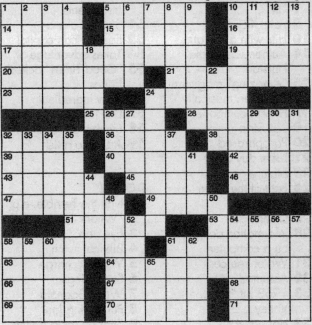

34 Fusses
35 Penny purchase, years ago
37 Model train layout, often
41 Not present: Abbr.
44 Gosh-awful
48 Pinpoint
50 Realtor's unit
52 Quotable catcher Yogi
54 Access the Net
55 Cockamamie
56 ___ fatale

57 No longer a slave
58 El ___, Tex.
59 Elementary particle
60 "Damn Yankees" vamp
61 Cro-Magnon's home
62 Frankfurt's river
65 Machine tooth

ACROSS

1 "In"
5 Faint flicker
10 Hits with a ray gun
14 Author ___ Neale Hurston
15 "Amazing" magician
16 Together, musically
17 Protein components
19 ___ Strip
20 Paraphrased
21 Latter-day Saint
23 Nature goddess
24 Fruit of the Loom competitor
25 Openings
28 Information accessed on a computer
31 Water sources
32 Assumed
33 1968 hit "Harper Valley ___"
34 Hangover?
35 Roebuck's partner
36 Mimic
37 Ryan's "Love Story" co-star
38 Observe Yom Kippur
39 Speck of land in the sea
40 Deserter
42 Coat of many colors wearer
43 Coeur d'___, Idaho
44 "Stand By Me" singer ___ King
45 Beefed
47 Xylophone-like instruments
51 Singer Falana
52 East African capital
54 Takes advantage of
55 "Good Times" actress Esther
56 Stew ingredient
57 Deli jarful
58 Symbol of freshness
59 Art Deco artist

DOWN

1 Ivan the Terrible, e.g.
2 "Where the heart is"
3 Eye part
4 Biblical hymn
5 Without charge
6 Shoestrings
7 Writer Bagnold
8 Put a wing (on)
9 Slips up, as a dating service
10 Croatian capital
11 It might bob up in conversation
12 "The Godfather" author
13 Penn name
18 Filling stations?
22 "Chestnuts roasting ___ open fire"
24 Le ___, France
25 Take an oath
26 Positive thinking proponent

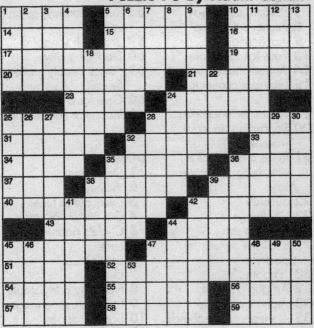

27 American Dance
    Theater founder
28 Steak ___
29 Pricey
30 Our planet
32 Crystal rock
35 Run of the mill
36 Come together
38 Pulitzer-winning writer
    James
39 Ancient part of Asia
    Minor
41 Rio Grande city

42 It's across the Hudson
    from New York
44 Jumps (out)
45 Dejected
46 Sub ___ (secretly)
47 1551, in monuments
48 1930's heavyweight
    champ Max
49 Aid in crime
50 Sushi bar drink
53 ___180 (turn around,
    in slang)

ACROSS

1 Pinkish, as a steak
5 Pitcher's boo-boo
9 Applications
13 Face-to-face exam
14 Annual theater award
15 Leg/foot connector
16 TIM
19 Airline to Stockholm
20 Regarding, in legal memos
21 Ruins a picnic or a Little League game, say
22 Subsidy
23 Challenge
24 Sheriff's star
27 It follows sunset, in poetry
28 "Phooey!"
32 Art photo shade
33 Alpha's opposite
35 A shepherd shepherds it
36 ERIC
39 Honest ___
40 ___ Ababa
41 Make pretty
42 Lipton and Twinings, e.g.
44 Actor Kilmer
45 Hearty steak
46 France's ___ des Saintes
48 ___ chi ch'uan
49 Give a damn?
51 Nuts (over)
52 By way of

55 OK
58 Runs smoothly, as an engine
59 Brownish songbird
60 Start for a kitty
61 "Black Beauty" author Sewell
62 Give for a while
63 Happy or sad feeling

DOWN

1 Steals from
2 Vicinity
3 Lively piano tunes
4 Gin maker Whitney
5 Clyde's partner in crime
6 Eat like ___
7 Queue
8 Fraternity party staple
9 Loose, as shoestrings
10 Body wrapper
11 "Desire Under the ___"
12 Notice
15 At a distance
17 Big honeymoon destination
18 Syracuse's team color
23 Considers
24 Deep-sea explorer William
25 Sleeper's woe
26 Dah's partner
27 90's-style letters
29 Scouting mission, informally
30 In the know

Puzzle 77 by Adam G. Perl

31 Where Memphis is: Abbr.
32 Improvise, musically
33 ___ Methuselah
34 The Black Stallion, e.g.
37 Adjective modifier
38 Bride's declaration
43 ___ Madres
45 Remnant
47 Puts (down)
48 Spoken for
49 Flabbergast
50 Frayed

51 Pierce with a tusk
52 Chianti, e.g.
53 Division word
54 Elderly
55 Health resort
56 Mouse catcher
57 Hydroelectric project

ACROSS

1 Shells, for short
5 "Not on ___!"
9 Mark left by Zorro?
13 Instrument for an étude
15 Pre-stereo
16 Dramatic entrance announcement
17 Blooper
18 Verve
19 Hertz rival
20 Little guy getting the third degree?
23 Wee, to Burns
25 "Gosh!"
26 Kind of crew
27 Neatly combed curmudgeon?
31 Hunter in the night sky
32 Lamp type
36 Filmmaker Jacques
37 Lesley of "60 Minutes"
39 ___ Penh, Cambodia
41 Ropes, as a dogie
43 Cartoon "Mr."
44 Gambling locale for the taciturn?
47 French dramatist Antonin ___
51 Sounds from Santa
52 Fishing aid
53 Bright-red unglazed china?
57 They may clash in business
58 Shower
59 Addicts
62 Letter for Gandalf
63 Tied
64 Sign up
65 Caddie's bagful
66 Withhold, as funds
67 Concerning

DOWN

1 Mimic
2 Russian space station
3 Tequila drink
4 ___ about (circa)
5 Sauntered
6 Word with crashing or tidal
7 Sir Geraint's wife
8 Like Cinderella's slipper, to her stepsisters
9 Jump involuntarily
10 Quibble
11 ". . . can you spare ___?"
12 Grating
14 Beginning
21 Jeans brand
22 Tramp
23 Robert Burns, for one
24 Subway artwork
28 Louis-Philippe and others
29 Gulf
30 "Yay, team!"
33 3.7 and 4.0, e.g.
34 Train V.I.P.'s
35 Nary a soul
37 Fused
38 4:00 gathering

Puzzle 78 by Susan Harrington Smith

40 No longer worth discussing
42 Hare's tail
43 Poe's "The ___ of the Red Death"
45 Climb, in a way
46 Fortune 500 listings: Abbr.
47 On the qui vive
48 Scamp
49 Dinner leftover for Bowser
50 Donkeys

54 Carry on
55 "Très ___!"
56 Annapolis sch.
60 Twaddle
61 ___-pitch softball

ACROSS

1 Thumb-twiddling
5 Leapfrogs
10 ___ Bator, Mongolia
14 Make airtight
15 ___ a time (singly)
16 "Cleopatra" backdrop
17 "Yes!"
19 Darling
20 Sendak's "Where the Wild Things ___"
21 Composer Satie
22 Soviet leader Brezhnev
24 Semiautomatic rifle
26 Land of the llama
27 Red-white-and-blue inits.
28 Information bank
32 Passing notice?
35 King of the jungle
37 What a lumberjack leaves behind
38 River to the Rio Grande
40 SSW's opposite
41 Like a haunted house
42 Skyward
43 Persian ___
45 Person to go out with
46 Round Table knight
48 C.I.O.'s partner
50 Skip
51 "Don't move!"
55 Snake-haired woman of myth
58 35-Across's sound
59 ___ de France
60 Walkie-talkie word
61 "Yes!"
64 Needles' partner
65 Train making all stops
66 Med school subj.
67 Otherwise
68 Manicurist's board
69 Optimistic

DOWN

1 Writer Asimov
2 Actress Winger
3 Tattoo remover
4 "Xanadu" rock grp.
5 Diary
6 Loosen, as a knot
7 Overly docile
8 Chum
9 Sharp-pointed instrument
10 "Yes!"
11 Mortgage
12 Jai ___
13 Uncool one
18 Arrival gifts in Honolulu
23 Remove, as marks
25 "Yes!"
26 See 51-Down
28 Coffee break snack
29 Glow
30 Slugged, old-style
31 Sportsman's blade
32 October's birthstone
33 Composer Bartók
34 PC picture
36 Fort Knox unit
39 Cherries' leftovers

Puzzle 79 by Gregory E. Paul

44 So as to cause death
47 Apt
49 Raise crops
51 With 26-Down, a rooftop energy device
52 Elton John's instrument
53 Arm bones
54 Not handling criticism well
55 Brood
56 Like Darth Vader
57 Cub Scout groups
58 Derby

62 ___ Kippur
63 Something to lend or bend

ACROSS

1 Auntie, dramatically
5 "La Classe de danse" artist
10 Birds in barns
14 Quizmaster Trebek
15 Humble
16 Cookie since 1912
17 Asset for 34-Across?
20 Bee activity
21 Classical lyric poet
22 Creative work
23 Book after Nehemiah: Abbr.
24 Sites of crosses
27 Meadow sounds
28 ___ Na Na
31 No longer on the plate
32 Doughnut shapes
33 Extent
34 Circus act
37 Place for a revival
38 Kind of desk
39 Flowerless plants
40 Before, in poetry
41 Rules out
42 Not yet sunk
43 Common hello or goodbye
44 Habeas corpus, for one
45 Spicy cuisine
48 Takes advance orders for
52 Liability for 34-Across?
54 The Urals are west of it
55 Dinner bird
56 Witty Bombeck

57 Put salt on, maybe
58 Bridge positions
59 Time of decision

DOWN

1 Handy computers
2 "There oughta be ___!"
3 Southwest sight
4 Glad-handing type
5 Father of Xerxes
6 Dark shades
7 Thieves' group
8 Numbskull
9 Leaves the dock
10 Zing
11 Saran, e.g.
12 Preyer
13 London or New York district
18 Be about to happen
19 Feedbag feed
23 Jumping the gun
24 Romantic adventure
25 More cold and wet
26 Agreeing (with)
27 Marina sights
28 Veep Agnew
29 ___-Barbera (big name in cartoons)
30 Feeling of apprehension
32 Coil
33 Took the heat badly
35 Search like wolves
36 Aloof
41 Island near Java

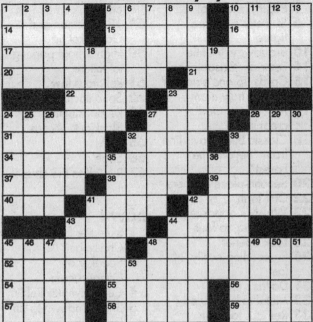

42 Rugged ridges
43 Actor Tom of "The Dukes of Hazzard"
44 Extract by force
45 Symbol of noncommunication
46 Trick
47 Oscar winner Jannings
48 Light: Prefix
49 Byron or Tennyson
50 Tibetan monk
51 Corset part
53 ___ fault (overly so)

ACROSS

1 Begin, as school
6 St. Peter's Square figure
10 Broadway "Auntie"
14 Peter of "Casablanca"
15 Cards up one's sleeve?
16 Muslim holy man
17 Any one of God's creatures
18 Classic Bette Davis line from "Beyond the Forest"
20 Second-place finishers
22 Call forth
23 WNW's opposite
24 DiCaprio, to fans
25 Lock opener
26 Proceeding easily, at last
31 Dallas's locale
32 Metal to be refined
33 Res ___ loquitur
37 Tempers
38 Flogged
40 Underground vegetable
41 Miss America wears one
42 ___ de Janeiro
43 Word on mail from Spain
44 Oscar-winning role for Tom Hanks
47 Greyhound, e.g.
50 Slalom curve
51 It's perpendicular to long.
52 Golden Delicious and others
54 1966 Simon and Garfunkel hit
59 High school parking lot fixture
61 Religious law
62 Soho socials
63 Responsibility
64 Blackjack phrase
65 Flubs
66 Sage
67 Run off to the chapel

DOWN

1 Exile site for Napoleon
2 Christmas
3 Speaker of Cooperstown
4 Cube inventor Rubik
5 Brief turndown to an invitation
6 Oklahoma Indian
7 Newspaperman Adolph
8 Stew morsel
9 Highly regarded
10 Skirt style
11 Frenzied: Var.
12 Mrs. Eisenhower
13 Running on ___
19 Not straight
21 Fire remnant
24 Tackle box item
26 Mayberry jail habitué
27 Actress Miles

Puzzle 81 by Randall J. Hartman

28 Alimony receivers
29 Poison ivy woe
30 Courtroom addressee, with "your"
33 "___ to differ!"
34 Lima's land
35 Appear
36 Surmounting
38 Medieval weapon
39 Broadcasts
43 Diplomat's aide
44 Corn, to chickens
45 Run out

46 Uncle ___
47 Sew with loose stitches
48 Certain berth
49 Weapon that's thrown
53 More or ___
54 Radio man Don
55 Train track
56 Word after catch or hang
57 Free ticket
58 Bouncing baby's seat
60 Single: Prefix

ACROSS

1 Nabisco cracker
5 Respond to seeing red?
9 Central highway
14 Brainstorm
15 Not taped
16 Former
17 Summon Warsaw citizens?
19 Hint of color
20 Opposite of masc.
21 F.B.I. workers
23 The I's have them
24 Mileage testing grp.
25 Undercover operation
27 Small change for a Brit
32 Unimagined
35 Broadcast studio sign
36 Any hit by Elvis
38 Hubbub
39 Artificial locks
40 Summon the elected?
42 Hit on the knuckles
43 Sorbonne summer
44 Bottle capacity
45 Common nest locale
47 Fine point
49 Under pressure
51 ___ Nile
53 Opponent of D.D.E.
54 Songstress Vikki
56 Dressed, so to speak
59 Trendy
62 Talk a blue streak
64 Summon actress Sharon?

66 ___ football (indoor sport)
67 Cartoonist Peter
68 "A Clockwork Orange" hooligan
69 Cattail's locale
70 Made a bubble, in a way
71 Crème de la crème

DOWN

1 Jazz phrase
2 Goofing off
3 Broncos or Chargers
4 Veer suddenly
5 Campaign ad feature
6 Scrabble piece
7 Broiling locale
8 Pains in the neck
9 To the point
10 The East
11 Summon Michael Jordan and John Stockton?
12 Take-out words
13 War god
18 Office fastener
22 Gravy spot
24 Prefix with center
26 Glaciers
27 Like illegally parked cars, sometimes
28 Get together
29 Summon a cable magnate?
30 Derby prospect

Puzzle 82 by Nancy Salomon

31 French fashion magazines
33 "Waste not, want not," e.g.
34 Ran
37 Malicious gossip
41 Was bedbound
46 Snaky letter
48 Chefs' wear
50 Was almost out of inventory
52 Get-well site
54 Study late

55 Ambiance
57 Baseball's Yastrzemski
58 German article
59 Links target
60 Washington bills
61 Student's book
63 "No dice"
65 Bill

ACROSS

1 Playwright William
5 Some Pennsylvania Dutch
10 Carol
14 That, in France
15 Division of a long poem
16 Hard rain?
17 Best Picture of 1995
19 Tex. neighbor
20 Car that was always black
21 Catch red-handed
22 Swerve
23 Arctic bird
25 Goalie's job
27 Bed turner?
31 ___ and anon
32 "I didn't know that!"
33 Appliquéd
38 Enticed
40 Crow's cry
42 Barber's work
43 ___ of Capricorn
45 Brit. fliers
47 Roman road
48 "Cracklin' Rosie" singer
51 "Shane," e.g.
55 "Last one ___ a rotten egg!"
56 Robust
57 Much of 35-Down's terr.
59 Melodious
63 With defects and all

64 Group that makes contracts
66 Fasting time
67 Drive away
68 "The African Queen" screenwriter James
69 Organization with a lodge
70 One of the Astaires
71 Slothful

DOWN

1 Part of a nuclear arsenal, for short
2 Fiddling emperor
3 Pleased
4 Listen in (on)
5 German warning
6 Fannie ___ security
7 ___ instant (quickly)
8 Italian road
9 Centers of activity
10 Push
11 Like some old buckets
12 Frasier's brother on "Frasier"
13 Harsh reflection
18 Actress Sommer
24 "Hold on ___!"
26 Payments to doctors
27 Moola
28 Assert
29 Fix up
30 Oyster's center
34 Capricious
35 Org. formed to contain Communism

Puzzle 83 by Frederick T. Buhler

36 Bread chamber
37 One who's socially clueless
39 Prime-time hour
41 Desert stream
44 Parts of brains
46 Wangle
49 Accustomed
50 Suffix with million
51 Humpback, e.g.
52 Stand for something
53 Go furtively

54 They may come in a battery
58 Ready to be picked
60 Korbut on the beam
61 Egyptian canal
62 Mind
65 The first of 13: Abbr.

ACROSS

1 Penniless
6 Frank of the Mothers of Invention
11 Pharmaceuticals overseer, for short
14 Whose 1961 record Mark McGwire beat
15 Hägar the Horrible's dog
16 ___ Lingus
17 Part 1 of a song parody
19 ___ tai
20 Funny old guy
21 Bog
22 Hilarious jokes
25 Book after Job
27 "Put a lid ___!"
28 Song parody, part 2
31 Cuban coins
33 "I don't believe it!"
34 Song parody, part 3
40 Tiny bit
41 Tartish plums
43 Song parody, part 4
48 Spy's secret
49 Kvetch
50 Stalemate
52 Pleasant tune
53 Clean the hands before dinner
55 A Gardner
56 End of the song parody
61 Singer Shannon
62 Jack of "The Great Dictator"
63 It's positively electric
64 Time in history
65 Stimulates
66 Attach a patch

DOWN

1 Maker of the 5-Series
2 "Yay!"
3 Dig it
4 Jamaica's capital
5 "Terminal Bliss" actress Chandler
6 A Gabor
7 Upfront amount
8 Equal
9 Start with school
10 Pac.'s counterpart
11 Zoological classification
12 "Stars above!"
13 Bold, impatient type, astrologically
18 Ginseng, e.g.
21 West of Hollywood
22 Republican
23 Once more
24 Enthusiastic reply in Mexico
25 Gasp
26 Snooty types
29 Attire at fraternity blasts
30 "Be still!"
32 Burlesque bits
35 After-bath cover
36 Resident: Suffix

Puzzle 84 by Kelly Clark

37 1931 convictee
38 Talks amorously
39 Shoes introduced by the United States Rubber Co.
42 Match in poker
43 Golf club
44 "How luxurious!"
45 Screwball
46 Snake sounds
47 Jewish youth org.
49 Forest clearing
51 Big cats

53 Boat follower
54 Arguing
56 Pull along
57 "That'll show 'em!"
58 It's one thing after another
59 Stir
60 Hankering

ACROSS

1 Entr' ___ (theater break)
5 Word repeated before "pants on fire"
9 Turns from ice to water
14 Daily delivery
15 Press for
16 Best
17 Italian wine province
18 Ring-tailed critter
19 Pause for a rest
20 Permanent military procedures
23 Lady of Lima
24 "___ geht's?" ("How goes it?"): Ger.
25 Plumbing convenience
32 Flower starter
35 They wrap their food well
36 Intake problem?
37 Part of a list
39 Coal box
41 Not a permanent employee
42 Reversible fabric
45 Wordsmith Webster
48 Wrestling site
49 Wishers' object
52 Chicken ___ king
53 Park features
57 Tree-to-tree traveler
62 Unearthly
63 Zap
64 "Othello" villain
65 Beatrice's adorer
66 Toward shelter
67 Threaded metal fastener
68 Recording sign
69 Fling
70 Puppy cries

DOWN

1 Pile up
2 Hindu social division
3 Giant
4 Romance novelist ___ Glyn
5 Tenor Pavarotti
6 Vitamin tablet supplement
7 Highly excited
8 Celebrity
9 Funguses
10 90's singer Brickell
11 Unpleasant look
12 Day planner features
13 Foxy
21 Clobber
22 Latvia's capital
26 Collar
27 Gershwin's "Of Thee ___"
28 Big inits. in long distance
29 Not us
30 Oscar winner ___ Thompson
31 Deeply absorbed
32 Auction actions
33 Orrin Hatch's state
34 It's just for show

Puzzle 85 by Fran and Lou Sabin

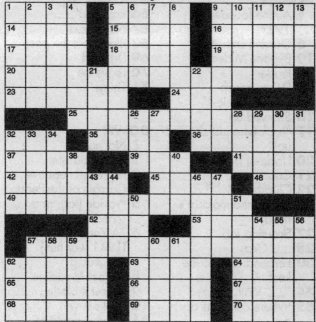

38 Longtime Chinese leader
40 Rebuffs
43 Dye worker
44 Brick oven
46 Puts into harmony
47 Mata ___
50 Pesters
51 Blue moon, e.g.
54 Teheran native
55 Slight advantage, so to speak
56 Atlantic City machines

57 Sweetened custard
58 Director Wertmüller
59 Abominable Snowman
60 D-Day invasion town
61 Opposite of an ans.
62 Ruckus

ACROSS

1 Airline founded in 1927
6 Garden smoother
10 Bygone Mideast leader
14 D-Day beach
15 "Make it quick!"
16 Showed up
17 "Look who just showed up!"
20 Uncle of rice fame
21 Court game
22 Cluckhead
25 Marooned motorist's need
27 Scouting job
28 ___ Gras
30 Perpendicular to the keel
34 "___ With a View"
35 Where cold cuts are cut
36 "This ___ fair!"
40 Popular basketball shoe
43 Midleg point
44 Rudely abrupt
45 Escape detection of
46 Expire
47 Eagle's home
48 Pitcher Hideo Nomo's birthplace
52 Popular oil additive
54 "Spy vs. Spy" magazine
55 Intern in the news
59 Spooky sighting
61 Rutgers, e.g.
66 Raison d'___
67 Numbskull
68 Blast from the past
69 Drifts off
70 Leave be
71 Thugs

DOWN

1 Not neg.
2 Sound booster
3 Highland negative
4 Captain of the Pequod
5 Provide (for), in a schedule
6 "A Yank in the ___" (1941 war film)
7 Regarding
8 Actress Madeline
9 Fencer's blade
10 Public row
11 Ruinous damage
12 Protein building block
13 Her face launched a thousand ships
18 Lennon's lady
19 Quad building
22 Impact sound
23 Baseball's Hank
24 Lying facedown
26 Crumples into a tiny ball
29 Peacenik
31 A round at the tavern, say
32 Delights
33 Do poorly

Puzzle 86 by Brendan Emmett Quigley

36 Castaway's spot
37 ___ und Drang
38 Gymnast Comaneci
39 In a corner
41 Company with a dog in its logo
42 Quaint children's game
46 Shady route
48 Sportscaster Merlin
49 Brawl
50 O. Henry, in the literary world
51 Toys with tails
53 Wed. preceder
56 Brewski
57 Shoelace problem
58 Cry of pain
60 1993 peace accord city
62 November honoree
63 Joining words
64 Food container
65 "Right"

ACROSS

1 "Damn Yankees" seductress
5 Thick piece
9 Where Rome is home
14 Frosted
15 Jay who chins with guests
16 Wanderer
17 Not much
18 Say positively
19 Brawls
20 Company with high personnel turnover
23 Dictation taker
24 "New Look" designer
25 Sweet potato
28 Graceful bird
31 Winnie-the-Pooh's creator
33 Lawyer: Abbr.
36 Regret
38 Mystery writer Gardner et al.
39 Eastern dancer
44 Bicker
45 Umpire's call
46 Home for Babe
47 Show, as a historic battle
50 Stands in the way of
53 Always, to a verse writer
54 Verse writer
56 Partner of pains
60 Yarn-making device

64 Pageant winner
66 Something the nose knows
67 Chorus syllables
68 Lovers' lane event
69 Popular sauce
70 Lacking bumps
71 Take care of
72 Messy dresser
73 Sprightly

DOWN

1 Whopper tellers
2 Eight-man band
3 "Get out!"
4 Extensions
5 Pole, e.g.
6 ___ Strauss & Co.
7 Put ___ to (finish)
8 Infamous Italian family name
9 Tattletale
10 Bullfight bull
11 Lilylike flower
12 Song played on a mandolin
13 Football gains: Abbr.
21 Daily temperature extreme
22 ___ good turn
26 "___ of robins in her hair"
27 Having an open weave
29 Jackie's second

Puzzle 87 by Dorothy Smitonick

30 Convent dweller
32 TV personality Kupcinet
33 Not in a fog
34 Perpetual time on the clock at Independence Hall
35 Ornamental stone
37 "I" problem
40 Operate
41 Enter full force
42 Nickname
43 Guesstimate letters

48 Jailbird
49 Pavarotti and Domingo
51 Green
52 Lug
55 Kind of wave
57 Throw
58 Specialist in fishing
59 Viewpoint
61 Botherer
62 Failed attempt
63 Chow
64 Parts of gals.
65 Suffix with press

ACROSS

1 Con game
5 Given an R or PG
10 60's do
14 Standard
15 Elicit
16 It may be entered in a court
17 Request for artist Georgia's forbearance?
20 ___ Tin Tin
21 Enticed
22 Washing jobs
23 They're apt to get into hot water
25 Sweetie
26 1952 and '56 campaign name
27 Grand
32 Like ___ out of hell
35 Drives off
36 Of the congregation
37 Mexico City portrait painter?
41 Behave
42 Western "necktie"
43 Revival meeting cry
44 Deficiency
46 Pale
48 OPEC export
49 Filled in
53 "Beat it!"
56 Plait
58 Eggs
59 "Georges paints as he pleases"?

62 Exploit
63 Appropriate
64 Marquis de ___
65 Recipe amts.
66 Schnozzes
67 Ogled

DOWN

1 [Hmmph!]
2 Newswoman Roberts
3 Scene of the action
4 Lady de la maison: Abbr.
5 Sanctuary
6 Swears
7 Heavy reading
8 ___ out a living (scraped by)
9 Org. involved in raids
10 Blacksmiths' wear
11 Kind of market
12 Study
13 Slow-growing trees
18 Antiaircraft fire
19 It may be worn under a sweater
24 Bridle parts
25 Catcall
27 Them there
28 Sharpen
29 Astringent
30 Specify
31 Actress Cannon
32 Epiphanies
33 "Art of the Fugue" composer

Puzzle 88 by Norma Steinberg

34 Choir part
35 Air apparent?
38 Punctual
39 Farm delivery
40 Author Grey
45 Lies in the summer sun
46 Places for watches
47 Adjutant
49 Shower
50 Incursion
51 Skirt
52 Saw
53 Room meas.

54 They're waited for at a theater
55 Glean
56 Vivacity
57 Tatters
60 Ashes holder
61 "___ as directed"

ACROSS

1 England's ___ Downs
6 Secluded vale
10 German philosopher Immanuel
14 Summa cum ___
15 Lifesaver, say
16 Hand cream ingredient
17 Tootsie
19 One of Columbus's ships
20 Implore
21 Pathetically inept person
23 Baptism, e.g.
25 Places for camels to drink
26 Two quarters
30 Kick-around shoes
33 Florida city
35 Sellout shows, for short
36 Building wing
39 Occasion for roses
43 Suffix with Canton
44 Country way
45 Sign by a free sample
46 Bullfighters
49 Nile vipers
50 Underway
53 March tourney sponsor
55 Way of thinking
58 Compel obedience to
63 Inter ___
64 Love note
66 Space on a schedule
67 Margarine
68 Delivery person's path
69 "Auld Lang ___"
70 Insect's home
71 Comic Johnson and others

DOWN

1 Otherwise
2 One on the way to a promotion?
3 Bird feeder food
4 River to the Baltic
5 Olympics measure
6 Area needing urban renewal
7 Meadow
8 Misses the mark
9 ___ care in the world
10 Topeka's home
11 Spy's name, possibly
12 Time being
13 Shipbuilding woods
18 Salute with enthusiasm
22 English county known for sheep
24 "We earn our wings every day" airline
26 Fire truck attachment
27 Book after John
28 Wash
29 Neighbor of Ga.
31 Thurs. follower
32 Long, long time
34 Apportions
36 Ice cream brand
37 Den light
38 Caustic materials

Puzzle 89 by Sidney L. Robbins

40 Order of corn
41 SSW's opposite
42 Mme., in Spain
46 Until now
47 Cousin of a leopard
48 Playing with a full deck
50 Stockpile
51 Colt's counterpart
52 Burger topper

54 Media workers' union
56 Black
57 Easy-to-clean floor
59 Scent
60 Win in a runaway
61 Baby-faced
62 Partners who called it quits
65 "___ Misérables"

ACROSS

1 Does a standard dog trick
5 Flock members
9 Actor Cary of "Twister"
14 To be, in Toulon
15 Ernie's "Sesame Street" pal
16 ___-lance (pit viper)
17 Kind of instrument
18 The "B" of N.B.
19 Nourishes
20 Country club employees
23 Ink for une plume
24 Sulky state
25 Lao-___
28 Originally named
29 Coral formation
33 Long John Silver, e.g.
35 Ironed
37 ___-majesté
38 Col. Klink player on "Hogan's Heroes"
43 Certain util.
44 Channel swimmer Gertrude
45 Remove the pits from
48 Capt. Hook's companion
49 Martians, e.g.
52 Glimpse
53 Animal doc
55 Assail
57 Peppermint liqueur
62 Hinder
64 Actress Campbell
65 "God shed His grace on ___"
66 News subject
67 Large number
68 Projector load
69 Gives up
70 They're seven positions after this theme
71 Scots Gaelic

DOWN

1 "Murphy Brown" star
2 Timeless, to a poet
3 Where Zeus was worshiped
4 Passover meal
5 Recedes
6 Time span
7 Sea eagle
8 Brew
9 Decadent
10 Playboy's gaze
11 Hulk Hogan, for one
12 Hall-of-Famer Roush
13 His or her, in France
21 Audacity
22 Energy
26 Late ruler Mobotu ___ Seko
27 River through Bavaria
30 Poetic contraction
31 Three-time speed skating gold medalist Karin
32 Circus impresario Irvin and others
34 Mirth

Puzzle 90 by Janet R. Bender

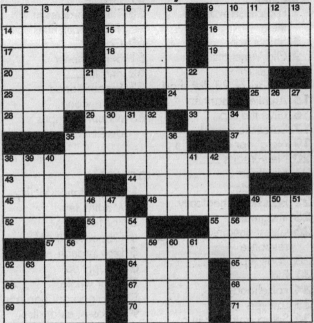

35 Suffix with exist
36 Consider
38 Joins in holy matrimony
39 Gen. Robt. ___
40 Completely excised, in surgery
41 G.I. chow in Desert Storm
42 Military academy freshman
46 Turns inside out
47 Rep. foe

49 Book after Nehemiah
50 Giggles
51 TV's "Remington ___"
54 High-strung
56 ___ nous
58 Actress Russo
59 Place for a farmer?
60 Daredevil Knievel
61 British stables
62 Jan. preceder
63 Night before

ACROSS

1 Pedicurists work on them
5 Ship's front
9 Old Venetian magistrates
14 Cutlass or 98, for short
15 Architect Saarinen
16 Give the slip
17 Sarcastic remark
19 Neighbor of Nigeria
20 New Year's ___
21 Mystique
22 Devastated
23 Backslide, medically
25 Imagination
26 Questionnaire response
28 Soak (up)
31 Bid
34 Falsehoods
35 Lawyers' org.
36 Select a winner in a sweepstakes
37 Base before home
39 Person whose name begins "Mc-," often
40 ___ Moines
41 Elvis's middle name
42 "Land ___!"
43 Word between ready and go
44 Hike
47 Pickup, e.g.
49 Stockpiled
53 Equality
55 Epithet
56 Actor Wallach
57 Precise
58 Title character in 1970's cult films
60 Corner
61 Skin softener
62 End in ___
63 Propositioned
64 Civil wrong
65 Mount Olympus dwellers

DOWN

1 Radio station facility
2 Martini item
3 Ford flop
4 Opposite NNW
5 Leaf through
6 Brought up
7 Killer whale
8 Moo goo gai pan pan
9 Exposes, as a false claim
10 Kind of acid
11 Grain holder on a farm
12 Chanteuse Adams
13 Dispatch
18 Prank
22 Competed at Daytona
24 Not many
25 Blond
27 Go on and off, as a light
29 Hand-held musical instrument
30 Butter servings

Puzzle 91 by Randall J. Hartman

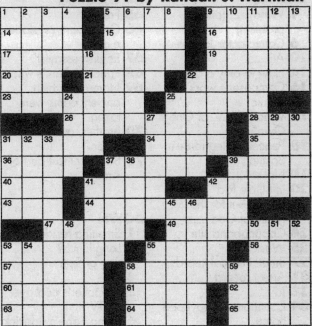

31 "What are the ___ . . . ?"
32 Gratis
33 Accelerated path to success
37 "Dick ___"
38 Leave at a pawnshop
39 ___ Fifth Avenue
41 Bordered on
42 Creepy
45 Whiteness
46 Lucky charm
48 Nouveau ___

50 Old defense pact
51 Spanish hero played on film by Charlton Heston
52 Dutch sights
53 Ex-Secretary Federico
54 Allies' foe
55 Farm building
58 Stand at the plate
59 Binge

ACROSS

1 Wind ___ (pilot's problem)
6 Comic actor Jacques
10 Ali ___
14 How to play a dirge
15 Composer's work
16 Mimic
17 Woolf's "___ of One's Own"
18 Peacekeeping force in Bosnia
19 Not strict
20 Infallible fact
23 "There but for the grace of God ___"
24 Copacabana site
25 Westerns
27 Small tropical lizards
31 Arrest record
33 Jai ___
34 Eisenhower's boyhood home
36 Biblical sin city
38 Klutz
39 Woods on the fairway
43 Paramaribo is its capital
46 Achy
47 Halite
50 "Paper Roses" singer Marie
52 Strands, as by a winter storm
53 Just ducky
54 Speed: Abbr.
55 Rural route
62 Pub stock
64 Calf's meat
65 Fret
66 Grandparents' stories, e.g.
67 English essayist
68 Prince Valiant's wife
69 Name on which ancient oaths were taken
70 Brother, aunt, etc.: Abbr.
71 Southernmost part of Arabia

DOWN

1 Smelting residue
2 Long lunch?
3 Son of Seth
4 On
5 The Joker's portrayer on TV
6 Kemo Sabe's sidekick
7 On ___ with
8 Ballerina's skirt
9 U-235 or C-14, e.g.
10 ___-relief
11 Orbital high point
12 Prior to
13 One who makes a scene?
21 Actress Bonet
22 Lacks, in brief
26 Belief in one God
27 Neon, e.g.
28 "Shine a Little Love" rock grp.
29 Ungentlemanly sort

Puzzle 92 by Randy Sowell

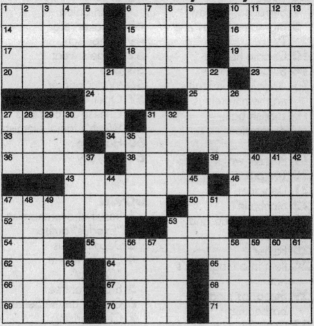

30 Newsstands
31 Laughing
32 Code word for A
35 Seethe
37 Orchestra output
40 Sticky stuff
41 Sea eagle
42 Badly chapped
44 Trampled
45 "The Hound of the Baskervilles" locale
47 Competes equally with

48 Yellow and black cat
49 Salad stalk
51 Bridge between buildings
53 Library volume
56 Congo river
57 Catch but good
58 Part
59 City near Provo
60 Museo holdings
61 Actress Cannon
63 Gender

ACROSS

1 Surrounding glow
5 Big name in daytime TV
10 Certain herring
14 Swamp critter
15 Appalachian Trail's northern terminus
16 Turkish bath decoration
17 Flee
19 Pulitzer writer James
20 Tee preceder
21 Deplaned
22 Stockpile
24 Actor Vigoda and others
25 Father
26 Item in a magician's hat
29 Steep, as meat for barbecuing
32 Over 21
33 Determined to follow
34 Apr. 15 letters
35 Bog
36 Flung
37 Like the world to pre-Columbians
38 Site of ink . . . or oink
39 Russian range
40 It's shown on a projector
41 Dutch Guiana, today
43 The "S" in O.A.S.
44 Loosen, as laces
45 Gush forth
46 Dry martini with a pearl onion
48 Sneaker, e.g.
49 Tempe sch.
52 Judge's wear
53 Flee
56 Water pourer
57 Open-eyed
58 Cheese on crackers
59 Witch's facial blemish
60 Hard up
61 Fax, say

DOWN

1 Result of overexercise
2 "Exodus" author
3 Decomposes
4 One of five in "Othello"
5 Brunch entree
6 Capital on the Seine
7 Civil uprising
8 Santa ___, Calif.
9 Living "fence"
10 ___ Island Ferry
11 Flee
12 Away from the storm
13 Bucks and does
18 Custom
23 Opposed to, in the boondocks
24 Skilled
25 "Psycho" motel name
26 Wheelchair-accessible routes
27 French farewell
28 Flee

Puzzle 93 by Gregory E. Paul

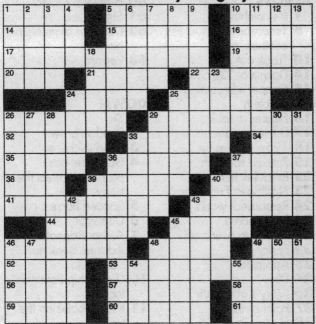

29 Haggard who sang "Okie From Muskogee"
30 Lifework
31 1950's candidate Kefauver
33 Embarrassment
36 Casey Jones, e.g.
37 Imperfection
39 "Do ___ others as . . ."
40 Animal in a roundup
42 Advertising section

43 Erratic
45 Piece of broken pottery: Var.
46 Sprouted
47 Des Moines is its capital
48 ___-Ball (arcade game)
49 Farm division
50 Scrape, as the knee
51 Like hand-me-downs
54 Pub pint
55 Stomach muscles

ACROSS

1 It's catching
5 Tenor-soprano combos, e.g.
10 "Look out . . ."
14 Downs of "20/20"
15 Sleeper's breathing problem
16 Figures in tables
17 B-1 insignia
18 1964 Beatles hit
20 Pressed for cash
22 Black-ink item
23 Northwest European
24 Rembrandt works
26 Royal home
29 Mosquito fleet craft
32 Fancy tie
33 Appraiser
34 Dine
36 Injury's aftermath
37 Paint base
38 El ___, Tex.
39 "2001" computer
40 Partner of onions
41 Ex-Gov. Cuomo
42 Adam Dalgliesh's creator
44 One very funny joke
45 ___ empty stomach
46 Microscopic
47 Mrs. Gorbachev
50 Bus passenger's request
54 Rating for the risqué
57 Yarn
58 Speechless
59 Target
60 Highland dialect
61 Simon ___
62 Divisions of municipal govt.
63 Repast

DOWN

1 Sic
2 Reddish-brown
3 Food thickener
4 How acid-base properties affect the body
5 Spotted horse
6 Discomfit
7 Author Bagnold
8 Address book no.
9 ___ Paulo
10 "Battleship Potemkin" locale
11 Makes bales on the farm
12 Western Indian
13 High, in the Alps
19 Heroism
21 Bombard
24 Sleek swimmer
25 Wild goat
26 Payment option
27 Songwriters' org.
28 Heat to just short of boiling
29 Crowns
30 Bygone dictators
31 "Wake Up Little ___" (1957 hit)
33 Poe visitor

Puzzle 94 by Robert Zimmerman

35 D
37 Andes capital
38 Auditorium fixture
40 Hawaiian isle
41 "Death in Venice" author Thomas
43 Kids
44 3Com Park team
46 Pick up the tab for
47 Tach readings
48 Spanish water
49 ___-bitty
50 Day worker, maybe

51 Bus token, e.g.
52 Hostess Maxwell
53 Lively dance
55 "Far out!"
56 Dead heat

ACROSS

1 Places to pitch tents
6 BMW rival
10 Dr. Pepper, for one
14 Dress fold
15 Restaurateur Toots
16 Golf or tennis championship
17 Designer Oscar de la ___
18 Slugger Sammy
19 For fear that
20 Deeply hurt
23 Nope's counterpart
24 Force
25 D.D.E.'s 1952 and '56 opponent
28 Award for a good student
31 Scorch
35 Blunder
37 Neighbor of Pakistan
39 Buenos ___
40 Visa alternative
43 Skylark, for one
44 ___ fide
45 Simplicity
46 What the fashion-savvy watch for
48 Cry at the doctor's office
50 Home for cubs
51 Goes out, as a fire
53 "Am ___ time?"
55 Gulliver's creator
61 Russian parliament
62 Scarlett's home
63 Pungent
65 Man with a spare rib?
66 Prepare for publication
67 River through Lyons
68 Exhausted, with "in"
69 Not bogus
70 "The Rehearsal" painter

DOWN

1 Paramedic's work, in brief
2 One of the Baldwins
3 Computer's option list
4 Raw quarter-pounder
5 Word with symbol or seeker
6 Mgr.'s aide
7 Apprehension expression
8 Administered medicine to
9 Invaders of Kuwait, 1990
10 Game in which players famously cheat
11 Oil cartel
12 Work space
13 Hill resident
21 Some nerve
22 Flip one's lid?
25 Make ___ buck
26 Fictional Gantry
27 Soft leather
29 Spirited horse
30 Talked and talked and talked
32 Auto tire necessity

33 Novelist Hermann
34 Ruhr industrial center
36 Subject of a trademark
38 Hawaiian goose
41 Neighbor of Pakistan
42 Horizontal line on a graph
47 Hunting dog
49 Facing
52 Sun protection
54 Recess for a statuette
55 Black belt's activity
56 Muscat is its capital

57 Diva's song
58 Part of N.F.L.: Abbr.
59 Budweiser ad creature
60 Actress Louise
61 June honoree
64 ___ Plaines, Ill.

ACROSS

1 Parachute ___
5 "Animal House" party wear
9 Ham it up
14 In midvoyage, maybe
15 "___ restless as a willow . . ." (1945 movie lyric)
16 Morocco's capital
17 Have on
18 Fissure
19 Ready for anything
20 Sage advice, part 1
23 Got fresh with
26 Pennsylvania city
27 "___, two, three, four . . ."
28 Wide shoe specification
30 One making picks and pans
35 The Little Mermaid
37 Bills and coins
40 Aborted mission words
41 Sage advice, part 2
44 Part of Q.E.D.
45 Not masc. or fem.
46 Uncomplaining servant
47 Sandwich meat
49 ___Tomé (island on the Equator)
51 Exist
52 Thingy
55 Abba's home country
57 Sage advice, part 3
62 Lasso
63 Thrilled
64 Jodie Foster's alma mater
68 Inquired
69 Author Wiesel
70 Say the paternoster
71 Pasta sauce with basil
72 Lairs
73 Test proctor's declaration

DOWN

1 Leno's got a big one
2 Exploit
3 ___ culpa
4 It was liberated in August 1944
5 Rant
6 Skip over
7 Faux pas
8 Moving
9 Pencil topper
10 Soda fountain choice
11 Follow the rules
12 Starch source
13 "___, Brute?"
21 Seems
22 Nouveau ___
23 Ray-Bans, e.g.
24 The dawn
25 Kind of cord
29 Behold, in old Rome
31 ___-European
32 "Tsk, tsk"
33 Tune out
34 Actor Joseph of "Citizen Kane"
36 Songstress James

Puzzle 96 by Stephanie Spadaccini

38 Prefix with pressure
39 Where movies are made
42 Togetherness
43 Go under for the third time
48 Gilbert and Sullivan emperor
50 Digressions
53 Bordered
54 A thousand, in France
56 Pharaoh's land
57 Police sting
58 Get up
59 Beasts of burden
60 Editor's direction
61 Stuck on oneself
65 Mr. Onassis
66 Leave in a hurry
67 CBS symbol

ACROSS

1 German river to the North Sea
5 Houston N.L.er
10 Fictional captain with an ivory leg
14 Fishing rod attachment
15 Oarsman
16 Malcolm X, for Denzel Washington
17 Where the President works
19 Minute amount
20 Jeans material
21 Regarding
22 Dick and Jane's dog
23 Skipped the wedding
25 Coin flips
27 High-hatter
29 Cockeyed
32 Seldom seen
35 Zoo inhabitants
39 Ill temper
40 Meyers of "Kate & Allie"
41 Sewing groups
42 L.B.J.'s successor
43 Bed-and-breakfast
44 Scrabble unit
45 Yards in passing, e.g.
46 Accepted doctrine
48 Shrink-____
50 Yellowbelly
54 Draw out
58 Auto racer A. J.
60 Sticky stuff
62 Hole-____ (ace)
63 "That hurts!"

64 Camelot fixture
66 Iwo Jima, e.g.
67 Hot coal
68 Study for finals
69 Lustful look
70 ____ Park, Col.
71 Makes bales for the barn

DOWN

1 Wear away, as earth
2 Carpenter's tool
3 Community gambling game
4 Area south of the White House, with "the"
5 Poodle's bark
6 Davenport
7 Chubby Checker's dance
8 Front of a sheet of paper
9 Nabisco cookies
10 Crops up
11 Dress for Scarlett O'Hara
12 Choir voice
13 Tuckered out
18 Harbinger
24 "The Many Loves of ____ Gillis"
26 Words of disrespect
28 Lahr of "The Wizard of Oz"
30 Humorous Bombeck
31 "What ____ wrong?"

Puzzle 97 by Gregory E. Paul

32 Narc's bust
33 Cartoonist Peter
34 Wagner work
36 Have work in Hollywood
37 Lot
38 ___ Haute, Ind.
41 Falcon feature
45 Popeye's muscle builder
47 May honoree
49 Came down to earth
51 Be in harmony

52 Motel units
53 Harbor suspicions
55 Snake charmer's snake
56 Dental filling
57 Abounds
58 Aluminum sheet
59 River in England
61 Where gramps jounces junior
65 A.M.A. members

ACROSS

1 Went airborne briefly
6 Sitcom set in Korea
10 Weary workers' exclamation
14 Eskimo home
15 Division word
16 "___ Rock" (Simon & Garfunkel hit)
17 Musician at a dance?
19 Egyptian cobras
20 Vitamin bottle info
21 Delaney of "N.Y.P.D. Blue"
22 Address part
24 Shade of blond
25 "No" vote from a horse?
28 Funky musical genre, for short
29 Rock singer ___ Bon Jovi
30 Julie in "Doctor Zhivago"
32 Needlefish
33 Jack who ate no fat
36 "What's your sign?," for example?
38 The hunted
39 Parson's home
40 Peruvian native
41 Booze for a 50's bash?
43 Fraternity man
44 Time of anticipation
45 Opening amount
46 Shoe part that may pinch

47 Gads about
49 Hells Canyon state
51 Modus operandi
54 Treat badly
56 "Praise be to ___!"
57 ___ brisk pace
58 Spring feature
59 Critique of an all-night teen dance?
63 Beheaded Boleyn
64 "Terrible" czar
65 MacLeod of "The Love Boat"
66 Relay segments
67 Superman's alter ego
68 Secluded valleys

DOWN

1 The Scales
2 "Holy smokes!"
3 Leader of Islam
4 Washington wheeler-dealer
5 Bun
6 Dolphins' home
7 Whichever
8 Sault ___ Marie
9 ___ d'oeuvre
10 Miss America's prize
11 Internal combustion device
12 Obstacle
13 Basketball strategy
18 Lender's claim
23 Cafeteria carrier
26 Peeked (at)
27 Unduly severe

Puzzle 98 by H. Estes and N. Salomon

29 Blue birds
31 66, e.g.: Abbr.
33 Sun-shaped
34 Smoked Italian cheese
35 Undoing an act
36 LuPone or LaBelle
37 Italian cabbage?
39 Back-to-work time: Abbr.
42 Singing Mama
43 Friendly, reliable sort
46 Norse bolt maker

48 Symbols of stubbornness
50 Publicity person
51 Forgo
52 Enjoyed home cooking
53 Shows signs of boredom
55 Estrada of "CHiPs"
60 Blvd.
61 Delivery vehicle
62 Kilmer of "At First Sight"

ACROSS

1 Cuba's Castro
6 Amo, ___, amat (Latin exercise)
10 Fishhook's end
14 Positive pole
15 70's-80's TV alien
16 Theater award
17 Place in the news, 3/28/79
20 Genesis son
21 Moderately slow, in music
22 Drink in a mug
23 Helen of ___
24 Shady retreat
28 Examiner
30 Shock
32 Duracell competitor
35 Bandleader Brown
36 They're hard to walk on
40 Mel's Diner waitress
41 Baby's room
42 Terriers and toy poodles, e.g.
45 Marvelous, in slang
49 Photographer Adams
50 Air conditioner capacity, for short
52 Scot's refusal
53 Marsh plant
56 Speaker's spot
57 Offside setback
61 Persia, now
62 Clumsy dancer's obstacles
63 Like a lot
64 Not straight
65 Not ___ eye in the house
66 Legislative aides

DOWN

1 Big shot
2 Fill the lungs
3 Boats with paddles
4 Genesis garden
5 Light-Horse Harry, for one
6 Kind of acid
7 Like stuff in the back of the fridge, maybe
8 Environs
9 Flesh
10 "10" music
11 Lawyers' org.
12 ___ Tin Tin
13 Retirement locale?
18 Getting hitched
19 Number on a baseball card
23 Sign of weeping
25 Torero's foe
26 Smallest bills
27 Country rtes.
29 Robert Morse Tony-winning role
30 Sounds of relief
31 Amtrak posting
33 Burden
34 TV hookup
36 Spanish custard
37 "Stupid me!"
38 Blows it

Puzzle 99 by Elizabeth C. Gorski

39 Iris's place
40 Neighbor of Ga.
43 Clothed, informally
44 Oil of ___
46 Not digital
47 ___ d'
48 Emphatic affirmative
50 Justice Ruth ___ Ginsburg
51 Sloshed
54 Socialite's "bye"
55 Walked (on)
56 Baby's first word

57 Prevaricate
58 Wrath
59 Vehicle with sliding doors
60 40 winks

ACROSS

1 Golf peril
5 South African author Alan
10 Impoverished
14 Latvia's capital
15 TV's Morgenstern
16 Witty Bombeck
17 Bartender's supply, squashed flat?
19 Jack-o'-lantern feature
20 Plunder
21 Working with a dragnet
23 Carpe ___
25 Actress Taylor of "The Nanny"
26 Apportioned, with "out"
29 Car safety device
33 Take in
34 Total, as an effort
35 G.I. address
38 Some scams, squashed flat?
41 Nile slitherer
42 Gladiatorial sites
43 Bona fide
44 Trattoria gadget
45 ___ Domingo
46 Zeno, notably
49 Actor Montand
51 Game with sticks
55 Brings a smile to
59 No longer mint
60 Meteorologist's study, squashed flat?

62 Catchall abbr.
63 Pacific nation since 1968
64 The life of Riley
65 January song ender
66 Muddleheaded
67 Common flag feature

DOWN

1 Remove the fat from
2 Costa ___
3 Ripening factor
4 Rose Bowl site
5 Victorian type
6 "So, it's YOU!"
7 Suit material, perhaps
8 River to the Baltic
9 Discovery grp.
10 Stereotypical pirate feature
11 Utah's Hatch
12 "Mother ___" (old standard)
13 Outfielder's asset
18 Pound sterling, informally
22 Vindictive anger
24 Gong hitter
26 Intro to physics?
27 Shuckers' units
28 Junket
30 Actress Graff
31 "Hail Mary" counter
32 Tampa Bay players, in headlines
34 Taj Mahal home

Puzzle 100 by Fred Piscop

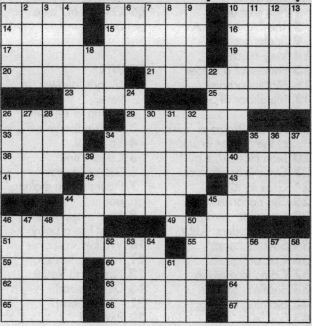

35 "Right on!"
36 Bog stuff
37 Capital on a fjord
39 Pusher's pursuer
40 Crossword solvers' smudges
44 Elasticized garment
45 Top Four matchup
46 Turns on an axis
47 Delicious
48 Neptune's realm
50 Empty spaces
52 Yemen's capital

53 P.D.Q., on "ER"
54 Six-foot avians
56 "Vamoose!"
57 Socialite Maxwell
58 Nostradamus, for one
61 Assayer's specimen

ACROSS

1 Not so much
5 The "A" in N.E.A.
9 Spelunker
14 Very much
15 Partner of potatoes
16 Martini garnish
17 Neighbor of Senegal
18 100%
19 Actress Braga of "Kiss of the Spider Woman"
20 Jean Harlow, e.g.
23 Goodyear product
24 Grassland
25 Gift decoration
28 Sawbuck
31 12th graders: Abbr.
34 Sailor's "stop!"
36 Cpl. or sgt.
37 Came to a perch
38 Beatles transport
42 Nothing but
43 Sun, e.g.
44 Wound up
45 Springsteen's "Born in the ___"
46 Aspen attire
49 Hair stiffener
50 Gorilla
51 Stiffly neat
53 Popular apple
61 Put up with
62 Chunks of history
63 Filly's father
64 Had a crush on
65 Trig function
66 Additionally
67 Skeptical
68 Popular sneakers
69 O'Neal of "Love Story"

DOWN

1 Mary's follower, in verse
2 Airline to Tel Aviv
3 Like Lindbergh's flight
4 Be frugal
5 Current unit
6 Deli sandwich
7 Plant used in making poi
8 Stern's opposite
9 Treat like a baby
10 Waikiki welcome
11 Tarzan's transport
12 Like Darth Vader
13 Down-to-earth
21 "Same here!"
22 Blossom
25 Louisiana marsh
26 Pizzeria fixtures
27 When repeated, a Washington city
29 Gives the brushoff, maybe
30 Toxic compound, for short
31 Broken arm holder
32 Post-wash cycle
33 Man of ___ (Superman)
35 Underhanded
37 "What ___ you getting at?"

Puzzle 101 by Gregory E. Paul

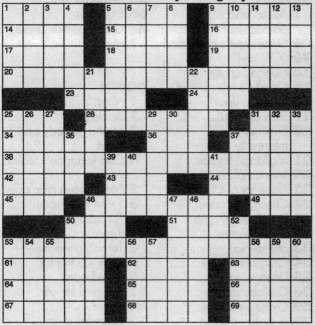

39 No longer asleep
40 ___ Lanka
41 Storage area
46 Rapid
47 Higher ground
48 Van Gogh painting that set an auction record in 1987
50 Puff snake
52 Scrooge, e.g.
53 Chutzpah
54 Instrument that's blown into

55 In person
56 Drawer site
57 Cleveland's lake
58 In need of a shampoo
59 ___ Major
60 Witnessed

ACROSS

1 Ayatollahs' predecessors
6 Gunslinger's command
10 "Oh, my!"
14 Hooded snake
15 Othello's false friend
16 "I'm ___ you!"
17 Start of a quip
20 Summer shirt, informally
21 Mallards' homes
22 Metric volume
23 Place for a 45
24 Clinch, as a deal
25 Part 2 of the quip
32 Son of Venus
33 Stiff denial
34 Old polit. cause
35 Dosage unit
36 Caribbean music
39 Ovine utterance
40 A major, maybe
41 Hydrocarbon suffix
42 Paris recreation area
44 Lucy's partner
45 Part 3 of the quip
50 Entanglement
51 Encumbrances
52 One who grins and bears it
55 Greek S
56 Biol., e.g.
59 End of the quip
62 Novelist Waugh
63 Tallow source
64 Words before sight and mind

65 Entanglement
66 Stumbles
67 Query before "Here goes!"

DOWN

1 "Out!"
2 Balderdash
3 Strong of body and mind
4 Charlemagne's realm: Abbr.
5 Early Greek lyric poet
6 1934 quintuplet
7 Forcefully stuff, as a throat
8 Turkish generals
9 Took the trophy
10 Chin beard
11 ___ and for all
12 Move
13 Place for a run
18 Warner Bros. creation
19 Resort island off Naples
23 Word in a price
24 Whit
25 "The Terminator" woman
26 Yemeni's neighbor
27 E-mail need
28 Play ___ with (damage)
29 Belgian composer Guillaume
30 Newspapers, with "the"

Puzzle 102 by Nathaniel Weiss

31 "Don't mince words!"
36 Oration
37 Henry Kissinger biographer Marvin
38 Canine cry
43 Thickness
44 Radio staff, for short
46 On/off ___
47 Tourist attractions
48 Prefix with spherical
49 Captivate
52 Defraud
53 It may be spun

54 Half of binary code
55 Disparagement
56 ___ good example
57 Oaf
58 Conjectural
60 Ethnic suffix
61 "So ___ me!"

ACROSS

1 Where Picassos hang in N.Y.C.
5 Baby buggy
9 Popular jeans
14 During
15 Four-star review
16 Defendant's excuse
17 Honored lady
18 Portent
19 St. Kitts and ___ (Caribbean nation)
20 Fashion slogan in the business world
23 Brooch
24 What's left after deductions
25 Palestinian chief Yasir
29 Trot or canter
31 Concert music blaster
34 Childbirth
35 "Schindler's ___"
36 Asterisk
37 Advice for the impulsive consumer
40 Pianist Myra
41 Bruins' sch.
42 "___ ho!"
43 Surgery sites, for short
44 Son of Seth
45 Food wrappers and such on the street
46 Slump
47 Response to a bad call
48 Catch phrase for the avid mallgoer
57 Approvals
58 Dinghy propellers
59 College in New Rochelle
60 Leader after Indian independence
61 Soothing agent
62 Runs (for)
63 Carpenter's device
64 Educator Horace
65 Helper: Abbr.

DOWN

1 Anti-D.W.I. group
2 Gen. Bradley
3 One who gives the silent treatment?
4 Summer quaffs
5 Loss's opposite
6 ___ Novarro, 1926 Ben Hur
7 Allege
8 Kind of room
9 Surgical instrument
10 Vote into office
11 On the qui ___
12 Wading bird
13 Snake sound
21 The fifth tire
22 Togetherness
25 Notwithstanding, informally
26 Pinker than pink
27 Bottomless pit
28 Watch chains
29 Cyndi Lauper's "___ Just Want to Have Fun"
30 On a deck, perhaps

Puzzle 103 by Bill Ballard

31 No longer on deck?
32 Purple shade
33 Snoop
35 Kooky
36 It's for the birds
38 Mushrooms, e.g.
39 State sch. in Athens
44 Completely consumes
45 Start to untie
46 ___ whale
47 "Don Juan" poet
48 In ___ (together)
49 Toe's opposite

50 Worker welfare org.
51 Rich soil
52 Kind of land
53 Woman who can carry a tune
54 French kings
55 Handy bills
56 History

ACROSS

1 Armed forces females
5 Like a whip?
10 Play parts
14 Fiery gem
15 Synagogue scroll
16 Combustible pile
17 ___ Sabe
18 Actress Verdugo
19 Israeli statesman
20 Gizmos for couch potatoes
23 Ace, e.g.
24 "You Are My Destiny" singer, 1958
25 Classic car
26 The "A" in NATO: Abbr.
27 Poem of praise
30 Feline hybrid
32 Constitutional Amendment that abolished slavery
34 Just barely places
38 1949 Bing Crosby hit
42 Puget Sound city
43 Quotation notation
45 "Grand" piece of furniture
48 Dancer Charisse
50 "The ___ Divorcee"
51 Mag. staffers
52 Infamous Rudolf
56 Hardly award-winning writing
58 Franklin and Eleanor Roosevelt, e.g.
62 Together, musically
63 Jetés, e.g.
64 Family problem
66 Stew bean
67 "L.A. Law" lawyer
68 Mother of twins, in myth
69 Watch part
70 Bury
71 Once, once

DOWN

1 Stir-fry pan
2 Preprandial potable
3 Evergreen with roselike flowers
4 Kind of replay
5 Undo a dele
6 Lawn pest
7 Betel palm
8 Didn't stop
9 Do an Oscar winner's job
10 Mimic
11 Six Million Dollar Man, e.g.
12 Town in County Kerry
13 Electric eye, e.g.
21 Oklahoma Indian
22 Shire who had a "Rocky" career
23 Bellum's opposite
28 Moist in the morning
29 Dutch cheese
31 Cuzco-centered empire
33 It smooths things over
35 Cheat
36 DeMille-type film

Puzzle 104 by Randy Sowell

37 Do in, as a dragon
39 Warm welcome
40 Casey Jones, e.g.
41 Tiny bubbles
44 Old-time humorist Bill
45 45-Across features
46 "Yippee!"
47 Take for granted
49 Sot's problem
53 Zhou ___
54 Back of a boat
55 Meager
57 Ransack and rob

59 "Go, ___!"
60 60's role for Ron Howard
61 Person with a PC
65 Lat. case

ACROSS

1 Big first for a baby
5 Fly high
9 Burns's "sweet" stream
14 Louisville's river
15 Years ago
16 Skiing locale
17 Inflexible
19 Game with straights and flushes
20 Be in the red
21 Best seller's number
22 Scholarship allowance
24 "Waiting for Lefty" playwright
26 Hans of Dadaism
27 Wyoming city
30 Crowd-pleasing basket
35 Throbs
36 Control knob
37 Writer ___ Stanley Gardner
38 Palindromic time
39 Long-winded
40 Detrained, e.g.
41 Apothecary's weight
42 ___ vera
43 Had control of the wheel
44 Witness
46 Junior high student
47 French article
48 Not be frugal
50 Kismet
54 Capone and Capp
55 "Steady as ___ goes"
58 Where Pocatello is
59 Having 20/20 vision
62 Emergency signal
63 Writer James from Tennessee
64 Holdup
65 Coin toss call
66 German mister
67 Brazilian booter

DOWN

1 Manhattan area with lots of galleries
2 Take out of the freezer
3 Emerald Isle
4 Pea container
5 Oklahoman
6 Get-go
7 Hotshot
8 Stoplight stop lights
9 Have hopes
10 Like a hound
11 Cigarette puff
12 ___ to suggestions
13 Dilbert, e.g.
18 Bumps
23 Add up
24 Gaping
25 Swabbies
27 Seabees' motto
28 Squirrel's prize
29 Sand bar
31 Water-skiing locale
32 Wrinkle-resistant fabric
33 Martini garnish
34 "___ and the Wolf"
36 Broad valley
39 Frost's "The Road Not ___"

Puzzle 105 by Gregory E. Paul

43 Crowded
45 Gazpacho ingredients
46 Person who handles bills
49 "On call" device
50 Potluck choice
51 Newswoman Magnus
52 Gilbert of "Roseanne"
53 "Uh-huh"
55 "Auld Lang ___"
56 Get better
57 Border
60 Application form info

61 Thought waves, for short

ACROSS

1 Shih Tzus, e.g.
5 One-time Chinese chairman
8 Hoopster Gilmore
13 A Great Lake
14 Zeus's wife
15 Stop
16 Dudley Do-Right's love
17 Apiece
18 Avignon's river
19 Quip about links lovers, part 1
22 Baseball bosses: Abbr.
23 Magazine income producers
24 Beads worn by a nun
27 Wish for a hot summer day
29 "What the ___!"
33 Keep away from
34 Gaels, etc.
36 Rap's Dr. ___
37 Quip, part 2
40 Consumed
41 Old photo color
42 Confiscate
43 Eliot's Adam ___
45 Lobsterlike
46 Made amends (for)
47 "___ nuff!"
49 Get-ready work
50 Quip, part 3
58 Dancer Ailey
59 Treaty preceders
60 "A Doll's House" heroine
61 Former Big Apple mayor Abe
62 Suffix with concession
63 St. Patrick's land
64 Goes it alone
65 Cagy
66 Wallop

DOWN

1 Successor to 5-Across
2 Chocolate-and-cream cookie
3 Part of a fish
4 Successful through one's own efforts
5 Beef, pork, etc.
6 St. Louis landmark
7 Hawaiian island
8 Bitter
9 Go over again
10 Town NNE of Santa Fe
11 "___ She Lovely?"
12 Understands
14 Husband to Catherine, Anne, Jane, Anne, Catherine and Catherine
20 Marsh birds
21 Big bag carrier
24 Therapeutic center, for short
25 Like some leaves
26 Used a piggy bank
27 Malodorous
28 ___ Romeo (Italian auto)

Puzzle 106 by Stephanie Spadaccini

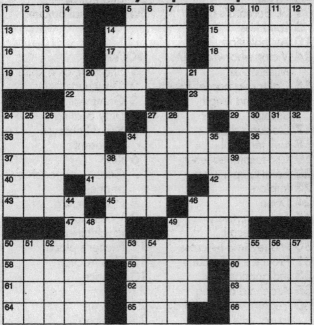

30 Newsman Newman
31 Fad
32 Atwitter, with "up"
34 Superhero accessory
35 Many a bridesmaid
38 Long-necked bird
39 Unlocked again
44 Alaska native
46 Get up
48 Dancer Gregory
49 Actor Luke
50 Bell ___
51 Butter substitute

52 Race track shape
53 "___ the night before . . ."
54 Honor, as a conquering hero
55 In days of ___
56 Skater Heiden
57 Went under

ACROSS

1 St. Bernard's bark
5 Loud kiss
10 Air pollution
14 Victor who wrote "Les Misérables"
15 California border lake
16 TV drama length, usually
17 Stocking shade
18 Cell terminal
19 Old-fashioned letter
20 Saint-Exupéry lad
23 Implore
24 Done
25 Moves furtively
28 Gun's recoil
30 Money in 31-Across
31 Province in Tuscany
33 Indignation
36 Arachnid of song
40 Vegetable that's hard to eat with a knife
41 Rich soils
42 Close
43 Engagement token
44 Olympic prizes
46 Football Hall-of-Famer Merlin
49 Unbroken
51 Nursery rhyme fellow
57 Etna output
58 Grocery section
59 Singer Turner
60 In any way
61 Look of disdain
62 The "E" of B.P.O.E.
63 Take care of
64 Shorebirds
65 Medicinal amount

DOWN

1 Sharpen, as a knife
2 "That hurts!"
3 Grimm villain
4 Dirty dealing
5 What Senators represent
6 Ray
7 Get ___ of (reach by phone)
8 Pig Latin, e.g.
9 Withhold
10 Psychiatrist
11 Pitcher's place
12 Cup fraction
13 Avarice
21 Sort
22 Sum up
25 Boo-boo
26 Paper-and-string flier
27 Celestial bear
28 Ivories
29 Election winners
31 For men only
32 Doctrine
33 Concept
34 Authentic
35 Goofs up
37 Pancakes served with sour cream
38 Charged particle
39 Like most paragraphs
43 First word on a "lost dog" sign

44 Lawn tools
45 Samuel's teacher
46 Young hooter
47 Sailor's time off
48 Deadly sins number
49 Not so dumb
50 Actress Hunt
52 Endure
53 Unemployment office
     sight
54 Metric weight
55 Signs, as a contract
56 Repose

ACROSS

1 False witnesses
6 Vocalizes like the Beastie Boys
10 Parks in 1955 news
14 Venezuela's ___ Falls
15 Clairvoyant's start
16 Has a tab
17 Suffix with sea or moon
18 Grocery vehicle
19 College course division
20 Production in a given period
22 Trait determinant
23 Pirouette point
24 MacNeil's longtime partner
26 Sombrero accompanier
30 Transparent
32 "___ 'Clock Jump"
33 Classic soft drink
35 Italian tourist center
39 Third-stringer
41 Sharpshooter's gift
42 Beat by a whisker
43 Use weasel words
44 Meat loaf serving
46 "Holy moly!"
47 Papa Doc ruled it
49 Stats for a porous defense
51 Battle site of 1916
54 Gulped down
55 Mideast bigwig
56 Pro-slavery Northerners, before the Civil War
63 Mission cancellation
64 Folklore fiend
65 Speechify
66 Lone Star State sch.
67 Chemicals giant
68 Hertz ___-Car
69 Slippery critters
70 Sit a spell
71 Alma ___

DOWN

1 In the cellar
2 Rainfall measurement
3 Lab gel
4 Bank takeback
5 Mr. Moto, e.g.
6 Nouveau ___
7 "Hurry, please!"
8 Pizarro conquest
9 Avoid a trial
10 Hero of 1898
11 Dog tag datum
12 Left Bank river
13 Autumn bloomer
21 Hoodlum
25 Move carefully (into)
26 Swanky
27 Years ago
28 Uncool sort
29 Cold comfort?
30 Burger or dog topper
31 Vegetable soup bean
34 All-star game side, often

36 Waffle brand
37 Warm, so to speak
38 States further
40 Belle's man
45 One of Alcott's "Little Women"
48 Like some pools or paint
50 ___ Judaism
51 Stage or stadium, say
52 Ham it up
53 Star in Orion
54 Insurance seller

57 Look lustfully
58 "QB VII" author
59 Field of study
60 Defeatist's word
61 Politically incorrect suffix
62 Mark with a branding iron

ACROSS

1 Lent activity
5 Ages and ages
9 Tin Pan Alley grp.
14 It connects to the wrist
15 ___ gin fizz
16 String quartet member
17 Trunk item
19 Bogeymen
20 Psychic power
21 Restroom, for short
22 Plains tribe
24 Mythological trio, with "the"
26 Grazing ground
27 Well-behaved
30 Lacking trees
35 Love, Italian-style
36 Workplaces for Edison
37 Dog biter
38 Veterans Day solo
39 Where trunks are
40 Boys
41 Newsman Huntley
42 Do a critic's job
43 Copenhageners
44 Severe scolding
46 Hang out on the line
47 Debtor's note
48 Ballet
50 Love ___
54 TV's "Science Guy" Bill
55 Maple fluid
58 "___ and Sing!" (1935 play by 65-Across)
59 Trunk item
62 Weekend wear
63 On the Aegean, say
64 Filly's father
65 See 58-Across
66 Crèche figure
67 Release, as lava

DOWN

1 Electrical safeguard
2 "The Sound of Music" backdrop
3 Ginger cookie
4 Part of cigarette smoke
5 Jefferson's Monticello, e.g.
6 Kind of branch offered in peace
7 Neither's partner
8 Trickle
9 Declared
10 Trunk item
11 Apple leftover
12 Out of the wind
13 Quarterback's option
18 Overjoy
23 At ___ for words
24 Trunk item
25 Went after houseflies
27 Quilt square
28 D-Day beach
29 Easygoing gazelle, e.g.
31 Sweet-toned musical instrument
32 Safari sighting
33 Passover meal
34 Pert

Puzzle 109 by Gregory E. Paul

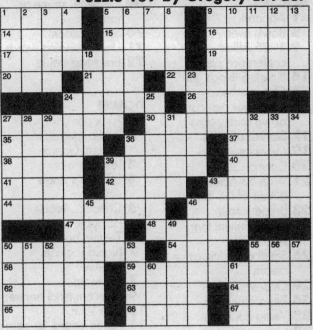

36 Meal accompanied by a hula
39 Debate
43 Kitchen gadget
45 As a surprising fact
46 No matter what
49 A deadly sin
50 Light ring
51 Overwhelmed
52 Pews' place
53 Cutting criticism
55 Use scissors
56 Farm unit

57 "That was close!"
60 Top medals winner at the 1996 Olympics
61 Swirly letter

ACROSS

1 Apparel
5 Bowls over
9 1945 Allied conference site
14 It makes things gel
15 Chowderhead
16 Messages that can arrive at any time
17 Start of a quote
19 Move laterally
20 Control ___
21 With 53-Across, author of the quote
23 Breadwinner
25 Impeachment trier: Abbr.
26 Small amounts, as of cream
29 One who's "out"
34 Restorative sites
38 Verne captain
40 Not a soul
41 Part 2 of the quote
44 Concerning
45 Highlander
46 Obscene
47 Verboten
49 Gambling game
51 ___ judicata
53 See 21-Across
58 Abduct
63 Baseball manager Joe
64 Port-au-Prince's land
65 End of the quote
67 Hand out
68 Part
69 ___ way, shape or form
70 Spring bloom
71 Understanding words
72 Breakfast staple

DOWN

1 Faux pas
2 Public square, in ancient Greece
3 Less common
4 80's-90's singer Adams
5 Critic ___ Louise Huxtable
6 Tequila bottle additive
7 Noted socialite Maxwell
8 Mixes up
9 Noncommittal answer
10 Gulf V.I.P.
11 Put on board, as cargo
12 Pinball problem
13 Bass, for one
18 Squeaked (out)
22 Prefix with political or logical
24 South African money
27 "All ___ are off"
28 Artist's wear
30 G.I. Joe, basically
31 Fashion
32 Once again
33 Internet addict, perhaps
34 Q-Tip, for one
35 Sunscreen additive

Puzzle 110 by Elizabeth C. Gorski

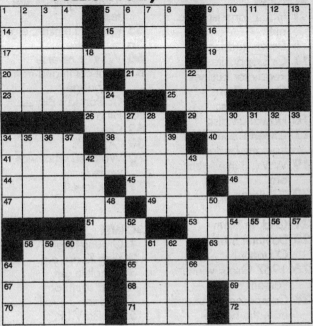

36 Shortly
37 Bowl over
39 Wind quintet member
42 Designer fragrance
43 Sicilian spewer
48 Ph.D., for example
50 Composer Luening
52 Puppeteer Lewis
54 "Gosh, will you look at that!"
55 Space shuttle part
56 Quite a swinger

57 Items sent to record companies
58 Real estate agent's goal
59 Hawaiian port
60 Huge amounts
61 Years in Havana
62 Not working
64 Accident
66 Born

ACROSS

1 In ___ land (spaced out)
5 Dawn goddess
11 Or's opposite
14 Ready for business
15 George Burns's foil ___ Allen
16 Hawaiian dish
17 Cheerful command from the bridge
19 W.W. II intelligence org.
20 "Children of a ___ God"
21 God, in Islam
23 Daytime host O'Donnell
26 1967 Oscar winner Parsons
28 Composed command from the bridge
32 Start of many German names
33 Deed
34 Boise's state: Abbr.
35 Furry companions
37 Great white ___
39 Bert of "The Wizard of Oz"
43 Equal: Prefix
45 Single, in Paris
46 Restroom at the Cock & Bull
47 Concerned command from the bridge
53 Most wicked

54 1936 Olympics star Jesse
55 Raise a hemline, e.g.
56 ___ d'etre
60 WSW's reverse
61 Final command from the bridge
66 California's Big ___
67 Fill a tank again
68 Over, in Berlin
69 "Amen!"
70 Watched what was wolfed
71 Look (over)

DOWN

1 Ground-level
2 King Kong, e.g.
3 Honolulu gift
4 Land south of Hadrian's Wall
5 Turkish V.I.P.'s
6 Coffee dispensers
7 Sprint
8 Orangeish shades
9 ___ Grande
10 Charged with gas
11 Space program to the moon
12 Cash register key
13 À la carte items
18 Listen to
22 By-the-book
23 Invitation inits.
24 Missouri River tribe
25 Dispatched
27 Black eye
29 Louts

Puzzle 111 by Robert Dillman

30 One-spot
31 Walk vainly
36 Walk laterally
38 ___ first-name basis
40 Wings: Lat.
41 Little Boy Blue's instrument
42 Fishing poles
44 Waitstaff overseer
47 Religious dissent
48 Madison, in Manhattan
49 Choirs may stand on them

50 Attack by plane
51 Blessing
52 Confesses (to)
57 "Sometimes you feel like ___ . . ."
58 ___ fixe
59 "Gone," at an auction
62 "___ Mir Bist Du Schön" (1930's hit)
63 Cable movie channel
64 Suffix with cash
65 Before: Prefix

ACROSS

1 Back tooth
6 Clash of clans
10 Coal-rich German region
14 Pueblo home
15 Bullets
16 Disassemble
17 Traveler's purchase, maybe
20 Art Deco notable
21 Not 'neath
22 Draws with acid
23 Hamelin critter
25 What's more
26 Playwright Burrows
29 Workshop machine
35 Soap brand since 1899
36 Projector items
37 Raines of filmdom
38 Slightest evidence
40 Camp sight
41 Einstein
42 Eyebrow shape
43 Skylit courts
45 "____ been had!"
46 Disappearing communication device
49 Nancy Drew's beau
50 Inlets
51 Major defense corp.
53 Spanking spot
56 Prospector's find
58 Way out there
62 NASA scientist's concern
65 Capture electronically
66 Obey
67 Where Goodyear's headquarters are
68 Puppeteer Tony
69 Part of A.D.
70 French river to the English Channel

DOWN

1 Stallion's mate
2 Polecat's defense
3 Oaf
4 One of the Yokums
5 Cincy player
6 Hack's customer
7 Kuwaiti bigwig
8 Diamond authority
9 "Go on!"
10 Giver of relief
11 Egyptian cross
12 "Zip-____-Doo-Dah"
13 Goes to waste
18 Comic Fields
19 "____ wrap!"
24 Vineyard measure
25 The ____-Prussian War (1866 conflict)
26 Wedding site
27 Pack animal
28 Right on
30 Summaries
31 Linen or denim
32 Assassinated
33 Still in the game
34 Tapered off
39 Explorer's activity

Puzzle 112 by Fred Piscop

41 30's boxing champ Max
44 Silicon Valley giant
47 Run amok
48 Popular motorcycle
52 Nutcase
53 Order (around)
54 Killer whale
55 Skier's transport
56 Baker's need
57 Overhaul
59 Al dente
60 Molecule part

61 Baseball's Sandberg
63 Novelist Deighton
64 Western treaty grp.

ACROSS

1 Keep ___ on (watch)
5 Largest city in Nebraska
10 Computer operator
14 Lifetime Oscar winner Kazan
15 Bars of soap
16 Botanical joint
17 "American Graffiti" actress
19 Thwart
20 Where bandits hole up
21 Caulking material
22 Hot rod
26 Steps that cross a fence
30 Mountain in Rio de Janeiro
34 Place for washing instructions
35 Ambulance personnel, for short
36 ___ Baba
37 Can't stop thinking about something
39 Vampire slayers
42 It may test the waters
43 Shade trees
47 Bring to bear
48 Newlyweds' trip
51 Army shelters
52 Rudolph and teammates
54 Gush
57 Flow (from)
62 Magnificent display
63 Like eyes during a boring speech
66 Subdivision
67 Sea duck
68 Swerve
69 Circus safety equipment
70 Woman's undergarment
71 Equips for war

DOWN

1 "Rambling Wreck From Georgia ___"
2 Jai ___
3 Fasten
4 Marquis de ___
5 Take place
6 Digestive enzyme
7 Letters before an alias
8 Part of H.M.S.
9 Inquire
10 Roll out
11 Combustion byproduct
12 Not leave alone
13 Have faith
18 Alpine songs
21 For each one
23 It comes in sticks
24 Three-striper: Abbr.
25 Soviet news agency
26 Indolence
27 No-no
28 "Peer Gynt" playwright
29 Businessman Iacocca

Puzzle 113 by Nancy Kavanaugh

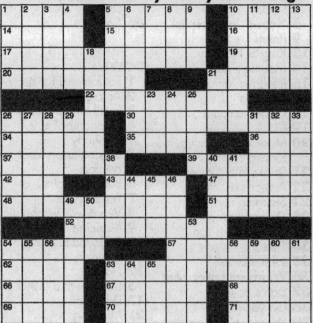

31 Like some sturdy furniture
32 Notify of danger
33 Punchers
38 Tractor-trailer
40 Foursome
41 Lizzie Borden used one
44 Creepy Chaney
45 "The ___ Squad"
46 Reacted to dust, maybe
49 Spews lava

50 Still
53 Nail file
54 Made a web
55 Corn bread
56 Leave out
58 Spectacular star
59 Declare
60 Swarm
61 Makes a boo-boo
63 Receive
64 Tell a tall tale
65 Build (on)

ACROSS

1 Daddy
5 "Now!" In a hospital
9 Points
13 King of Norway
14 Mountain lion
15 It follows larval
16 Cunning
18 Of any amount
19 Chit
20 Music and painting, for two
21 Drinks in big amounts
22 Author's assistant
24 Spinning toys
25 Quick-thinking
31 Cain was his son
34 Thin
35 John, abroad
36 Words said at an altar
37 Dah's go-with
38 Go yachting
39 Words said at an altar
40 Zoo inhabitant
43 Paquin or Magnani
44 Gibraltar-ish?
47 Long cut
48 Patchwork works
52 Curt
55 Clock division
57 "Gotcha!"
58 Balloon
59 Chubby plus
61 Favors sought
62 Got off
63 Popular insulator
64 Start with boy or girl
65 "Mahogany" vocalist Diana
66 Solicits

DOWN

1 Put forward for study
2 Amalgam
3 Fulfill an obligation
4 "Mogambo" star, familiarly
5 Lacking luxury and comfort
6 Bunch of hairs
7 Famous ___
8 Word with withholding
9 Musician of old
10 It's found in a ring
11 Summon
12 Harms
15 Shrub with a tasty fruit
17 Door part
21 Middling
23 Philosophical holdings
24 Tooth buildup
26 Bit in a salad bar
27 ___ donna
28 Comic King
29 Half-dollar, say
30 Kind of nut
31 Company with cars
32 Dummy
33 Army no-show
38 Alias of H. H. Munro
40 Conforms
41 Cartoonist Thomas
42 Asian fruits
45 Common lizard

Puzzle 114 by Gayle Dean

46 Junkyard dogs
49 ___ lazuli
50 Not too brainy
51 Historical writings
52 "S.O.S." pop group
53 Rorschach stain
54 Applaud (for)
55 Luminous ring
56 Football's ___
Armstrong
59 ___ and away
60 Dr.'s org.

ACROSS

1 Hearty kiss
5 "To thine own ___ be true"
9 Showy success
14 Woodwind
15 Shakespearean king
16 Michelangelo masterpiece
17 Used up
18 Diva's song
19 Ritz-Carlton, e.g.
20 1934 film starring 58-Across, with "The"
23 Dry, as wine
24 Sedate
25 Prepared for battle
27 Croquet area
30 Teeter-totters
33 Stork's delivery
36 Lout
38 Stretched the neck to look
39 The works
40 1935 film starring 58-Across
42 Spy's org.
43 Finnish baths
45 Tony winner Caldwell
46 Brighten, with "up"
47 Solemnly affirm
49 Slight advantage
51 Bethlehem product
52 Makes eyes at
56 Pan in Chinese cooking
58 Star born May 10, 1899

62 Excuse
64 Verdi opera or heroine
65 Stash away
66 "Don't You Know" singer Della
67 Bridle strap
68 Pakistani language
69 Teary 1960 Everly Brothers hit
70 Egg foo ___
71 Ooze

DOWN

1 Baseball's Wade
2 German sub
3 "Crime and Punishment" heroine
4 In a shabby way
5 Croat, e.g.
6 Architect Saarinen
7 Lion's den
8 Rhubarb
9 Items of short-lived use
10 A.F.L.'s partner
11 1950 film starring 58-Across
12 To ___ (exactly)
13 Locker room powder
21 Gilbert and Sullivan princess
22 Built
26 That, in Mexico
28 Ohio town or its college
29 Collar
31 Small river dam
32 Pierre's state: Abbr.

Puzzle 115 by Frances Hansen

33 Lowest pitch
34 "There oughta be ___!"
35 1946 film starring 58-Across
37 Casbah headgear
40 Lofty
41 Caviar
44 Slave Turner
46 Winged horse of myth
48 Mrs. whose cow started the Chicago Fire

50 Acquired
53 Petrol unit
54 Wear away
55 Make final, as a deal
56 Treaties end them
57 Butter alternative
59 "Mon ___!"
60 Tennis score after deuce
61 Warbled
63 Jamboree grp.

ACROSS

1 Hair in need of a barber
5 Salamanders
9 "Good ___!"
14 Accident-preventing org.
15 Spoils
16 Kind of down
17 Understands
18 Moon goddess
19 Honshu city
20 Certainly not the life of the party
23 Neil Simon's "___ in Yonkers
24 Schlep
25 Animation frame
28 1953 A.L. M.V.P. Al
31 Give relief to a thief
33 Deputy
34 Exclamation of discovery
35 Mint plant
37 Andy of "The Untouchables"
39 Box office sensation
42 Drive-in employee
43 Courteous chap
44 ___ v. Wade
45 Ess molding
46 ___ Ed. (H.S. course)
48 Computer pix
50 Suffix with pamphlet
51 Make a knot
52 ___-American relations
54 Soap interruption?
59 Bow or Barton
62 Handyman's need
63 Deli jarful
64 Wall Street woe
65 Highest European volcano
66 Declare with certainty
67 Saying
68 Word with cheeks or picture
69 Avian haunt

DOWN

1 Pear type
2 Net-surfer
3 Stadium seen from the Van Wyck Expressway
4 Annoyance
5 Bret who wrote "Less Than Zero"
6 Plaza feature
7 Half a picker-upper
8 Riding ___
9 Conductor Solti
10 Yeast's effect on cake
11 Wyo. neighbor
12 "Omigod!"
13 Italian monk
21 Boss
22 Defeat in battle
25 "O tempora! O mores!" orator
26 Inventor who saw the light
27 Rental agreements
28 Gat
29 Resistance measurement

30 Eagle, for one
32 Like many 90's trousers
33 It's measured in degrees
36 Beads and headband wearer
38 Job for a thespian
40 "___-Devil" (1989 Streep film)
41 Congressional periods
47 Gat
49 Swindler

51 Vestige
53 Dental filling
54 Jail for a sailor
55 Japanese zither
56 Place for a gutter
57 They follow exes
58 Photocopier function
59 Tax preparer, for short
60 Stripling
61 Literary collection

ACROSS

1 Cereal serving
5 Easy basketball shot
10 Ninny
13 Blows it
14 Senseless
15 Voice below soprano
16 Oriental Avenue neighbor, in Monopoly
19 Elite
20 Person who gets picked on
21 Prefix with red
22 Minuscule
23 Subjects of wills
25 Dishes out
28 Fall over in a faint
29 Invent, as a phrase
30 Christmas dinner bird
31 Plopped down
34 Journalists who don't have desk jobs
38 United
39 Furious
40 Cause a stench
41 Occurrences on icy roads
42 Steamy places
44 Jane Eyre, e.g.
47 Teen spots
48 On the ball
49 Pesky insect
50 French friend
53 Weapons since the late 19th century
57 December 24 and 31
58 "And thereby hangs ___"
59 Watch feature, perhaps
60 Blanc who was the voice of Bugs Bunny
61 Coolidge's Veep
62 1975 Wimbledon champ

DOWN

1 "Sesame Street" regular
2 Nabisco cookie
3 Tin foil, e.g.
4 It'll make you see things
5 Tablecloths and such
6 Furious
7 Small football gain
8 Acapulco article
9 Province east of N.B.
10 In the sky
11 Goggle
12 Drinks with straws
15 Desi of "I Love Lucy"
17 "What's ___ for me?"
18 Environmentalist's annoyance
22 Novelist Morrison
23 Get hitched quick
24 Mediocre
25 High: Prefix
26 Crazy as a ___
27 Like most sports telecasts
28 Homer and others
30 A+ or C−
31 Laid eyes on

Puzzle 117 by Ethan Cooper

32 Vicinity
33 Sounds of disapproval
35 Premier Khrushchev
36 Sheepish look
37 Loyal
41 Tender spots
42 Terrorizes
43 Voting no
44 Ladies' room?
45 Student at the Sorbonne
46 Ward off
47 Viewpoint

49 Chew, like a beaver
50 Dramatic wail
51 The "M" in S.M.U.: Abbr.
52 "Understood"
54 Small amount
55 Give ___ shot
56 Medicine regulators: Abbr.

ACROSS

1 Sound of thunder
5 Word with apple or dessert
9 Spray
13 A flower in Florence
14 Burn balms
16 Absorbed by
17 Martial ___
18 Defeat decisively
19 Fraudulent operation
20 Keeps a travel log?
23 Colorful wrap
24 Popular cookie
25 Tatters
28 When repeated, an 80's-90's pop group
32 House shader
35 Egg: Prefix
36 Ventilate
37 One who pays low auto insurance?
41 Pooh's pal
42 Early second-century date
43 Not-so-desirable bread slice
44 Form of Alexander
45 Medicinal amount
48 Currency worth a little over a dollar
50 Soup kitchen needs
54 Pulled off the job?
59 Quattro maker
60 A real looker
61 Heavenly glow
62 Ukraine's capital
63 River past St.-Germain

64 Hilarious comedian
65 Feminine suffix
66 Dam up
67 Expunge

DOWN

1 Animal stomachs
2 Peter of "Casablanca"
3 Up and about
4 Orzo and rotelli
5 Pot luck dinner staple
6 Start of some cloud names
7 Mouth part
8 Largo and lento
9 Truman's home state
10 Member of a bygone empire
11 Like bachelor parties
12 São ___
15 Debate (with)
21 Book between Gal. and Phil.
22 Exodus commemoration
26 Second person
27 "Saturday Night Fever" setting
29 Certain review
30 Egyptian solar deity
31 Unlikely candidate for prom king
32 Comes up short
33 Zone
34 Accordion parts
36 Kind of tax, as on property

38 Unified
39 Weiner topping
40 Sibling, in brief
45 Evades
46 School of whales
47 The Black Prince
49 Antique autos
51 Cab dispatcher on "Taxi"
52 Flynn of film
53 Play in the N.H.L.
54 Rouse
55 Archeologist's site

56 Never-never land
57 Dart
58 Lacoste of the courts

ACROSS

1 Ice unit
5 College QB or student body pres., maybe
9 Go bad
14 Unlock
15 Overhaul
16 Parts of British pounds
17 Part of a hippie's attire
19 Indy 500 and others
20 "___ luck?"
21 Took part in a 10K
22 Visible bullets
24 Dukes
26 Needle hole
27 Tiny village
30 Vehicle for reporters
35 Standoffish
36 Jungle squeezers
37 Cosmonaut Gagarin
38 10 miles per hour, say
39 Barracks boss
40 Nick at Nite rerun
41 Uniroyal product
42 Sampras of tennis
43 Die down
44 Pep up
46 Eats away at, as support
47 Cedar Rapids college
48 Prince of Darkness
50 Soldier's shelter near the front line
54 West of "My Little Chickadee"
55 The Righteous Brothers, e.g.
58 Self-titled #1 album of 1956
59 1969 event attended by hippies
62 Light-footed
63 Art Deco designer
64 Earthen pot
65 Military incursions
66 Oboe, e.g.
67 VCR button

DOWN

1 Fizzy drink
2 Stratford-___-Avon
3 Group, as of beauties
4 U-turn from WSW
5 Chicken piece
6 Intended
7 Unorthodox
8 Amount to pay
9 Uses a hose
10 Hippie emblem
11 As soon as
12 Bakery implement
13 Sale-priced
18 Short-winded
23 Pee Wee of the Dodgers
24 Hippie
25 Wore, showily
27 Waste maker
28 Pooped
29 Connery's successor as 007
31 Foam at the mouth
32 Band-Aid rival
33 Rocky ridge

Puzzle 119 by Gregory E. Paul

34 Carnival attractions
36 59-Across performer
39 Sales pitch
43 Sign after Pisces
45 Quickly increases
46 Got around
49 Overact
50 Terror
51 Gymnast Korbut
52 17, in old Rome
53 Drink server
55 Cabbage Patch Kid, e.g.

56 U.S.C. rival
57 Passable
60 Smelter input
61 Outdo

ACROSS

1 "Wow!"
7 Doll's cry
11 Film director's cry
14 "Shoulda listened to me!"
15 Smudge
16 From ___ Z
17 Darn good looking
18 Movie critics' approval
20 Cultural underwriting org.
21 Companies selling stock, e.g.
22 Speakers' aids
27 Manhattan address: Abbr.
28 Pitch's partner
29 ___ Dhabi (Gulf emirate)
30 Partake of
32 Wallach of "The Associate"
33 "Time ___ the essence"
34 Milk, in Madrid
38 Not extreme
42 Future predictors
43 Rainbow goddess
44 Flavor enhancer, for short
45 Big, fat mouth
47 Not do well
48 Greek cheese
49 BMW competitor
52 Chief plotter
55 Movie that rates 0 stars
57 Wild blue yonder
58 Comic who had a 1950 sitcom
60 "Relax, and that's an order!"
63 Man in a lodge
64 Orange cover
65 Windshield clearer
66 Juan Carlos, e.g.
67 Spy Aldrich ___
68 Gumption

DOWN

1 Game finales: Abbr.
2 Skip preceder
3 Hit, seemingly from nowhere
4 Payments to Madison Avenue firms
5 One way to reach someone
6 Happy cheer
7 Colo. clock setting
8 Plant sucker
9 Hairstylist's stuff
10 Bill producers, briefly
11 Mudville's most famous batter
12 About-face
13 ___-turvy
19 Sacrifice offerer?
22 Articles
23 "And that's ___" ("Believe you me")
24 Part of a judge's docket

Puzzle 120 by Philip Lew

25 Ending with bug or peek
26 Brute
31 Porters
33 ___ Lund of "Casablanca"
35 It's good for a laugh
36 Rush
37 Mystery writer's prize
39 Photocopier toner, e.g.
40 H.S. math
41 ___ Valley ("Back to the Future" locale)

46 Early round
48 Put on an act
49 According to
50 Being of value
51 Pint-sized
53 Cara of "Fame"
54 ___ Lauder
56 Actress Sedgwick
59 Wynn and Koch
60 Naval off.
61 French seasoning
62 Before, in verse

ACROSS

1 Spigot
4 Last in the class
9 Rug fiber
14 Hosp. area for emergency cases
15 Big name in video arcades
16 Singer Bryant
17 Sci-fi villains, for short
18 Supposed aid for finding water
20 The "D" of C.D.
22 Not so believable, as an excuse
23 Descartes, who said, "I think, therefore I am"
24 Rubes
26 Thinks
28 M-16, e.g.
30 Had
32 German sub
33 Negatively charged particle
34 Devotee
37 Résumé, of a sort
38 That special touch, briefly
40 Print measures
41 Fish eggs
42 Concorde, notably
43 Auto seen way too much in an auto shop
45 Graphic symbols
47 Dissuade
48 Barn toppers
49 Overly showy
52 Newspaper advertising piece

55 Gain ___ (get ahead in a race)
56 Prefix with -plasty or -gram
58 Tinted
61 Big-time
64 Copy
65 Boxer Griffith
66 Make ___ (befoul)
67 Sleep phenomenon
68 Exercised one's wanderlust
69 Runs out of energy
70 In excelsis ___

DOWN

1 Like a 4-4 score
2 It follows a curtain-raising
3 Move cautiously
4 Scoutmaster, often
5 Serviceable
6 Like engagements at sea
7 Harvard color
8 "___ kleine Nachtmusik"
9 ___ Quentin
10 Actress Bergman
11 Woman with a come-hither look
12 Joined (with)
13 Puts on cargo
19 Like patches or decals
21 7-Up alternative
25 Brewing sites
27 Quietly thinking

Puzzle 121 by Joey Crumley

28 Burnishes
29 Cousin of a heron
31 Austria's capital, to the locals
33 High point
34 Visible play area
35 Super-duper
36 Monster's loch
39 Deadly
44 It might be gotten from a folder
46 Cutup
47 Two-rod antenna

49 Player
50 Memorable 1836 battle site
51 One of the Gandhis
53 Africa's third-longest river
54 Drunkard
57 Spiffy
59 Sporting blade
60 Test-driver's car
62 7-Down, basically
63 Squiggly letter

ACROSS

1 Plays in alleys, maybe
6 Broad valley
10 ___ the Hyena of "Li'l Abner"
14 Actor Milo
15 Bard's river
16 Savings plans
17 Peck, illegally?
19 Drop a line?
20 Op. ___ (footnote abbr.)
21 "___ the night before . . ."
22 Hummable, perhaps
24 Less deliberate
26 Conclusion
27 In addition
28 Tiebreakers
31 Quench
34 Ford Motor product, informally
35 Press
37 It must be cast
38 High nest: Var.
39 Husband of Poppaea
40 Theta-kappa go-between
41 Rock's Mötley ___
42 Poet Nash
43 Filmgoer's purchase
45 Before, in verse
46 It may be minced
47 Decorative craft
51 Take a wrong turn
54 Poland's Walesa
55 ___ Victor
56 Surrounded by

57 Make breakfast, illegally?
60 Wait
61 Many a miniseries
62 Rajah's wife
63 Military award
64 Watery fluids
65 Discourage

DOWN

1 "Garden of Earthly Delights" artist
2 Ancient city at the mouth of the Tiber
3 Stimulates
4 Meadow
5 Soup cracker
6 Senegal's capital
7 "We try harder" company
8 ___ Altos, Calif.
9 Settle snugly
10 Assist, illegally?
11 Late CBS newsman Sevareid
12 Rambler maker
13 Pale
18 Impressed
23 Fuss
25 Flee, illegally?
26 1911 Chemistry Nobelist
28 Any "Seinfeld," now
29 A Flintstone
30 None too happy
31 ___ Lanka

32 Roller coaster maneuver
33 Part in an ensemble
34 Gift of the Wise Men
36 Oui's opposite
38 Groups that have adapted to their environments
42 Site for an apple press
44 Ford Motor product
45 Apiece
47 Tourist magnet
48 "___ you glad you did?"
49 Old radio's Fibber ___
50 Enthusiastic
51 Yaks
52 Leave out
53 Verdi slave girl
54 Cougar's retreat
58 Unlock, poetically
59 Scot's negative

ACROSS

1 Duelist's steps
6 Rogue
11 Likely
14 Run off to get hitched
15 Peace, Justice and Order, in Greek myth
16 What to call a knight
17 Come-on to those who are broke
19 Word before "I told you so!"
20 Spring or summer
21 Ore testers
23 Stir up
25 Windborne deposit
26 Move backward
30 Flabbergast
31 "Don't get any funny ___!"
32 Article in Harper's or The Atlantic
35 Dunce
38 Mention
39 Whimsically humorous
40 A check, one might hope: Abbr.
41 W.W. II inits.
42 Bridal path
43 The "U" of UHF
44 "Blue" or "White" river
46 Animate
48 Rocket type
50 ___ Park, Colo.
52 Seine's south side
54 Like some controversial plants
59 Saloon
60 Come-on to those who are patient
62 Prior to, in old times
63 "The Godfather" author Puzo
64 With whom Juliet 14-Acrossed
65 WNW's reverse
66 "___ we all?"
67 Chicago's ___ Tower

DOWN

1 Writes
2 Lotion ingredient
3 1978 movie thriller
4 Poetry studied in Greek class
5 Men, in La Mancha
6 Not bold
7 Musical endings
8 Stood up
9 Gaping mouths
10 Result of an infraction
11 Come-on to couch potatoes
12 Where ships come in
13 Lock of hair
18 1940's Cardinal ___ Slaughter
22 Who's solving this puzzle
24 Consumers
26 Serving with sushi
27 Rephrase
28 End of a come-on to bargain hunters
29 "Norma ___"

Puzzle 123 by Robert O. Dillman

30 Mule of song
33 The Sun
34 Ugly winter forecast
36 Land unit
37 Spanish dessert
39 Go kaput
40 ___ Lilly and Co.
42 Namath's alma mater
43 Heavy coats
45 Lender's income: Abbr.
47 Within view

48 Pulitzer winner for "Seascape"
49 They may be shifted or stripped
50 ___ nous
51 Tangle
53 At a distance
55 Double reed
56 Doll's cry
57 Roman route
58 Corp. heads
61 Nonsense

ACROSS

1 Torcher's misdeed
6 Means of secret knowledge?
9 Fuzzbuster's detection
14 Art print, for short
15 Bossy utterance?
16 Draw out
17 Genesis weaponry?
19 Prepared to fire
20 Crown jewels and such
21 Transport to Oz
23 Toothpaste type
24 Toothpaste unit
25 Get the pot going
28 Genesis actor?
34 Three Musketeers unit
35 La ___ Tar Pits
36 Tabloid worker
37 Taper off
39 J.F.K. posting
41 Novelist Zola
42 Individuals, so to speak
44 Fictional hunchback
46 Family heads
47 Genesis military force?
49 Book-lined rooms
50 Unlikely to bite
51 Serpent's tail?
53 Base for cheese
57 Most imperturbable
61 Sci-fi visitor
62 Genesis agricultural product?
64 Mark up or mark down

65 Gold-record earner
66 Deposed leader, perhaps
67 Leaps for Lipinski
68 Poet's preposition
69 Neuter

DOWN

1 Banned apple spray
2 Hitchhiker's quest
3 For men only
4 Electrical resistance
5 Barnes's partner
6 Austen heroine
7 Melodramatic cartoon word
8 Coffee substitute
9 Freeway mishap
10 Score after deuce
11 Russian parliament
12 Got 100 on
13 Decorate anew
18 Persian Gulf ship
22 Long, slender instrument
24 Londoner's break
25 Addis ___
26 Wealthy one
27 Sports deal
29 Neckline shape
30 Crippled Cratchit
31 "One Day at ___"
32 Strikeout king Ryan
33 Get decked out
35 Occupational hazards for apiarists
38 "Shop ___ you drop"

Puzzle 124 by Fred Piscop

40 Improve, as beef
43 Penn or Connery
45 Pungent bulb
48 Don of "Cocoon"
49 Top-shelf
52 Snooped (about)
53 Poet Teasdale
54 Author Haley
55 Dietary, in ads
56 Mallard's cousin
57 Give a ticket to
58 Auspices: Var.
59 Marketer's aim

60 Fearsome dinosaur, for short
63 Go public with

ACROSS

1 Clublike weapon
5 Mutual of ___
10 "Now!"
14 A magnet attracts it
15 Salvaged
16 Kind of straits
17 Use a stopwatch
18 Witch
19 Legal paper
20 Cook in the microwave
21 Significant other, in the gossip columns
23 Dancer Duncan
25 French article
26 Hoodwinks
27 Eccentric
32 The "U" of UHF
34 Telephone location
35 Letter before sigma
36 Bumpkin
37 Charlotte ___ (dessert)
38 Clark of Superman fame
39 Actress Thurman
40 Churchill Downs event
41 Money in Monterrey
42 Equine pest
44 Bucks' mates
45 Capote, to friends
46 It's spotted in a zoo
49 Garden gourd
54 "Fancy that!"
55 One of Pandora's finds
56 Also, in Arles
57 1965 movie with an exclamation point in its title
58 It's between Huron and Ontario
59 Eyelid cosmetic
60 Motel room
61 Bump into
62 Ten pins on two tries
63 Draw with acid

DOWN

1 Gaynor of "South Pacific"
2 Operatic songs
3 It's good for curbside parking
4 WSW's reverse
5 Academy Awards
6 Newswoman Shriver
7 Stratford's stream
8 Egg producers
9 Good enough
10 Reading matter along Madison Avenue
11 Father
12 Neighbor of Mex.
13 N.F.L.'s ___ Rozelle Award
21 "___ Lisa"
22 Neither up nor down, as a stock price: Abbr.
24 Mr. Uncool
27 Culp's "I Spy" co-star
28 Optimistic
29 Publicist
30 Cry of woe
31 Rug rats
32 "No way!"

Puzzle 125 by Norma Steinberg

33 Transportation to the 5-Down
34 Singer Ives
37 Noes
38 Retain
40 Hollywood's Bruce or Laura
41 Milne bear
43 Avenue
44 Covet
46 Cutting light
47 Archeologist's find
48 The third "D" of 3-D

49 "Um, pardon me"
50 Center
51 Sheriff Taylor's kid
52 Witticism
53 Annapolis initials
57 Color

ACROSS

1 Minnesota ___
5 Neighbor of Cameroon
9 ___ Alpha Epsilon fraternity
14 1997 Peter Fonda role
15 Despise
16 Subsequently
17 Start of a quip about weight loss
20 Minnesotan
21 "Heavens!"
22 Soissons saison
23 Kind of code or drive
25 Classic TV brand
26 Where St. Pete is
29 Mover and shaker
31 Household name
33 Scarlett's first love
35 Ants, in dialect
38 Make fun of
39 Middle of the quip
41 In the lead
43 Kissy-kiss
44 Popular carpet style
46 Nearly worthless coin
47 Biblical country
51 "Evita" character
52 Ump
54 Kind of particle
56 Comic Philips
57 Trap
59 Michael of Disney
61 End of the quip
65 Spanish port from which Columbus sailed, 1493
66 Window part
67 Robt. ___
68 "Voilà!"
69 Actress Lamarr
70 Feel sorry for

DOWN

1 Wasn't 100% honest
2 Former San Francisco Mayor Joseph
3 Crow's home
4 Clockmaker Thomas
5 J.F.K. appeal
6 Laugh sound
7 "Up and ___!"
8 Put off
9 Like some humor
10 Uncertain
11 Car that's "really lookin' fine," in a 1960's song
12 Danny's "Lethal" co-star
13 Biblical boat
18 "___ who?"
19 Killer whale
24 Wharves
26 Criticism
27 "___ Miz"
28 Yachtie's "yes"
30 Curative center
32 Flower holders?
34 Actress Anne
36 Update
37 Posture problem
39 "As you ___"
40 Swatter's target

Puzzle 126 by Stephanie Spadaccini

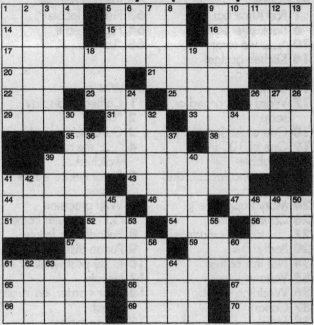

41 Agatha Christie's "The
 ___ Murders"
42 Laugh sound
45 Bring up
48 Mt. McKinley's Indian
 name
49 Bad place to find shells
50 Newsman Safer
53 Unwilted
55 "Richard ___"
57 Ado
58 Singer Adams
60 Dance instructor's call

61 Deed
62 "Uh-uh!"
63 Presidential inits.
64 Archaic

ACROSS

1 Fort Knox bar
6 Book after Joel
10 "___ we forget"
14 Kitchen gadget
15 Way to go
16 Declare
17 Word after grand or soap
18 One of the Jackson 5
19 One of 100 in Scrabble
20 Mary Lincoln ___ Todd
21 Coward
24 Mary Poppins, e.g.
26 Cartoon frame
27 ___ to one's madness
29 Portly
34 Not this or that
35 Valiant
36 Wedding words
37 Cohort
38 Moisten, as a roast
39 Microscopic organism
40 Haw's companion
41 Corkwood
42 Old ___ tale
43 Tree-planting occasion
45 Most outspread
46 Four-footed friend
47 More levelheaded
48 Combat award
53 "Phooey!"
56 Butter substitute
57 Bona fide
58 Sidestep
60 Snake eyes
61 La ___, Calif.

62 Kitchen gadget
63 Fishing locale
64 Hightailed it
65 "Land ___!"

DOWN

1 Cathedral display
2 "Uh-uh"
3 Gardener's asset
4 "___ the ramparts we watched . . ."
5 Pie of the 20's-30's Pirates
6 With precision
7 G.I.'s link with home
8 Palindromic fellow
9 Put on display
10 In the past week or so
11 Unholy
12 Bear's order, on Wall Street
13 Deuce topper
22 Sign off
23 Group of birds
25 "Pardon me"
27 Coffee shop order
28 Old anesthetic
29 Brazen one
30 Sundance Kid's girlfriend
31 Head gorilla, with distinctive coloring
32 Noses (out)
33 B.L.T. base
35 Festive
38 No longer speaking, after "on"

Puzzle 127 by Gregory E. Paul

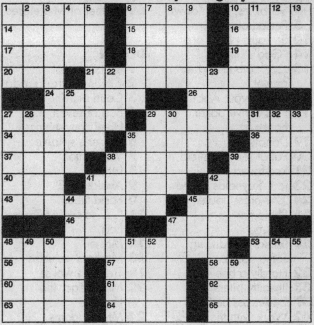

39 Man Friday
41 Belgian composer Jacques
42 Cold times . . . or times for colds
44 Be against
45 "Saving Private Ryan" subject
47 Meal starter, often
48 Sunbathing locale
49 Elbow-wrist connection
50 Really smell
51 Dickens's Uriah

52 Relaxation
54 "Zip-___-Doo-Dah"
55 Towel stitching
59 By way of

ACROSS

1 Scribbles, with "down"
5 Purse holder
10 St. Louis N.F.L.'ers
14 "God's Little___"
15 ___ football (indoor game)
16 Slanty type: Abbr.
17 First of five poker hands
19 Donate
20 Pal of Jerry Seinfeld
21 Red-faced
23 R. J. Reynolds brand
24 17-Across beater
26 Photo tint
28 ___-mo
29 Letters introducing some names
32 Hardly a beeline
33 Itty-bitty biters
37 24-Across beater
42 Work with the hands
43 John of England
44 Delivery from Santa
45 Fond du ___, Wis.
47 Methuselah's father
50 37-Across beater
54 Coffee order
58 Charms
59 Uncover, with "out"
60 Part of a magic incantation
61 Winner!
64 Dino's tail?
65 In flames
66 Conductor Klemperer
67 Enterprise doings
68 Sri ___
69 Partner of wherefores

DOWN

1 Makes fun of
2 City in central Florida
3 Court activity
4 Best of seven, e.g.
5 Hotel convenience
6 Singer's syllable
7 VCR button
8 Lend ___
9 Avoids an F
10 Pasta tubes
11 "___ to every purpose": Eccl.
12 Master
13 Mushers' vehicles
18 Treater's words
22 Mrs. Hägar the Horrible
24 Mrs. Addams, to Gomez
25 Major headaches
27 Tent holder
29 Plead
30 Blood, so to speak
31 Bough breaker
34 A.T.F. employee: Abbr.
35 E'en if
36 Place to wallow
38 Distinguishing trait
39 Quality potato
40 Voice quality
41 Milne marsupial
46 Pen in

Puzzle 128 by Nancy Salomon

48 Staff symbol
49 Jean of "Bombshell"
50 Thanksgiving celebration
51 Open, as a gate
52 Lash of old westerns
53 Good ol' country, for short
55 Firm fact
56 Snappish
57 Cultural credo
59 Kind of market or circus

62 The feminine side
63 It was made of gopher wood

ACROSS

1 Physics Nobelist Niels
5 Site for lashes
11 Huge bunch
14 Canal to the Hudson
15 The "D" in F.D.R.
16 Tree-felling tool
17 Notorious Prohibition-era gangster
19 C.E.O.'s degree
20 Items worn with shorts
21 Matt of "Saving Private Ryan"
23 Auto's tankful
24 Raccoon's hands
27 Sportscaster Musberger
30 Sahara, e.g.
31 Oxen's harness
32 City northeast of Indianapolis
33 Successors of LP's
36 Trussed up
39 Antiquity, once
40 Ducks renowned for their down
41 Gumbo ingredient
42 Starers
43 Cloudless
44 Bus passengers without seats
47 Antlered animal
48 Horrible
49 Chowhound
53 Burning
54 Military sanction
58 Heading opposite WSW
59 "Semper fidelis" person
60 Airy tune
61 Mal de ___
62 Annoy
63 Sporting sword

DOWN

1 Holdup device?
2 Mine finds
3 Mighty's partner
4 Left a job voluntarily
5 Reviews and corrects
6 Pro votes
7 Shade maker
8 Vientiane native
9 Traveler's stopover
10 Moved unsteadily
11 Beta's follower
12 "The ___ Incident" (1943) Fonda film)
13 Word after jelly or coffee
18 "Phooey!"
22 Fitting
24 Sites of auto dents
25 Prized statuettes
26 Bridle attachments
27 Group of bits, in data storage
28 Stir up
29 Supplemented, with "out"
30 Scottish port on the Firth of Tay
32 Indian corn
33 Pepsi rival

34 "Dumb ___"
("Blondie" forerunner)
35 Film's lead
37 Miner's or caver's light generator
38 "Paul Bunyan," for one
42 Wildebeest
43 "Join the ___"
44 Witchcraft trials city
45 Strong string
46 Following
47 Fudd of cartoons
49 Heredity transmitter

50 Excursion
51 Eye up and down
52 Memo
55 "Norma ___"
56 Bride's new title
57 Command to Fido

ACROSS

1 What a test driver test-drives
5 Adventuresome story girl
10 Dutch treat
14 Nabisco favorite
15 Coup ___
16 Balcony section
17 Founding member of a 60's-80's pop trio
19 Santa soiler
20 Back-to-work time: Abbr.
21 English ___
22 Broaden
24 Lad who drew a sword from a stone
26 Intense hatred
27 Desktop communication
29 Jalopies
33 Nine inches
36 "This Gun for Hire" star
38 Use energetically
39 Delta city
41 Sgt., e.g.
42 Low area of land
43 Comic Joslyn of "The Eve Arden Show"
44 Actress Thompson
46 Kind of sch.
47 Snacked
49 Wheel on a spur
51 Apartments, in real estate talk
53 Gives as one's share
57 English cheese
60 65-Down, to us
61 "You ___ There"
62 Some wines
63 "That'll Be the Day" star, 1974
66 Ship that sailed in quest of the Golden Fleece
67 Site of French learning
68 Split
69 ___ Mawr, Pa.
70 Asked for Friskies?
71 Sale condition

DOWN

1 You'd better believe it
2 Miscue
3 Intended
4 La-la preceder
5 Large, colorful butterfly
6 Fast time
7 Call ___ day
8 Examined before robbing
9 Italian-American, say
10 Old-time journalist-socialite
11 "Let's Make a Deal" option
12 In a state of excitement
13 Distribute, with "out"
18 Astringent
23 Artificial bait
25 Half Moon captain
26 This puzzle's theme
28 Fleming and McKellen

Puzzle 130 by Arthur S. Verdesca

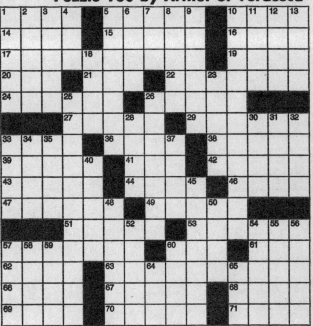

30 Freshwater duck
31 ___ Stanley Gardner
32 Banana stalk
33 Examination by remote camera
34 ___ Alto, Calif.
35 Is unwell
37 A genius? No
40 Ceaselessly
45 Bestowed
48 Crown
50 Alternative word
52 Vestige

54 Where to get a date?
55 Fountain locale
56 Male and female
57 Grumble
58 Mister, in Bonn
59 Nervous
60 Marathon unit
64 Promise
65 Mme., in Sonora

SOLUTIONS

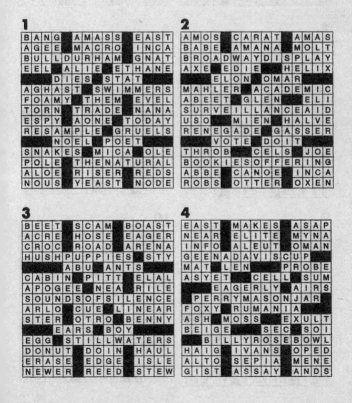

1

B	A	N	G		A	M	A	S	S		E	A	S	T
A	G	E	E		M	A	C	R	O		I	N	C	A
B	U	L	L	D	U	R	H	A	M		G	N	A	T
E	E	L		A	L	I	E		E	T	H	A	N	E
			D	I	E	S		S	T	A	T			
A	G	H	A	S	T		S	W	I	M	M	E	R	S
F	O	A	M	Y		T	H	E	M		E	V	E	L
T	O	R	N		T	R	A	D	E		N	A	N	A
E	S	P	Y		A	O	N	E		T	O	D	A	Y
R	E	S	A	M	P	L	E		G	R	U	E	L	S
			N	O	E	L		P	O	E	T			
S	N	A	K	E	S		M	I	C	A		O	L	E
P	O	L	E		T	H	E	N	A	T	U	R	A	L
A	L	O	E		R	I	S	E	R		R	E	D	S
N	O	U	S		Y	E	A	S	T		N	O	D	E

2

A	M	O	S		C	A	R	A	T		A	M	A	S
B	A	B	E		A	M	A	N	A		M	O	L	T
B	R	O	A	D	W	A	Y	D	I	S	P	L	A	Y
A	X	E		E	D	I	E			H	E	L	I	X
			E	L	O	N		O	M	A	R			
M	A	H	L	E	R		A	C	A	D	E	M	I	C
A	B	E	E	T		G	L	E	N			E	L	I
S	U	R	V	E	I	L	L	A	N	C	E	A	I	D
U	S	O			M	I	E	N		H	A	L	V	E
R	E	N	E	G	A	D	E		G	A	S	S	E	R
			V	O	T	E		D	O	I	T			
T	H	R	O	B		C	E	L	S		J	O	E	
B	O	O	K	I	E	S	O	F	F	E	R	I	N	G
A	B	B	E		C	A	N	O	E		I	N	C	A
R	O	B	S		O	T	T	E	R		O	X	E	N

3

B	E	E	T		S	C	A	M		B	O	A	S	T
A	C	R	E		H	O	S	E		E	A	G	E	R
C	R	O	C		R	O	A	D		A	R	E	N	A
H	U	S	H	P	U	P	P	I	E	S		S	T	Y
			A	B	U		A	N	T	S				
C	A	B	I	N		P	I	T	T		E	L	A	L
A	P	O	G	E	E		N	E	A		R	I	L	E
S	O	U	N	D	S	O	F	S	I	L	E	N	C	E
A	R	L	O		C	U	E		L	I	N	E	A	R
S	T	E	R		O	T	R	O		B	E	N	N	Y
			E	A	R	S		B	O	Y				
E	G	G		S	T	I	L	L	W	A	T	E	R	S
D	O	N	U	T		D	O	I	N		H	A	U	L
E	R	A	S	E		E	D	G	E		I	S	L	E
N	E	W	E	R		R	E	E	D		S	T	E	W

4

E	A	S	T		M	A	K	E	S		A	S	A	P
N	E	A	R		E	L	I	T	E		M	Y	N	A
I	N	F	O		A	L	E	U	T		O	M	A	N
G	E	E	N	A	D	A	V	I	S	C	U	P		
M	A	T		L	E	N			P	R	O	B	E	
A	S	Y	E	T		C	E	L	L		S	U	M	
			E	A	G	E	R	L	Y		A	I	R	S
P	E	R	R	Y	M	A	S	O	N	J	A	R		
F	O	X	Y		R	U	M	A	N	I	A			
A	S	H		M	O	S	S			E	X	U	L	T
B	E	I	G	E			S	E	C		S	O	I	
			B	I	L	L	Y	R	O	S	E	B	O	W	L
H	A	I	G		I	V	A	N	S		O	P	E	D
A	L	T	O		S	E	P	I	A		M	E	N	E
G	I	S	T		A	S	S	A	Y		A	N	D	S

5

```
CROW  PUPS  NOBLE
LEIA  OMIT  ONEAL
EELY  WATERWORKS
AVENGE TEEN  TEA
REDEALT  PLOW
   SELES  AWAKEN
SCOWL  SHOT  LIRA
OHNO  PLANE  TWIT
NEER  RANT  SWINE
GRILLE  EARTH
   DALE  PELICAN
SSE  DAVE  POTATO
WILLYWONKA  MILL
IMBAD  KIEV  ARAT
MIAMI  EDGE  NOSE
```

6

```
KHAN  MOMA  PACER
NODE  ERIC  ADALE
OLDASMETHUSELAH
XES  COMEON  NAPE
   FRI  SOFT  ISM
OCULARS   ERASE
NEWAMSTERDAM
TEEM  AGO   YEAR
  BORROWEDTIME
GRETA  SNEAKIN
IRE  OKLA  CNN
NIPS  ELLIOT  ZIG
BLUEGRASSREGION
ALTAR  MOLE  ANNA
DEERE  APES  SCAT
```

7

```
RUSH  BRIM  CLEFT
ATTA  EASE  RATER
PAIN  ASIS  ITALY
THROUGHTHEMILL
    ISLE  DEN
FDA  HERALDS  ATT
LUNGE  DOI  ACRE
UNDERTHEWEATHER
TEEM  HOP  TEENS
ESS  CONTEST  DDE
   FOR  THIS
AROUNDTHECLOCK
CLEAR  ERIE  IRAN
BOILS  PICT  CARE
SENSE  TOSS  ELSE
```

8

```
ENCLAVE  UGH  ARE
FRAILER  BRO  RON
TALKEDABOUT  CUD
DECI  OLE  CATO
GIRLSCOUTLEADER
AMOY  MTS  CBERS
PAN  NONO  GROSSE
   HIDINGOUT
OCTANE  NUTS  SAP
BREST  TIS  SEMI
SOUTHVIETNAMESE
CUTE  OER  ALIT
ETO  WIDEMOUTHED
NON  ICY  IMMERSE
ENS  GEE  TISSUES
```

9

```
ABBOT  RAJAS  GEL
CORNS  ERATO  ANO
QUICKDRAWMCGRAW
URGE  RUBS  CIRCE
ISH  HENS  HELOTS
TETRA  MAR  TET
  ORACLES  BED
  SWIFTYLAZAR
 BUS  ORESTES
GAR  ARS  REELS
ADMIRE  FARO  DEO
FLING  ELLE  FINN
FASTEDDIEFELSON
ENE  NIGER  MOORE
RDS  TRYST  TENET
```

10

```
MAMAS  FROM  FAME
AGILE  RARA  OLEG
RONEE  EGAN  UPTO
KNUCKLEUNDER
SYS  EAR  GYN  CAB
  ARNESS  ATRIA
ACED  DIE  SCROLL
THROWINTHETOWEL
TIARAS  TEA  ODDS
ANSEL  ROLLUP
RAE  LIE  PAN  ALL
  EATHUMBLEPIE
BRED  SERA  EXACT
RANG  MEAT  SPRIG
AHOY  ELLE  SOTTO
```

11

```
S L O T _ P R A M _ S C A L P
L I V E _ R A R E _ T A B O O
A M E N _ A S I S _ O B E S E
V E R O N I C A S C L O S E T
_ _ _ R O S A _ _ L I T _ _ _
N A W _ R E L A T E D _ L A P
O P A R T _ N R A _ D E C A
M A R T H A S V I N E Y A R D
A C M E _ L A I _ N E V E R
D E S _ C O L L A R D _ E S E
_ _ R A F _ _ _ R O O T _ _
C H R I S T I N A S W O R L D
R O A S T _ D E B T _ T O U R
A N G E L _ E R I E _ A L V A
G E E S E _ S O A R _ L E S T
```

12

```
S H A W _ S C A T S _ V A S T
H O L O _ C O R O T _ O N T O
O R E M _ A D I M E _ O D E S
O N E A R M E D B A N D I T S
_ _ _ N A P _ _ _ D O O _ _
L I C I T _ S A S _ T O S C A
I R R S _ A U D I T S _ O R B
T W O H A N D E D V O L L E Y
R I O _ S T A L L S _ O T T S
E N N U I _ N E E _ I V I E S
_ _ S D S _ _ _ N N E _ _
T H R E E L E G G E D R A C E
H O E S _ O V A L S _ B U L L
U R D U _ B E G O T _ O R E L
G A S P _ S L A B S _ Y A M S
```

13

```
L I S P S _ S P E C _ D I V A
E C L A T _ T I L E _ O B I S
S O U P A N D S A N D W I C H
E N G A G E _ A T T E N D E E
_ _ L E A R _ _ E R A S _ _
C B S _ S T E M _ I N T A K E
O U T S _ E E O C _ N A M E D
M E A T A N D P O T A T O E S
E N D E R _ S E C S _ E R L E
T O T E M S _ D O E S _ Y S L
_ _ L A L A _ _ A T U B _ _
R E S I D I N G _ S C A L P S
C A K E A N D I C E C R E A M
A S I S _ G U L P _ O R A T E
S E N T _ S P A R _ R E N E W
```

14

```
C A P R I _ E G G _ P A T T Y
U N I O N _ S I R _ O M A H A
S T E M S _ A L I _ L A X E R
P E R P E T U A L M O T I O N
_ _ _ S C I _ _ S L I P _ _
I S H _ T A X _ E X O T I C A
N C A A _ R I G _ N O N O S
F O U N T A I N O F Y O U T H
R U N T O _ U N E _ K I T E
A T T I M E S _ A L F _ T A N
_ _ O P I E _ _ O U R _ _
P R O G R A M M I N G A V C R
E E L E R _ I A N _ E V E R Y
A M I N O _ L I T _ E E R I E
S I N E W _ E L O _ S L O B S
```

15

```
P I T H _ M O R A L _ I P S O
S O H O _ C R A T E _ F U N K
S W I N G I N G O N A S T A R
T A S K S _ A G L O W _ O P A
_ _ Y E A _ M E L _ E O N _ _
F E E D _ B E D S _ S T A R T
A L A _ E E N Y _ K O S H E R
G E R _ N E T _ D I M _ A M I
I N S I S T _ C O D E _ P U P
N I K O N _ C O B S _ A P S E
_ _ I N A _ A M A _ P L Y _ _
A S S _ R E M I T _ R E F E R
I T S A L L I N T H E G A M E
N O E L _ A N G L E _ A C M E
T A S S _ N O S E S _ R E A L
```

16

```
A H A B _ L I M P _ P L A N B
N O L A _ A R I A _ O A S E S
K N O B _ P O N T _ S C H W A
A G E O F A N X I E T Y _ _ _
_ _ _ O R L Y _ O N A _ J O G
V E N O M _ _ _ I G N O R E
M I A _ M A U V E D E C A D E
A R T S _ G E T _ O N E S
G A S L I G H T E R A _ N A E
I G U A N A _ _ _ E Q U A L
C O P _ T N T _ S T U N
_ _ M E G E N E R A T I O N
K A Z A N _ N O T A _ O S L O
A D A M S _ E P I C _ L E G O
T E P E E _ T E N T _ D E A R
```

17

```
S U M   M O A T     S T R A W
E R I   U N B A R   Q U I C K
D A M   S E A T O   U R G E S
U N O W H A T I M E A N
C U S H Y       E B B   I M A
E S A I   R E S O W   B R A G
    P E E L E   H O R A C E
  D O S O F M E D I C I N E
J E J U N E   D I T T O
R E A P   R H Y M E   C R I B
S R I   T E A   S H A N E
    T R E S E L E M E N T S
A R M E Y   T R U C E   C U T
L I A R S   E R R O L   O N E
T A I N T     S E N T   R E D
```

18

```
D E C A F   A D L I B   L U V
E L I S E   D I A N A   A S A
L O O S E L I P P E D   M E T
          L A O S   L E E D S
F A S T E N S   C R U M B
E N T I R E   E L E C T R O N
L Y R E S   P L U N K   A C E
L O O S   F I L E D   M I T T
A N N   P I N E S   S E N A T
S E G M E N T S   S E R E N E
    A T S E A   S E C E D E D
V E R S E   P A R T
C A M   T I G H T F I S T E D
R T E   A T R E E   O R O N O
S A D   S T O W S   N O N E T
```

19

```
S E R F S   L I R A   S C A M
T R A I T   O D O R   P O L E
R A C E R   T E A T   A L I T
A S K F O R H E R H A N D
W E S   K E A   A R C   W P A
    H E A R T T O H E A R T
A R T E   C I O   E N T E R
R O W S   T O W I T   S E E A
M O O S E   E N E   U R N S
  O N B E N D E D K N E E
R E Y   D A Y   S T L   G A B
    F O O T E D T H E B I L L
C O O L   E L I A   C A L L A
T H U D   R E M I   T I D E S
S O R E   S T E N   S L A N T
```

20

```
S L A T   C R A M   D O O N E
H A I R   R I G A   U P T O N
U S D A   I T E R   R A T I O
T H E L A S T E M P E R O R
      A L T E   O A S T
A R G   F O R E S T S   K I M
L E R O I   A E C   N A N A
A L I F E F O R T H E C Z A R
R E S T   R U T   L O O P Y
M E T   B E T H U N E   O T S
      T E A R   R O N S
  C H I C K E N A L A K I N G
P L I N K   A O N E   O N I N
C A D G E   C P U S   A T T A
S W E E T   H E S S   L O S T
```

21

```
G A S P   E L V I S   P E C K
I T T O   C O I N S   E V A N
J O I N T O W N E R   N E R O
O M E G A   M E D   S H R E W
E S S   L E A D I N T O
    C O R N   B E E L I N E
O C T A N E   B L E N D S I N
T O R N   C R E E D   E I N E
T O O O F T E N   L O R N E S
O L D P R O S   H E S S
    E A R L I E S T   A G E
S C A N T   A L A   E B B E D
P A C E   S T I R F R Y I N G
O V E R   T E A S E   E D I E
T E D S   A D D E R   S E E S
```

22

```
P L U M B   C L V   B L A H
R E S A Y   L A I   B O I S E
I M A D E H I M A N O F F E R
A M I   A M P   I N F E A R
M A R L O N B R A N D O
      A R K   E T E   Y E S
A L E N E   D Y E R   C O R P
W E L C O M E   A S T O R I A
R A K E   A B A T   A M E N S
Y R S   B U D   A R E
    T H E G O D F A T H E R
S P I R A L   R I A   O D E
H E C O U L D N T R E F U S E
A L E U T   J E T   P A N E S
W E S T   S R O   A D D L E
```

23

```
T I L E   B E L L   A N G R Y
A V E R   O D I E   M E L E E
M I N I   G N A W   I D E A L
P E A C E G A R D E N   E L L
A S S A I L       R O T C
      G E R M A N   O L G A
R A J A H   E A S E   Q U I D
A P O R T   L I S   B U B B A
K A Y E   H A Z E   Y E S E S
E L B A   E X E T E R
    U S E R   L O C A L E
B I Z   L O V E H A N D L E S
O O Z E D   A R A T   R I M S
S T E V E   S I T E   O B O E
C A R E R   T E E D   M I N N
```

24

```
O L D S   C O L I C   T A C K
D A R T   A F A C T   E L H I
D R E S S B L U E S   R I A L
S K A   L I A R   S M E L T
    M O U N T A I N P I N K S
C H I N E S E   S E A N
P O E T S   A I R R I F L E
A S S   A L L T O   L E N
S T T H O M A S   F R I T Z
    O M E N   A G R E E T O
C O L L A R D G R E E N S
O S I E R   A C R E   A A A
S H O O   H A S H B R O W N S
M E N U   E L S I E   D A T E
O A S T   P A Y E R   E Y E S
```

25

```
S P I T   M A B E L   D I A L
T O D O   O P E R A   I D L E
D O O M   C H E A T   M E A T
  F L A S H I N T H E P A N
      H E A D   E L L
P L E A T   S U B   F E T C H
A I R W A Y   T A P   S O U
S N A K E I N T H E G R A S S
S E T   P E E   A L E R T S
E R O D E   O R B   A S S A Y
    E T S   A C R E
  S T I C K I N T H E M U D
C H I C   A B A T E   B R I M
S I D E   T I M E S   L A V A
A V E R   E D E N S   E L A N
```

26

```
L A P P   W E D G E   A S A P
A L L Y   A X I A L   R A C E
H O U R G L A S S F I G U R E
R E S E A R C H   R Y D E R
      R U T   B A I L
C A L A I S   F A L S E T T O
A W A C S   K A T E   R E P
W A T C H O N T H E R H I N E
E K E   L E E S   E A T O N
D E R A N G E D   A N G E R S
      F O A L   A N D
M E N L O   A S T E R O I D
C L O C K W O R K O R A N G E
A L I I   A L I E N   S T O P
N E R O   R E A D Y   P O R T
```

27

```
I O W A   R E S T   L O N E
M A I L   I N T O   S A V E D
E T R E   F R O G   A M E N D
T H E C O L O R O F M O N E Y
      H E L M   I O U
S I N B A D   A N A R C H Y
A R O A R   O L L A   R I O
D O L L A R D I P L O M A C Y
I N T   A D E S   P I N K O
E Y E L I D S   S T R E S S
    O R A   M A L I
I F I W E R E A R I C H M A N
R I S E N   M R E D   E A S E
A D E L E   M I N E   I C E R
N O E L   A N T S   R E A D
```

28

```
S P A M   N O T E R   C H A D
L O B E   O C H R E   H A L E
A C E S   S H I N E   A L A N
T O L O V E O N E S E L F I S
      N O R   S E A L
B O S   W I L D   S T E I N S
O T T O   N O O K   I N G O T
T H E B E G I N N I N G O F A
H E R O D   S T E M   E R A T
A R N E S S   S E P T   S T S
      R E M S   L A M
L I F E L O N G R O M A N C E
A B L E   O A R E D   N E A R
D E E D   C R O N E   N E R O
E T E S   H E W E D   A D D S
```

29

```
A B H O R . S E G A . S O L E
B L A R E . C R O W . I N O N
B E L E T T E R P E R F E C T
R U S S I A N S . . A T T A R
. . . E X T . U S S . O L E .
M A M A S . . S P A S . . . .
O B I S . S C H E L L . R A J
P U S H T H E E N V E L O P E
S T S . I O D I D E . O D E S
. . . . P E E K . . Q U E S T
U N I . T D S . T A U . . . .
P I N T O . . H O R I Z O N S
S T A M P O F A P P R O V A L
E R N E . W I N S . E L E V E
T E E N . E G G Y . D A R E D
```

30

```
E S T O P S . P R O M . O D D
R A H R A H . O O N A . V I A
S H O R T E N E D S T R E E T
E L M . C R I M E . A O R T A
. . . P A R T . . F D A . . .
P A R I S I A N P R O N O U N
S L A S H . A J A R . C H I .
Y O D A . G A S S Y . S C U T
C H A . O L L A . C O U R T .
H A R M F U L L I G H T R A Y
. . . A F T . . B A A S . . .
A S P I C . W H E L P . S R O
G E R M A N A U T O M A K E R
E V A . S O N G . R A V I N E
D E Y . T R E E . E N A M E L
```

31

```
S I L A S . S A T . L U S H
A T A L L . P S I . R E N T E
C A C T I . A H A . E N D E R
S L E E P E R . R E L O O P S
. . . R U Y . D A D A . . . .
E R A . P E T E . S I N N E D
P A C T . O I L S . D E U C E
O V E R . F L I P S . I D L E
D E R E K . E V I E . L E A D
E L B E R T . E T N A . S T S
. . . A V E R . A N S . . . .
G A T E M A N . S T I N K E R
I N A W E . A D O . M A N G O
G O N E R . C O D . A R E A S
I N K S . T W A . L E E D S
```

32

```
M A R C . D O G M A . M A L T
A R I A . A C R E S . A L O E
W E L L . M E A N S . R A G E
. A L I E N A B D U C T I O N
. . . E V E N . M R I . . . .
V E I N E D . O R I E N T A L
I N S T . S T A N D . A V A .
C E L E B R I T Y G O S S I P
. A R A . O O Z E S . A S A P
R O M A N C E R . L E M O N S
. . . K K K . S A M S . . . .
E L V I S S I G H T I N G S .
L O O M . T O R A H . E L A L
B U L B . A L O N E . A U N T
A S T O . R A W E R . D E E D
```

33

```
C O P S E . S A G . S P A T S
A P R I L . H E E . T A G U P
G U A R D P O S T . E P O D E
E S T . E U R O . B E A R O N
. . . S T E P F O R W A R D .
M I D S T S . . . R N A . . .
I D E A . I S E E . G U I D E
C O M M U N I T Y C E N T E R
A L I E N . R O A R . I L K S
. . . E W E . . O U T L E T .
. F O R W A R D P A S S . . .
A P I A R Y . E L B A . I C E
R E S I N . B O D Y G U A R D
C R E T E . U N E . E G G E D
E A R E D . S Y R . S H O W Y
```

34

```
O W N E R . G L E E . B A D
T R A L A . R A F T . G O B I
H E S I N C O N F E R E N C E
O N T O . O V A L . E R N S T
. . . T I L E . U M P S . . .
T E A . S A L I V A . H A G S
A T R I A . S I R . W H O A .
S H E S W I T H A C L I E N T
. K E N O . R H O . I N A N E
S L A P . K E T T L E . D A D
. . . R O S S . E I N E . . .
S H O E R . T A T I . L E A S
H E S N O T A T H I S D E S K
E A S E . A N N E . P E R K Y
A D O . O D O R . A R O S E
```

35

```
S O C K   F I A T S   A P T S
A C H E   A N D R E   T R O T
T H I N K A G A I N   E E R O
Y E N T A   E Y E S H A D O W
R R S   P A S   S O U S A
    J U S T F O R G E T I T
D E P O T S   R U S E   I R A
E R L E   S E T   S N A G
M I A   J O I E   V S I G N S
I N Y O U R D R E A M S
    A N K L E   R N A   C U B
L I P R E A D E R   S H A N E
E S A U   N O T A C H A N C E
M E R S   D O N N E   R O U T
S E T H   O R A T E   P E T S
```

36

```
A L P S   A R A L   S A F E R
T O U T   F A R E   O C A L A
T A L E   C H E V Y C H A S E
A T L A S     N I E C E
C H U M P C H A N G E   A S U
H E P   A P O   G R E G O R
A R O M A S   L E A N
C H I N E S E C H E C K E R S
A E O N   S T E R E O
M A N I A C   L E D   W B A
E T S   C H A R L I E C H A N
    S C O P E   D R A N G
C H O K E C H A I N   A L T O
D I D I N   I T S Y   Z E A L
S P E N T   D A M E   E R M A
```

37

```
R I B S   A V I A S   A M M O
O M O O   R I N G O   R A I N
Y O U R P L A C E O R M I N E
A N N E H E C H E   E E N
L I C   I S O   S L E D G E
S T E T   M A T T E   R U M
    R A E   P H E A S A N T
W H A T S Y O U R S I G N
D I A M E T E R   N E T
A N Y   C E N T S   S H E A
R E F E R S   E P A   I T S
    E X O   A R E A C O D E S
H A V E W E M E T B E F O R E
E W E R   L E A H S   F U N T
P E R T   I N L E T   S T E S
```

38

```
S A G S   F A D S   D E C A Y
P U R E   A L I T   E C O L E
O R A N   R A N I   B O X I N
N O H A R M N O F O U L
G R A T I S   L U G   O D E
Y A M   S O L V E R   A V E R
    A Q U A E   A R E N A
N O G U T S N O G L O R Y
G E N R E   A R L E N
A N Y A   A S L E E P   E B B
L E X   A S H   A P O L L O
    N O P A I N N O G A I N
U L C E R   G L E E   D I N G
M O N E T   G E A R   E N D O
P A N D A   Y A P S   N E S S
```

39

```
A B E T   B A A S   F A T A L
L O P E   A B L E   U T I L E
A L E X   B L I P   R O L L S
S T E A M B O A T W I L L I E
    S O L O     E E L
V C R   N E M E S I S   S A G
E R O D E   L A G   P A R R
G O O D T I M E C H A R L I E
A C M E   L E N   L E A S E
S K Y   S I N A T R A   D E N
    A T A   H E M S
S T A G E D O O R J O H N N Y
C A D R E   A B O O   R I C O
A R I E L   T O N I   E T A L
M O N E Y   S E E N   W E A K
```

40

```
S T I F F   G A G A   O N T O
C H O I R   A L E X   R A I L
A U N T I E M A M E   I N R E
M G S   E D E N S   T O N E S
    A N D       O I L Y
D A D D Y L O N G L E G S
O A S E S   A P O R T   O P S
A T T N   U N T I E   P A L O
F U R   U R G E S   G O T I N
M O M M I E D E A R E S T
    L O P S     N O T
C L O D S   S E E T O   O D E
R A G E   U N C L E V A N Y A
O V E R   S A H L   E L M E R
W A R N   E G O S   D E E D S
```

41

```
STOMP BIOS SHAH
PACER RSVP MAXI
EXTREMEMEASURES
DIS SAW RNA ESS
    PERU HIGH
GUILTYPLEASURES
OHNO  ORR  GARP
LUC MANED  ZOO
FRAS ACE  HOST
SUNKENTREASURES
   ARTS VIED
ARF MIA ERA AIR
SUREASSURECANBE
OBEY SILT OWNED
FETE AFTS WESTS
```

42

```
MODEM IRAQ GELT
EBOLI SITU UVEA
DIGIN AOTI YIPS
  FASHIONPLATES
CVI TAD  SNARE
RIGORS FONDA
OCHRE JANE  SHA
SATELLITEDISHES
SRS IVES  SUOMI
   CREED LABREA
APPLY CUB  TNN
FLYINGSAUCERS
LURE ROCK LITUP
AMEN AMMO LOOSE
TEXT BEER ASPEN
```

43

```
ARID  PITY  PAAR
REDUB OREO AXLE
COOKIESANDCREAM
 SLEAZE SARA
   NEUT ADAGE
 BLACKRASPBERRY
BALSA METS  COD
LIBS JAPES ETUI
ALE TAKE  PRICE
HEATHBARCRUNCH
SENOR  SPAR
  POGS SNEEZE
PEPPERMINTSTICK
OKIE AUTO TNOTE
WEED STOW ANON
```

44

```
FLAP STAY SALTS
LIME URGE EMAIL
ATOP POOL NASTY
SHOPPINGLISZT
KENYAN  REELIN
   GEWGAWS ADA
 SHEA INRI LUAU
HAYDNPLAINSIGHT
ALPS ALTA ECHO
ISE STASSEN
GARLIC  LAOTSE
 BACHSCRATCHER
STORK PLOP COMA
SOLVE AIMS URIS
SMEAR MOPE ROSE
```

45

```
BLTS LAMAR RIOT
EIRE ABODE ANNA
EMIT MEALS WALK
FITTOBETIED LYE
STELLA  BERRA
  EDSEL NATTER
OAFS TOAD NEHRU
NIL HENPECK ELS
EDUCE SILO FRET
RESENT NINER
  TONES CLEATS
SHE ALLWORKEDUP
LORD LARGE MANE
OBEY EVERT AGEE
BODE RENEE NERD
```

46

```
LAVA BASS MASKS
OBIT ACHE ONEAL
COVERGIRL UNITE
ADIEU DIMES ZIP
LED SPREADSHEET
  STEAK SEA
MARTINIS  LOIN
AZTECAN SILENCE
COEN EASESOUT
  CHI GLOAT
AFGHANHOUND SGT
TOE SCOTT USHER
BRASH WRAPPARTY
AGREE LIRA NEMO
TESTS SPYS GWEN
```

47

```
C A S H   C A S T   P S H A W
U L N A   O L I O   O C A L A
B O O M E R A N G   P R Y O R
S E W   T R I   A T T E S T S
      G H A N A   H O W
P A T R O L   S L A P D A S H
A L I A S   O P E N   R E N E
R I B S   D R I N K   I R O N
E V E S   H A R D   A V I O N
D E T H R O N E   S L E E P Y
      O I L   S T A I R
S T E P P E S   E B B   S K Y
C A R P E   H U R R I C A N E
A L I E N   A N N E   A R E A
B E E R S   M O S S   P I E R
```

48

```
M O O L A   S P E C   P I P S
A D H O C   T A P A   O S H A
T O N Y C U R T I S   N A I F
S R O   U S A   S P A C K L E
      A R U N   T I S H
O S C A R D E L A H O Y A
P R E T T Y   L E N   A N T
R A I S E   S I S   C O N D O
O T S   A C H   C A G N E Y
E M M Y L O U H A R R I S
      I A G O   A R T E
B R A C K E T   V O S   J I B
R O C K   R I T A M O R E N O
E T R E   I N O N   F I E R Y
W H E Y   A G R A   F A Z E D
```

49

```
A L E C   S W A M P   B A J A
D I A L   T I B I A   E V I L
A E R O   A L I S T   L E V I
M U L T I P L E C H O I C E
      H O L Y   E N E
B O V I N E   A C T O F G O D
A R E N A   I N A I R   A M A
S O N G   A B O R C   M E E K
I N A   S P O D E   H E L G A
C O L L A P S E   Q U A S A R
      A F R   C U L T
N O N E O F T H E A B O V E
G O D A   V I R U S   A L S O
A N K H   A R E N T   L I O N
S O S O   L E E K S   L O P S
```

50

```
A S S N   A D D U P   I S L E
T U N E   M O O L A   N L E R
B R O W N B E T T Y   S O A R
A L O H A   S E R E   T P K S
T Y P I N G   A E S O P
      R O U N D S   T R Y O N
S A V E   L O U   D E E J A Y
P I E   S L I M J I M   O R E
A D A P T S   B O X   B E S T
M E L E E   C O Y O T E
      O S T E R   N O R M A L
P O S T   A I R S   A R I S E
O N C E   S T E A K D I A N E
O M A R   T I B I A   E M E R
H E R S   S C A L Y   S I R S
```

51

```
A R T S   G R U B   A S T A B
L U A U   E A S E   N O O S E
P I C S   O N E A   A L F I E
O N T H E F I R S T C O U N T
      I N F   T A O
A L I   D R A M   G N E I S S
N A D A   E L I S   D A N C E
G U I L T Y A S C H A R G E D
E R O S E   S H O O   P O N G
L A M O N T   A W L S   T E E
      O R E   L I L
O R D E R I N T H E C O U R T
M A U D S   D O E R   C L E O
A R E N A   O G R E   K A N T
R E L A X   W A R D   E N T O
```

52

```
B E A M   M T G   R E D A T E
A B B A   I W O   E R I C H S
J A C K A R O O   M A D M E N
A N D O R R A   C A T S E Y E
            C O C K A T O O
M S G   A R T I S T   A L B
A C H E D   P E E K A B O O
C R A N I A   D I A L I N
K A N G A R O O   N A U R U
S P A   T A R I F F   E E S
B U C K A R O O
T O T A L L Y   A R L B E R G
A F R I C A   K I C K A P O O
G L A Z E S   A L E   L I M A
S A Y E R S   L S D   I C E D
```

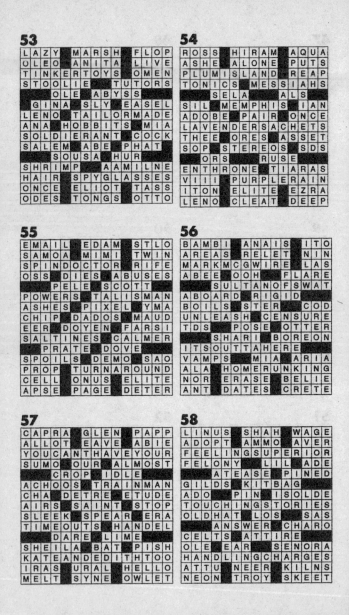

53

L	A	Z	Y		M	A	R	S	H		F	L	O	P
O	L	E	O		A	N	I	T	A		L	I	V	E
T	I	N	K	E	R	T	O	Y	S		O	M	E	N
S	T	O	O	L	I	E			T	U	T	O	R	S
			O	L	E		A	B	Y	S	S			
	G	I	N	A		S	L	Y		E	A	S	E	L
L	E	N	O		T	A	I	L	O	R	M	A	D	E
A	N	A		H	O	B	B	I	T	S		M	I	A
S	O	L	D	I	E	R	A	N	T		C	O	C	K
S	A	L	E	M		A	B	E		P	H	A	T	
			S	O	U	S	A		H	U	R			
S	H	R	I	M	P			A	A	M	I	L	N	E
H	A	I	R		S	P	Y	G	L	A	S	S	E	S
O	N	C	E		E	L	I	O	T		T	A	S	S
O	D	E	S		T	O	N	G	S		O	T	T	O

54

R	O	S	S		H	I	R	A	M		A	Q	U	A
A	S	H	E		A	L	O	N	E		P	U	T	S
P	L	U	M	I	S	L	A	N	D		R	E	A	P
T	O	N	I	C	S		M	E	S	S	I	A	H	S
			S	E	L	A			A	L	S			
S	I	L		M	E	M	P	H	I	S		I	A	N
A	D	O	B	E		P	A	I	R		O	N	C	E
L	A	V	E	N	D	E	R	S	A	C	H	E	T	S
T	H	E	E		O	R	E	S		A	S	S	E	T
S	O	P		S	T	E	R	E	O	S		S	D	S
			O	R	S			R	U	S	E			
E	N	T	H	R	O	N	E		T	I	A	R	A	S
V	I	I	I		P	U	R	P	L	E	R	A	I	N
I	T	O	N		E	L	I	T	E		E	Z	R	A
L	E	N	O		C	L	E	A	T		D	E	E	P

55

E	M	A	I	L		E	D	A	M		S	T	L	O
S	A	M	O	A		M	I	M	I		T	W	I	N
S	P	I	N	D	O	C	T	O	R		R	I	F	E
O	S	S		D	I	E	S		A	B	U	S	E	S
			P	E	L	E		S	C	O	T	T		
P	O	W	E	R	S		T	A	L	I	S	M	A	N
A	S	H	E	S		P	I	X	E	L		Y	M	A
C	H	I	P		D	A	D	O	S		M	A	U	D
E	E	R		D	O	Y	E	N		F	A	R	S	I
S	A	L	T	I	N	E	S		C	A	L	M	E	R
			P	R	A	T	E		D	O	V	E		
S	P	O	I	L	S		D	E	M	O		S	A	O
P	R	O	P		T	U	R	N	A	R	O	U	N	D
C	E	L	L		O	N	U	S		E	L	I	T	E
A	P	S	E		P	A	G	E		D	E	T	E	R

56

B	A	M	B	I		A	N	A	I	S		I	T	O
A	R	E	A	S		R	E	L	E	T		N	I	N
M	A	R	K	M	C	G	W	I	R	E		L	A	S
A	B	E	E		O	O	H		F	L	A	R	E	
			S	U	L	T	A	N	O	F	S	W	A	T
A	B	O	A	R	D		R	I	G	I	D			
B	O	I	L	S		S	T	E	R			C	O	D
U	N	L	E	A	S	H		C	E	N	S	U	R	E
T	D	S			P	O	S	E		O	T	T	E	R
			S	H	A	R	I		B	O	R	E	O	N
I	T	S	O	U	T	T	A	H	E	R	E			
V	A	M	P	S		M	I	A		A	R	I	A	
A	L	A		H	O	M	E	R	U	N	K	I	N	G
N	O	R		E	R	A	S	E			B	E	L	I	E
A	N	T		D	A	T	E	S		C	R	E	T	E

57

C	A	P	R	A		G	L	E	N		P	A	P	P
A	L	L	O	T		E	A	V	E		A	B	I	E
Y	O	U	C	A	N	T	H	A	V	E	Y	O	U	R
S	U	M	O		O	U	R		A	L	M	O	S	T
			C	R	O	P		I	D	L	E			
A	C	H	O	O	S		T	R	A	I	N	M	A	N
C	H	A		D	E	T	R	E		E	T	U	D	E
A	I	R	S		S	A	I	N	T		S	T	O	P
S	L	E	E	K		S	P	E	A	R		E	R	A
T	I	M	E	O	U	T	S		H	A	N	D	E	L
			D	A	R	E		L	I	M	E			
S	H	E	I	L	A		B	A	T		P	I	S	H
K	A	T	E	A	N	D	E	D	I	T	H	T	O	O
I	R	A	S		U	R	A	L		H	E	L	L	O
M	E	L	T		S	Y	N	E		O	W	L	E	T

58

L	I	N	U	S		S	H	A	H		W	A	G	E
A	D	O	P	T		A	M	M	O		A	V	E	R
F	E	E	L	I	N	G	S	U	P	E	R	I	O	R
F	E	L	O	N	Y		L	I	L		A	D	E	
			A	T	E	A	S	E		P	I	N	E	D
G	I	L	D	S		K	I	T	B	A	G			
A	D	O		P	I	N		I	S	O	L	D	E	
T	O	U	C	H	I	N	G	S	T	O	R	I	E	S
O	L	D	H	A	T		L	O	S			S	A	S
			A	N	S	W	E	R		C	H	A	R	O
C	E	L	T	S		A	T	T	I	R	E			
O	L	E		E	A	R		S	E	N	O	R	A	
H	A	N	D	L	I	N	G	C	H	A	R	G	E	S
A	T	T	U		N	E	E	R		K	I	L	N	S
N	E	O	N		T	R	O	Y		S	K	E	E	T

59

```
E W E R   A S P S   G O M E R
F A D E   M O L T   I N T R A
T W E N T Y F O U R S E V E N
S A N T A   A W A I T S
      A R S   R O S I E S T
N E I L   H I N T S   D X I I I
O R D   T A C O   D E T R E
O N E E I G H T H U N D E R D
S E A M S   E A S Y   A N Y
E S T S   B A D G E   E S S E
S T E R O I D   S O X
      G R A D E S   S P A R K
S E V E N S I X T Y S E V E N
I R A N I   N I L E   L O D E
P A N T S   G T O S   S N O W
```

60

```
  A L A E   I L S A   C A S H
G L E N N   D O W N   A R T E
M E A N T   E X I T   R E A L
S C H I R R A   S H E P A R D
      E E E   S H E R E
M A T   E T N A   M I N D E D
O S H A   A I L S   E T U D E
T H E M E R C U R Y S E V E N
H O T E L   E T T A   R E N T
S T A T I C   E A S E   T S E
      H O O K S   I D A
S L A Y T O N   G R I S S O M
H I P S   P A L E   S I T U P
E A S T   E V E N   O D O R S
A R E S   R E N E   N E W S
```

61

```
M O A T   F O B S   W H A L E
E L L A   O R E O   A E G I S
S E A M   R E A L   G L U E S
A G I A N T A M O N G M E N
      R O A D S   O L E
M E D A L S   P O E T I C S
E R E C T   R O A N   C U T
Y A N K E E I N G E N U I T Y
E T E   N I T E   O N E I L
R O B E R T S   S T E R E O
      U A R   A S K E D
A N C I E N T M A R I N E R
D I A L S   O B I T   T U B A
E D D I E   S A L E   E D A M
B E A D S   E Y E S   D E N S
```

62

```
H E A P   P A P E R   S L E D
O L L A   I D A H O   M A D E
D A V Y   N O I S E   E M I R
S N A P   U R N   E L I T E
      H O P E L E S S T A S K
A C T O R   S E G O S
C R A N E S   S O P   S I L O
H O M E L E S S S H E L T E R
E W E S   L A D   S T E E V E
      E L M E R   C U R I O
E N D L E S S N I G H T
P E R I L   T A R   H O W E
E R A S   A G I L E   I N O N
E V I L   B A S T E   N E R D
S Y N E   S I T O N   G A M S
```

63

```
S T A I R   E C H O   S O F A
H A N O I   G O O P   E L L S
A P I N G   G R E E K W E E K
L E S   A G E E   R A N G E S
T R E A T E D   D E N
      T O T   L A T E P A S S
L O G O N   A I N T   E L M O
I T A L I A N S T A L L I O N
M O L L   B I T E   E L E G Y
P E A S A N T S   O W E
      L O A   U N I T I N G
E A S I E R   A N O N   N O R
S W I S S M I S S   S A N T A
T O L L   A C H E   K N E E S
A L O E   L E E R   Y A R D S
```

64

```
O H G O D   S I T S   H A L T
D E U C E   E D I T   A B I E
A W F U L   R O T E   M O N A
      F L I P F L O P S I D E S
      A L A S   S E L E N E
F A R R A R   S P U R T
E N A   H I P H O P B O O T S
A T M S   E A R   N O R A
T I P T O P S H E E T   Z E N
      O D E T S   R I B E Y E
M A G P I E   A G R A
C L I P C L O P B O A R D
C O V E   E L A N   D R I P S
O N E R   R I P E   E E R I E
Y E N S   S O A R   S L E P T
```

65

```
T A L L   A S P E N   A B L E
I D E A   S H A R I   A L E X
G O O D D A Y S U N S H I N E
E R N I E   O P E N   N O S
R E A D E R S   T R E A D
      A D U L T   S E T S T O
A D S   H E A P   Z I P U P
B E T T E R P L A C E T O B E
C L E A N   T E L L   T A R
D E V I L S   S L A P S
    E L I O T   S W A T T E D
O W N   S P A S   L O R N A
B E S T T H I N G F O R Y O U
I R O N   I N U S E   K I L N
T E N T   A T B A Y   S T A T
```

66

```
W A G E D   M O T O   G L U M
A L O N E   A S A P   L I N E
S L A V S   C L U E   O B I S
  L O C K H O R N S   W I T H
P A P Y R I   U S E   D E E
A G O   Y O W L S   P L O D S
M E S S   S E A   S T Y
  S T O C K E X C H A N G E
A H A   L O U   N U L L
K A F K A   L Y O N S   A L I
O D E   S A Y   T E H R A N
B A R R E L C H E S T E D
O G R E   P E A R   T W I L L
L I E N   H U L A   L E A V E
D O T E   A M E S   E R N I E
```

67

```
P A R T S   R A T A   S M O G
A T A R I   E D A M   T A B U
S E C O N D M O R T G A G E S
S A I D   E A R S   R I N D
E S S   A N N E   H E R E I N
R E T R E A D   D I S   S E A
    A R T   C U D   I N T
T H E F O U R T H E S T A T E
H E Y   R E S   A A A
O R E   W E D   A W K W A R D
R E P A I D   A L A I   P O I
  H I N T   O D A Y   L E S S
B E E T H O V E N S S I X T H
A R C O   D E L I   I S E R E
S E E N   E R A S   C A S A S
```

68

```
S R S   C Z A R   H I L T O N
T E C   R A T E   A M O E B A
I S H   A N T S   U B O A T S
G O O D B Y E C O L U M B U S
M U L E S   N U R S E   A S E
A R A B   I D E S   A G E R
S C R A M M E D   C P R
  E S C A P E   F R O M L A
L P S   T O A P O I N T
P O M E   D E N Y   I T T O
U N E   F A U L T   A R I E L
L E A V I N G L A S V E G A S
S I D I N G   S I T E   A T T
A D O N I S   O N O R   N E O
R A W E S T   N E W T   T R Y
```

69

```
S T A T   P E R M A   A N O N
P A I R   A V O I R   L O B O
A X L E   M E A T C U T T E R
M I S S P E N D   T O A S T
    T A L E   T R U S T E E
M A I L C A R R I E R
E G R E T   A D E N   P P S
L E O S   R A V E D   C O O T
T E N   S O L E   G A M M A
    N A I L C L I P P E R
C O N C E R T   O A R S
A W A R E   S H U T T E R S
U N D E R L I N E R   O M I T
S E E S   I N U R E   N I L E
E R R S   B A B E L   E L E M
```

70

```
A L P S   P E T S   P A N E L
M O R T   I R A E   A D O R E
B O O R   N A U T   S E N S E
I T M A R K S T H E S P O T
  S O P H I E   D O T
    P I E   E R I N   W I G
S I T I N   I S O N   S H O W
U N K N O W N Q U A N T I T Y
M O O G   A G U E   O R G A N
O N S   T H E E   P R E
  S A O   R O M A N O
S Y M B O L F O R A K I S S
S N A I L   E A S T   E C H O
M A P L E   A M I E   R H E A
U P S E T   P E E R   S E A R
```

71

B	O	L	D		T	S	A	R		K	M	A	R	T
O	H	I	O		H	E	R	A		H	A	N	O	I
S	O	M	E		R	U	I	N		A	N	O	D	E
C	H	A	R	L	E	S	D	I	C	K	E	N	S	
			O	S	S				A	I	D			
A	T	T	A	C	H		L	A	P	S		D	D	E
P	A	R	M	A		S	A	A	R		O	R	A	L
T	H	E	P	L	O	T	T	H	I	C	K	E	N	S
L	O	S	S		D	U	H	S		I	R	A	T	E
Y	E	S		C	E	D	E		E	V	A	D	E	S
			B	O	O				C	L	I			
	S	P	R	I	N	G	C	H	I	C	K	E	N	S
L	I	E	O	N		A	L	E	X		I	D	E	A
A	L	A	M	O		P	A	R	I		W	A	R	S
S	T	R	O	P		E	W	E	R		I	M	O	K

72

	O	D	R	A		S	U	S	A	N		B	R	A
	P	I	E	S		C	H	O	K	E		R	E	N
W	E	A	R	Y	W	I	L	L	I	E		O	P	A
A	R	G	A	L	I		A	I	M		R	I	L	L
B	A	R	N	U	M	A	N	D	B	A	I	L	E	Y
E	T	A		M	P	S		S	O	R	B	E	T	S
E	M	S		L	I	Z			C	A	D	E	T	
			T	H	E	F	A	T	M	A	N			
	M	A	G	E	E		P	G	A		D	O	M	
A	D	E	L	I	N	A		I	L	L		R	O	E
S	A	R	A	S	O	T	A	F	L	O	R	I	D	A
S	P	A	R		R	O	B		E	C	H	O	E	S
A	T	L		E	M	M	E	T	T	K	E	L	L	Y
G	O	D		M	A	I	L	S		I	M	E	T	
E	R	O		U	N	C	L	E		N	E	S	S	

73

P	A	I	R		S	L	I	D		A	M	A	Z	E
A	L	S	O		T	I	M	E		L	A	M	E	R
B	A	L	L		E	M	I	T		P	R	U	N	E
S	M	A	L	L	P	O	T	A	T	O	E	S		
T	O	M	E	I		A	I	R			E	M	S	
		L	I	T	T	L	E	W	O	M	E	N		
S	H	A	D		D	O	E		P	I	E	T	A	
P	I	N	E	F	O	R		E	D	A	S	N	E	R
A	T	O	N	E		A	L	I		E	T	R	E	
T	I	N	Y	B	U	B	B	L	E	S				
S	T	Y		P	I	A		S	I	M	B	A		
	M	I	N	I	A	T	U	R	E	G	O	L	F	
O	P	I	N	E		S	I	N	O		A	L	I	A
F	A	T	S	O		E	N	I	D		V	A	S	T
T	R	Y	O	N		S	G	T	S		E	R	S	E

74

W	E	E	D		A	M	A	S	S		K	A	Y	
A	B	L	E	R		R	O	B	O	T		I	V	E
N	E	W	B	O	R	N	B	A	B	Y		L	E	T
T	R	A	I	N	E	E	S		M	A	O	R	I	
S	T	Y		A	N	S		K	E	I	T	H		
			B	L	E	S	S	E	D	E	V	E	N	T
S	H	A	R	D		O	N	E	S		R	I	O	
P	O	L	O		C	A	N	O	N		I	T	L	L
A	Y	E		A	U	D	I		F	A	Z	E	D	
T	A	X	D	E	D	U	C	T	I	O	N			
		H	O	R	S	E		I	S	R		A	S	K
	A	L	A	M	O		E	L	E	G	A	N	C	E
G	A	L		B	U	N	D	L	E	O	F	J	O	Y
E	V	E		I	M	A	G	E		T	O	O	N	E
D	A	Y		C	A	G	E	D		R	U	E	D	

75

S	A	G	A		R	O	L	L	O		B	E	G	S
E	D	E	N		O	N	E	A	L		U	T	A	H
P	O	S	T	A	L	C	A	R	D		B	A	B	A
A	R	T	I	C	L	E		G	A	R	B	L	E	D
L	E	E	C	H		M	O	G	U	L				
			E	T	T	A		E	N	E	R	G	Y	
F	L	A	N		O	H	N	O		A	G	E	N	A
A	I	D	E		G	U	A	V	A		U	N	U	M
C	R	O	W	D		S	T	A	B		M	O	S	S
T	A	S	S	E	L		E	L	S	A				
			P	R	O	B	E		C	L	I	F	F	
P	A	L	A	N	C	E		C	O	R	O	N	E	R
A	T	O	P		A	R	C	A	D	E	G	A	M	E
S	O	L	E		T	R	O	V	E		O	N	M	E
O	M	A	R		E	A	G	E	R		N	E	E	D

76

C	H	I	C		G	L	E	A	M		Z	A	P	S
Z	O	R	A		R	A	N	D	I		A	D	U	E
A	M	I	N	O	A	C	I	D	S		G	A	Z	A
R	E	S	T	A	T	E	D		M	O	R	M	O	N
			I	S	I	S		H	A	N	E	S		
S	P	A	C	E	S		D	A	T	A	B	A	S	E
W	E	L	L	S		G	I	V	E	N		P	T	A
E	A	V	E		S	E	A	R	S		A	P	E	R
A	L	I		A	T	O	N	E		I	S	L	E	T
R	E	N	E	G	A	D	E		J	O	S	E	P	H
		A	L	E	N	E		B	E	N	E			
G	R	I	P	E	D		M	A	R	I	M	B	A	S
L	O	L	A		A	D	D	I	S	A	B	A	B	A
U	S	E	S		R	O	L	L	E		L	E	E	K
M	A	Y	O		D	A	I	S	Y		E	R	T	E

77

R	A	R	E		B	A	L	K			U	S	E	S
O	R	A	L		O	B	I	E			A	N	K	L	E
B	E	G	I	N	N	I	N	G	O	F	T	I	M	E
S	A	S		I	N	R	E		R	A	I	N	S	
			A	I	D		D	A	R	E				
	B	A	D	G	E		E	E	N		D	R	A	T
S	E	P	I	A		O	M	E	G	A		E	W	E
C	E	N	T	R	A	L	A	M	E	R	I	C	A	N
A	B	E		A	D	D	I	S		A	D	O	R	N
T	E	A	S		V	A	L		T	B	O	N	E	
			I	L	E	S		T	A	I				
	S	W	E	A	R		G	A	G	A		V	I	A
S	T	O	R	Y	B	O	O	K	E	N	D	I	N	G
P	U	R	R	S		W	R	E	N		A	N	T	E
A	N	N	A			L	E	N	D		M	O	O	D

78

A	M	M	O		A	B	E	T		S	C	A	R	
P	I	A	N	O		M	O	N	O		T	A	D	A
E	R	R	O	R		B	R	I	O		A	V	I	S
			G	R	I	L	L	E	D	S	H	R	I	M	P
S	M	A		G	E	E			M	O	T	L	E	Y
C	U	R	R	I	E	D	C	R	A	B				
O	R	I	O	N			H	A	L	O	G	E	N	
T	A	T	I		S	T	A	H	L		P	N	O	M
	L	A	S	S	O	E	S			M	A	G	O	O
			C	L	A	M	S	C	A	S	I	N	O	
A	R	T	A	U	D			H	O	S		N	E	T
L	O	B	S	T	E	R	B	I	S	Q	U	E		
E	G	O	S		R	A	I	N		U	S	E	R	S
R	U	N	E		E	V	E	N		E	N	R	O	L
T	E	E	S		D	E	N	Y		A	S	T	O	

79

I	D	L	E		J	U	M	P	S		U	L	A	N
S	E	A	L		O	N	E	A	T		N	I	L	E
A	B	S	O	L	U	T	E	L	Y		D	E	A	R
A	R	E		E	R	I	K		L	E	O	N	I	D
C	A	R	B	I	N	E		P	E	R	U			
			U	S	A		D	A	T	A	B	A	S	E
O	B	I	T		L	I	O	N		S	T	U	M	P
P	E	C	O	S		N	N	E		E	E	R	I	E
A	L	O	F	T		G	U	L	F		D	A	T	E
L	A	N	C	E	L	O	T		A	F	L			
			O	M	I	T		S	T	A	Y	P	U	T
M	E	D	U	S	A		R	O	A	R		I	L	E
O	V	E	R		B	Y	A	L	L	M	E	A	N	S
P	I	N	S		L	O	C	A	L		A	N	A	T
E	L	S	E		E	M	E	R	Y		R	O	S	Y

80

M	A	M	E		D	E	G	A	S		O	W	L	S
A	L	E	X		A	B	A	S	E		O	R	E	O
C	A	S	T	I	R	O	N	S	T	O	M	A	C	H
S	W	A	R	M	I	N	G		S	A	P	P	H	O
			O	P	U	S		E	S	T	H			
G	R	A	V	E	S		B	A	A	S		S	H	A
E	A	T	E	N		T	O	R	I		S	P	A	N
S	W	O	R	D	S	W	A	L	L	O	W	I	N	G
T	E	N	T		C	I	T	Y		F	E	R	N	S
E	R	E		B	A	N	S		A	F	L	O	A	T
			W	A	V	E		W	R	I	T			
C	R	E	O	L	E		P	R	E	S	E	L	L	S
L	U	M	P	I	N	T	H	E	T	H	R	O	A	T
A	S	I	A		G	O	O	S	E		E	R	M	A
M	E	L	T		E	A	S	T	S		D	D	A	Y

81

E	N	T	E	R		P	O	P	E		M	A	M	E
L	O	R	R	E		A	C	E	S		I	M	A	M
B	E	I	N	G		W	H	A	T	A	D	U	M	P
A	L	S	O	R	A	N	S		E	L	I	C	I	T
			E	S	E		L	E	O		K	E	Y	
O	V	E	R	T	H	E	H	U	M	P				
T	E	X	A	S		O	R	E		I	P	S	A	
I	R	E	S		C	A	N	E	D		B	E	E	T
S	A	S	H		R	I	O		A	E	R	E	O	
			F	O	R	R	E	S	T	G	U	M	P	
B	U	S		E	S	S		L	A	T				
A	P	P	L	E	S		I	A	M	A	R	O	C	K
S	P	E	E	D	B	U	M	P		C	A	N	O	N
T	E	A	S		O	N	U	S		H	I	T	M	E
E	R	R	S		W	I	S	E		E	L	O	P	E

82

R	I	T	Z		S	T	O	P		A	O	R	T	A
I	D	E	A		L	I	V	E		P	R	I	O	R
F	L	A	G	P	O	L	E	S		T	I	N	G	E
F	E	M		A	G	E	N	T	S		E	G	O	S
			E	P	A			S	T	I	N	G		
T	U	P	P	E	N	C	E		A	C	T	U	A	L
O	N	A	I	R		O	L	D	I	E		A	D	O
W	I	G		C	A	L	L	I	N	S		R	A	P
E	T	E		L	I	T	E	R		H	E	D	G	E
D	E	T	A	I	L		S	T	R	E	S	S	E	D
			U	P	P	E	R		A	E	S			
C	A	R	R		D	E	C	E	N	T		H	O	T
R	U	N	O	N		H	A	I	L	S	T	O	N	E
A	R	E	N	A		A	R	N	O		A	L	E	X
M	A	R	S	H		B	L	E	W		B	E	S	T

83

```
I N G E   A M I S H   S O N G
C E L A   C A N T O   H A I L
B R A V E H E A R T   O K L A
M O D E L T   N A B   V E E R
      S K U A   D E F E N S E
G A R D E N S P A D E
E V E R   G E E   S E W N O N
L E D O N   C A W   S H A V E
T R O P I C   R A F   I T E R
      N E I L D I A M O N D
W E S T E R N   I N I S
H A L E   E U R   A R I O S O
A S I S   B R I D G E C L U B
L E N T   R E P E L   A G E E
E L K S   A D E L E   L A Z Y
```

84

```
B R O K E   Z A P P A   F D A
M A R I S   S N E R T   A E R
W H E N T H A T E E L   M A I
      G E E Z E R   M I R E
G A S S E R S   P S A L M S
O N I T   B A T S A N E Y E
P E S O S   O H N O
W I N K R I G H T B A C K
      I O T A   S L O E S
D O N T B E S H Y   C O D E
G R O U S E   I M P A S S E
L I L T   W A S H U P
A V A   T H A T S A M O R A Y
D E L   O A K I E   A N O D E
E R A   W H E T S   S E W O N
```

85

```
A C T E   L I A R   M E L T S
M A I L   U R G E   I D E A L
A S T I   C O O N   L I E B Y
S T A N D I N G O R D E R S
S E N O R A   W I E
    R U N N I N G W A T E R
B U D   B O A S   A S T H M A
I T E M   B I N   T E M P
D A M A S K   N O A H   M A T
S H O O T I N G S T A R
      A L A   T R A I L S
F L Y I N G S Q U I R R E L
A L I E N   S T U N   I A G O
D A N T E   A L E E   T N U T
O N A I R   T O S S   Y I P S
```

86

```
P A N A M   R A K E   S H A H
O M A H A   A S A P   C A M E
S P E A K O F T H E D E V I L
      B E N   O N E O N O N E
S A P   T O W   R E C O N
M A R D I   A B E A M
A R O O M   D E L I   I S N T
C O N V E R S E A L L S T A R
K N E E   C U R T   E L U D E
      L A P S E   A E R I E
O S A K A   S T P   M A D
L E W I N S K Y   U F O
S T A T E U N I V E R S I T Y
E T R E   D O P E   O L D I E
N O D S   S T E T   G O O N S
```

87

```
L O L A   S L A B   I T A L Y
I C E D   L E N O   N O M A D
A T A D   A V E R   F R A Y S
R E V O L V I N G D O O R
S T E N O   D I O R   Y A M
      S W A N   A A M I L N E
A T T   R U E   E R L E S
W H I R L I N G D E R V I S H
A R G U E   O U T   S T Y
R E E N A C T   B A R S
E E R   P O E T   A C H E S
    S P I N N I N G W H E E L
Q U E E N   O D O R   L A L A
T R Y S T   R A G U   E V E N
S E E T O   S L O B   P E R T
```

88

```
S C A M   R A T E D   A F R O
N O R M   E V O K E   P L E A
O K E E F F E M E A B R E A K
R I N   L U R E D   L O A D S
T E A B A G S   H O N
    I K E   T H O U S A N D
A B A T   S H O O S   L A Y
H A L S O F M O N T E Z U M A
A C T   N O O S E   A M E N
S H O R T A G E   W A N
    O I L   B R I E F E D
S C R A M   B R A I D   O V A
Q U E S E U R A T S E U R A T
F E A T   R I G H T   S A D E
T S P S   N O S E S   E Y E D
```

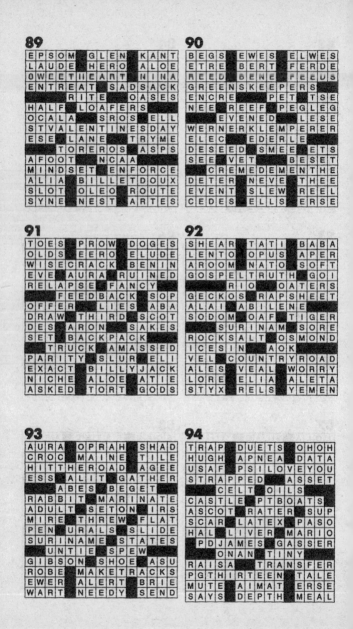

89

```
E P S O M   G L E N   K A N T
L A U D E   H E R O   A L O E
S W E E T H E A R T   N I N A
E N T R E A T   S A D S A C K
      R I T E     O A S E S
H A L F   L O A F E R S
O C A L A   S R O S     E L L
S T V A L E N T I N E S D A Y
E S E   L A N E   T R Y M E
      T O R E R O S   A S P S
A F O O T     N C A A
M I N D S E T   E N F O R C E
A L I A   B I L L E T D O U X
S L O T   O L E O   R O U T E
S Y N E   N E S T   A R T E S
```

90

```
B E G S   E W E S   E L W E S
E T R E   B E R T   F E R D E
R E E D   B E N E   F E E D S
G R E E N S K E E P E R S
E N C R E   P E T     T S E
N E E   R E E F   P E G L E G
      E V E N E D   L E S E
W E R N E R K L E M P E R E R
E L E C   E D E R L E
D E S E E D   S M E E   E T S
S E E   V E T     B E S E T
      C R E M E D E M E N T H E
D E T E R   N E V E   T H E E
E V E N T   S L E W   R E E L
C E D E S   E L L S   E R S E
```

91

```
T O E S   P R O W   D O G E S
O L D S   E E R O   E L U D E
W I S E C R A C K   B E N I N
E V E   A U R A   R U I N E D
R E L A P S E   F A N C Y
      F E E D B A C K   S O P
O F F E R   L I E S   A B A
D R A W   T H I R D   S C O T
D E S   A R O N   S A K E S
S E T   B A C K P A C K
      T R U C K   A M A S S E D
P A R I T Y   S L U R   E L I
E X A C T   B I L L Y J A C K
N I C H E   A L O E   A T I E
A S K E D   T O R T   G O D S
```

92

```
S H E A R   T A T I   B A B A
L E N T O   O P U S   A P E R
A R O O M   N A T O   S O F T
G O S P E L T R U T H   G O I
      R I O     O A T E R S
G E C K O S   R A P S H E E T
A L A I   A B I L E N E
S O D O M   O A F   T I G E R
      S U R I N A M   S O R E
R O C K S A L T   O S M O N D
I C E S I N   A O K
V E L   C O U N T R Y R O A D
A L E S   V E A L   W O R R Y
L O R E   E L I A   A L E T A
S T Y X   R E L S   Y E M E N
```

93

```
A U R A   O P R A H   S H A D
C R O C   M A I N E   T I L E
H I T T H E R O A D   A G E E
E S S   A L I T   G A T H E R
      A B E S   B E G E T
R A B B I T   M A R I N A T E
A D U L T   S E T O N   I R S
M I R E   T H R E W   F L A T
P E N   U R A L S   S L I D E
S U R I N A M E   S T A T E S
      U N T I E   S P E W
G I B S O N   S H O E   A S U
R O B E   M A K E T R A C K S
E W E R   A L E R T   B R I E
W A R T   N E E D Y   S E N D
```

94

```
T R A P   D U E T S   O H O H
H U G H   A P N E A   D A T A
U S A F   P S I L O V E Y O U
S T R A P P E D   A S S E T
      C E L T   O I L S
C A S T L E   P T B O A T S
A S C O T   R A T E R   S U P
S C A R   L A T E X   P A S O
H A L   L I V E R   M A R I O
P D J A M E S   G A S S E R
      O N A N   T I N Y
R A I S A   T R A N S F E R
P G T H I R T E E N   T A L E
M U T E   A I M A T   E R S E
S A Y S   D E P T H   M E A L
```

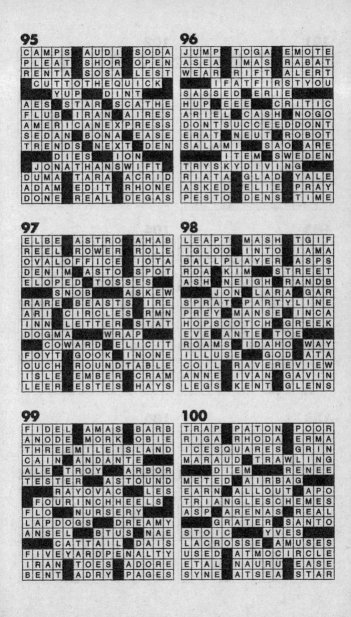

95

C	A	M	P	S		A	U	D	I		S	O	D	A
P	L	E	A	T		S	H	O	R		O	P	E	N
R	E	N	T	A		S	O	S	A		L	E	S	T
	C	U	T	T	O	T	H	E	Q	U	I	C	K	
			Y	U	P			D	I	N	T			
A	E	S		S	T	A	R		S	C	A	T	H	E
F	L	U	B		I	R	A	N		A	I	R	E	S
A	M	E	R	I	C	A	N	E	X	P	R	E	S	S
S	E	D	A	N		B	O	N	A		E	A	S	E
T	R	E	N	D	S		N	E	X	T		D	E	N
			D	I	E	S		I	O	N				
	J	O	N	A	T	H	A	N	S	W	I	F	T	
D	U	M	A		T	A	R	A		A	C	R	I	D
A	D	A	M		E	D	I	T		R	H	O	N	E
D	O	N	E		R	E	A	L		D	E	G	A	S

96

J	U	M	P		T	O	G	A		E	M	O	T	E
A	S	E	A		I	M	A	S		R	A	B	A	T
W	E	A	R		R	I	F	T		A	L	E	R	T
	I	F	A	T	F	I	R	S	T	Y	O	U		
S	A	S	S	E	D		E	R	I	E				
H	U	P		E	E	E		C	R	I	T	I	C	
A	R	I	E	L		C	A	S	H		N	O	G	O
D	O	N	T	S	U	C	C	E	E	D	D	O	N	T
E	R	A	T		N	E	U	T		R	O	B	O	T
S	A	L	A	M	I		S	A	O		A	R	E	
			I	T	E	M		S	W	E	D	E	N	
	T	R	Y	S	K	Y	D	I	V	I	N	G		
R	I	A	T	A		G	L	A	D		Y	A	L	E
A	S	K	E	D		E	L	I	E		P	R	A	Y
P	E	S	T	O		D	E	N	S		T	I	M	E

97

E	L	B	E		A	S	T	R	O		A	H	A	B
R	E	E	L		R	O	W	E	R		R	O	L	E
O	V	A	L	O	F	F	I	C	E		I	O	T	A
D	E	N	I	M		A	S	T	O		S	P	O	T
E	L	O	P	E	D		T	O	S	S	E	S		
			S	N	O	B			A	S	K	E	W	
R	A	R	E		B	E	A	S	T	S		I	R	E
A	R	I		C	I	R	C	L	E	S		R	M	N
I	N	N		L	E	T	T	E	R		S	T	A	T
D	O	G	M	A			W	R	A	P				
	C	O	W	A	R	D		E	L	I	C	I	T	
F	O	Y	T		G	O	O	K		I	N	O	N	E
O	U	C	H		R	O	U	N	D	T	A	B	L	E
I	S	L	E		E	M	B	E	R		C	R	A	M
L	E	E	R		E	S	T	E	S		H	A	Y	S

98

L	E	A	P	T		M	A	S	H		T	G	I	F
I	G	L	O	O		I	N	T	O		I	A	M	A
B	A	L	L	P	L	A	Y	E	R		A	S	P	S
R	D	A		K	I	M		S	T	R	E	E	T	
A	S	H		N	E	I	G	H		R	A	N	D	B
			J	O	N		L	A	R	A		G	A	R
S	P	R	A	T		P	A	R	T	Y	L	I	N	E
P	R	E	Y		M	A	N	S	E		I	N	C	A
H	O	P	S	C	O	T	C	H		G	R	E	E	K
E	V	E		A	N	T	E		T	O	E			
R	O	A	M	S		I	D	A	H	O		W	A	Y
I	L	L	U	S	E		G	O	D		A	T	A	
C	O	I	L		R	A	V	E	R	E	V	I	E	W
A	N	N	E		I	V	A	N		G	A	V	I	N
L	E	G	S		K	E	N	T		G	L	E	N	S

99

F	I	D	E	L		A	M	A	S		B	A	R	B
A	N	O	D	E		M	O	R	K		O	B	I	E
T	H	R	E	E	M	I	L	E	I	S	L	A	N	D
C	A	I	N		A	N	D	A	N	T	E			
A	L	E		T	R	O	Y		A	R	B	O	R	
T	E	S	T	E	R		A	S	T	O	U	N	D	
			R	A	Y	O	V	A	C		L	E	S	
	F	O	U	R	I	N	C	H	H	E	E	L	S	
F	L	O		N	U	R	S	E	R	Y				
L	A	P	D	O	G	S		D	R	E	A	M	Y	
A	N	S	E	L		B	T	U	S		N	A	E	
	C	A	T	T	A	I	L		D	A	I	S		
F	I	V	E	Y	A	R	D	P	E	N	A	L	T	Y
I	R	A	N		T	O	E	S		A	D	O	R	E
B	E	N	T		A	D	R	Y		P	A	G	E	S

100

T	R	A	P		P	A	T	O	N		P	O	O	R
R	I	G	A		R	H	O	D	A		E	R	M	A
I	C	E	S	Q	U	A	R	E	S		G	R	I	N
M	A	R	A	U	D		T	R	A	W	L	I	N	G
			D	I	E	M			R	E	N	E	E	
M	E	T	E	D		A	I	R	B	A	G			
E	A	R	N		A	L	L	O	U	T		A	P	O
T	R	I	A	N	G	L	E	S	C	H	E	M	E	S
A	S	P		A	R	E	N	A	S		R	E	A	L
			G	R	A	T	E	R		S	A	N	T	O
S	T	O	I	C			Y	V	E	S				
L	A	C	R	O	S	S	E		A	M	U	S	E	S
U	S	E	D		A	T	M	O	C	I	R	C	L	E
E	T	A	L		N	A	U	R	U		E	A	S	E
S	Y	N	E		A	T	S	E	A		S	T	A	R

101

```
L E S S   A R T S   C A V E R
A L O T   M E A T   O L I V E
M A L I   P U R E   S O N I A
B L O N D E B O M B S H E L L
      T I R E     L E A
B O W   T E N S P O T   S R S
A V A S T   N C O   A L I T
Y E L L O W S U B M A R I N E
O N L Y   O R B   T E N S E
U S A   S K I S U I T   G E L
      A P E   P R I M
G O L D E N D E L I C I O U S
A B I D E   E R A S   S I R E
L O V E D   S I N E   E L S E
L E E R Y   K E D S   R Y A N
```

102

```
S H A H S   D R A W   G O S H
C O B R A   I A G O   O N T O
A K L E P T O M A N I A C I S
T E E   P O N D S   S T E R E
      P H O N O   I C E
S O M E O N E W H O H E L P S
A M O R   N O T I   E R A
R A D   S K A   B A A   K E Y
A N E   P A R C   D E S I
H I M S E L F A S H E J U S T
      W E B   L I E N S
S T O I C   S I G M A   S C I
C A N T H E L P H I M S E L F
A L E C   S U E T   O U T O F
M E S H   E R R S   R E A D Y
```

103

```
M O M A   P R A M   L E V I S
A M I D   R A V E   A L I B I
D A M E   O M E N   N E V I S
D R E S S F O R S U C C E S S
      P I N   N E T
A R A F A T   G A I T   A M P
L A B O R   L I S T   S T A R
T R Y B E F O R E Y O U B U Y
H E S S   U C L A   H E A V E
O R S   E N O S   L I T T E R
      S A G   B O O
S H O P T I L L Y O U D R O P
Y E S E S   O A R S   I O N A
N E H R U   A L O E   V I E S
C L A M P   M A N N   A S S T
```

104

```
W A C S   S M A R T   A C T S
O P A L   T O R A H   P Y R E
K E M O   E L E N A   E B A N
R E M O T E C O N T R O L S
P I L O T   A N K A   R E O
A T L   O D E     L I G E R
X I I I   E D G E S I N
  F A R A W A Y P L A C E S
    O L Y M P I A   A N O N
P I A N O   C Y D   G A Y
E D S   H E S S   T R I P E
D I S T A N T C O U S I N S
A D U E   L E A P S   F E U D
L I M A   A R N I E   L E D A
S T E M   I N T E R   E R S T
```

105

```
S T E P   S O A R   A F T O N
O H I O   O N C E   S L O P E
H A R D N O S E D   P O K E R
O W E   O N E   S T I P E N D
      O D E T S   A R P
C A S P E R   A L L E Y O O P
A C H E S   D I A L   E R L E
N O O N   T A L K Y   A L I T
D R A M   A L O E   D R O V E
O N L O O K E R   T E E N E R
      U N E   S P E N D
D E S T I N Y   A L S   S H E
I D A H O   E A G L E E Y E D
S I R E N   A G E E   S N A G
H E A D S   H E R R   P E L E
```

106

```
D O G S   M A O   A R T I S
E R I E   H E R A   C E A S E
N E L L   E A C H   R H O N E
G O L F E N T H U S I A S T S
      M G R S   A D S
R O S A R Y   F A N   H E C K
E V A D E   C E L T S   D R E
H A V E T H A T F A I R W A Y
A T E   S E P I A   S E I Z E
B E D E   R E D   A T O N E D
      S H O   P R E P
L O O K I N T H E I R E Y E S
A L V I N   W A R S   N O R A
B E A M E   A I R E   E R I N
S O L O S   S L Y   D E C K
```

107

W	O	O	F		S	M	A	C	K		S	M	O	G
H	U	G	O		T	A	H	O	E		H	O	U	R
E	C	R	U		A	N	O	D	E		R	U	N	E
T	H	E	L	I	T	T	L	E	P	R	I	N	C	E
			P	L	E	A	D		E	N	D	E	D	
S	K	U	L	L	S		K	I	C	K				
L	I	R	A		S	I	E	N	A		I	R	E	
I	T	S	Y	B	I	T	S	Y	S	P	I	D	E	R
P	E	A		L	O	A	M	S		N	E	A	R	
	R	I	N	G		M	E	D	A	L	S			
O	L	S	E	N		W	H	O	L	E				
W	E	E	W	I	L	L	I	E	W	I	N	K	I	E
L	A	V	A		A	I	S	L	E		T	I	N	A
E	V	E	R		S	N	E	E	R		E	L	K	S
T	E	N	D		T	E	R	N	S		D	O	S	E

108

L	I	A	R	S		R	A	P	S		R	O	S	A
A	N	G	E	L		I	S	E	E		O	W	E	S
S	C	A	P	E		C	A	R	T		U	N	I	T
T	H	R	O	U	G	H	P	U	T		G	E	N	E
			T	O	E		L	E	H	R	E	R		
P	O	N	C	H	O		C	L	E	A	R			
O	N	E	O		N	E	H	I		S	I	E	N	A
S	C	R	U	B		A	I	M		E	D	G	E	D
H	E	D	G	E		S	L	A	B		E	G	A	D
			H	A	I	T	I		E	R	R	O	R	S
V	E	R	D	U	N		A	T	E					
E	M	I	R		D	O	U	G	H	F	A	C	E	S
N	O	G	O		O	G	R	E		O	R	A	T	E
U	T	E	P		O	L	I	N		R	E	N	T	A
E	E	L	S		R	E	S	T		M	A	T	E	R

109

F	A	S	T		E	O	N	S		A	S	C	A	P
U	L	N	A		S	L	O	E		V	I	O	L	A
S	P	A	R	E	T	I	R	E		O	G	R	E	S
E	S	P		L	A	V		P	A	W	N	E	E	S
			F	A	T	E	S		L	E	A			
P	O	L	I	T	E		W	O	O	D	L	E	S	S
A	M	O	R	E		L	A	B	S		F	L	E	A
T	A	P	S		A	U	T	O	S		L	A	D	S
C	H	E	T		R	A	T	E		D	A	N	E	S
H	A	R	A	N	G	U	E		A	I	R	D	R	Y
			I	O	U		D	A	N	C	E			
H	A	N	D	L	E	S		N	Y	E		S	A	P
A	W	A	K	E		L	U	G	W	R	E	N	C	H
L	E	V	I	S		A	S	E	A		S	I	R	E
O	D	E	T	S		M	A	R	Y		S	P	E	W

110

G	A	R	B		A	W	E	S		Y	A	L	T	A
A	G	A	R		D	O	L	T		E	M	A	I	L
F	O	R	Y	E	A	R	S	I		S	I	D	L	E
F	R	E	A	K		M	A	R	G	A	R	E	T	
E	A	R	N	E	R		S	E	N					
			D	A	B	S		O	D	D	M	A	N	
S	P	A	S		N	E	M	O		N	O	O	N	E
W	A	N	T	E	D	T	O	B	E	O	L	D	E	R
A	B	O	U	T		S	C	O	T		L	E	W	D
B	A	N	N	E	D		K	E	N	O				
			R	E	S		A	T	W	O	O	D		
S	H	A	N	G	H	A	I		T	O	R	R	E	
H	A	I	T	I		A	N	D	N	O	W	I	A	M
A	L	L	O	T		R	O	L	E		I	N	N	O
P	E	O	N	Y		I	S	E	E		E	G	G	S

111

L	A	L	A		A	U	R	O	R	A		A	N	D
O	P	E	N		G	R	A	C	I	E		P	O	I
W	E	I	G	H	A	N	C	H	O	R		O	S	S
	L	E	S	S	E	R		A	L	L	A	H		
R	O	S	I	E			E	S	T	E	L	L	E	
S	T	E	A	D	Y	A	S	S	H	E	G	O	E	S
V	O	N		A	C	T		I	D	A				
P	E	T	S		H	E	R	O	N		L	A	H	R
			I	S	O		U	N	E		L	O	O	
H	A	R	D	T	O	S	T	A	R	B	O	A	R	D
E	V	I	L	E	S	T		O	W	E	N	S		
R	E	S	E	W		R	A	I	S	O	N			
E	N	E		A	B	A	N	D	O	N	S	H	I	P
S	U	R		R	E	F	U	E	L		U	B	E	R
Y	E	S		D	I	E	T	E	D		P	O	R	E

112

M	O	L	A	R		F	E	U	D		S	A	A	R
A	D	O	B	E		A	M	M	O		U	N	D	O
R	O	U	N	D	T	R	I	P	T	I	C	K	E	T
E	R	T	E		O	E	R		E	T	C	H	E	S
			R	A	T		A	L	S	O				
A	B	E		C	I	R	C	U	L	A	R	S	A	W
L	U	X		R	E	E	L	S		E	L	L	A	
T	R	A	C	E		C	O	T		B	R	A	I	N
A	R	C	H		A	T	R	I	A		I	V	E	
R	O	T	A	R	Y	P	H	O	N	E		N	E	D
			R	I	A	S		T	R	W				
B	O	T	T	O	M		O	R	E		A	F	A	R
O	R	B	I	T	A	L	V	E	L	O	C	I	T	Y
S	C	A	N		H	E	E	D		A	K	R	O	N
S	A	R	G		A	N	N	O		S	O	M	M	E

113

T	A	B	S		O	M	A	H	A		U	S	E	R
E	L	I	A		C	A	K	E	S		N	O	D	E
C	A	N	D	Y	C	L	A	R	K		F	O	I	L
H	I	D	E	O	U	T		P	U	T	T	Y		
			D	R	A	G	S	T	E	R				
S	T	I	L	E		S	U	G	A	R	L	O	A	F
L	A	B	E	L		E	M	T	S		A	L	I	
O	B	S	E	S	S		S	T	A	K	E	S		
T	O	E		E	L	M	S		E	X	E	R	T	
H	O	N	E	Y	M	O	O	N		T	E	N	T	S
			R	E	I	N	D	E	E	R				
S	P	O	U	T		E	M	A	N	A	T	E		
P	O	M	P		G	L	A	Z	E	D	O	V	E	R
U	N	I	T		E	I	D	E	R		V	E	E	R
N	E	T	S		T	E	D	D	Y		A	R	M	S

114

P	A	P	A		S	T	A	T			L	O	C	I
O	L	A	V		P	U	M	A		P	U	P	A	L
S	L	Y	A	S	A	F	O	X		A	T	A	L	L
I	O	U		A	R	T	S		S	W	I	L	L	S
T	Y	P	I	S	T			T	O	P	S			
			S	H	A	R	P	A	S	A	T	A	C	K
A	D	A	M		N	A	R	R	O	W		L	O	O
V	O	W	S		D	I	T		S	A	I	L		
I	D	O		A	N	I	M	A	L		A	N	N	A
S	O	L	I	D	A	S	A	R	O	C	K			
			G	A	S	H		Q	U	I	L	T	S	
A	B	R	U	P	T		H	O	U	R		A	H	A
B	L	O	A	T		F	A	T	A	S	A	P	I	G
B	O	O	N	S		A	L	I	T		M	I	C	A
A	T	T	A		R	O	S	S		A	S	K	S	

115

B	U	S	S		S	E	L	F		E	C	L	A	T
O	B	O	E		L	E	A	R		P	I	E	T	A
G	O	N	E		A	R	I	A		H	O	T	E	L
G	A	Y	D	I	V	O	R	C	E	E		S	E	C
S	T	A	I	D		A	R	M	E	D				
			L	A	W	N		S	E	E	S	A	W	S
B	A	B	Y		O	A	F		C	R	A	N	E	D
A	L	L		R	O	B	E	R	T	A		C	I	A
S	A	U	N	A	S		Z	O	E		P	E	R	K
S	W	E	A	R	T	O		E	D	G	E			
			S	T	E	E	L		O	G	L	E	S	
W	O	K		F	R	E	D	A	S	T	A	I	R	E
A	L	I	B	I		A	I	D	A		S	T	O	W
R	E	E	S	E		R	E	I	N		U	R	D	U
S	O	S	A	D		Y	U	N	G		S	E	E	P

116

B	U	S	H		E	F	T	S		G	R	I	E	F
O	S	H	A		L	O	O	T		E	I	D	E	R
S	E	E	S		L	U	N	A		O	S	A	K	A
C	R	A	S	H	I	N	G	B	O	R	E			
			L	O	S	T		L	U	G		C	E	L
R	O	S	E	N		A	B	E	T		A	I	D	E
O	H	O		C	H	I	A		G	A	R	C	I	A
S	M	A	S	H	I	N	G	S	U	C	C	E	S	S
C	A	R	H	O	P		G	E	N	T		R	O	E
O	G	E	E		P	H	Y	S		I	C	O	N	S
E	E	R		T	I	E		S	I	N	O			
			B	R	E	A	K	I	N	G	N	E	W	S
C	L	A	R	A		T	O	O	L		M	A	Y	O
P	A	N	I	C		E	T	N	A		A	V	E	R
A	D	A	G	E		R	O	S	Y		N	E	S	T

117

B	O	W	L		L	A	Y	U	P			A	S	S
E	R	R	S		I	N	A	N	E		A	L	T	O
R	E	A	D	I	N	G	R	A	I	L	R	O	A	D
T	O	P		N	E	R	D		I	N	F	R	A	
			T	I	N	Y		E	S	T	A	T	E	S
A	L	L	O	T	S		P	L	O	T	Z			
C	O	I	N		G	O	O	S	E		S	A	T	
R	O	V	I	N	G	R	E	P	O	R	T	E	R	S
O	N	E		I	R	A	T	E		R	E	E	K	
			S	K	I	D	S		S	A	U	N	A	S
H	E	R	O	I	N	E		A	C	N	E			
A	L	E	R	T		G	N	A	T		A	M	I	
R	E	P	E	A	T	I	N	G	R	I	F	L	E	S
E	V	E	S		A	T	A	L	E		D	A	T	E
M	E	L		D	A	W	E	S		A	S	H	E	

118

C	L	A	P		C	A	R	T			M	I	S	T
R	O	S	A		A	L	O	E	S		I	N	T	O
A	R	T	S		S	T	O	M	P		S	C	A	M
W	R	I	T	E	S	O	F	P	A	S	S	A	G	E
S	E	R	A	P	E			O	R	E	O			
			S	H	R	E	D	S		D	U	R	A	N
O	A	K		O	V	I		A	E	R	A	T	E	
W	R	E	C	K	L	E	S	S	D	R	I	V	E	R
E	E	Y	O	R	E		C	I	V		E	N	D	
S	A	S	H	A		D	O	S	A	G	E			
			E	U	R	O		L	A	D	L	E	S	
W	R	E	S	T	E	D	F	R	O	M	W	O	R	K
A	U	D	I		O	G	L	E	R		A	U	R	A
K	I	E	V		S	E	I	N	E		R	I	O	T
E	N	N	E		S	T	E	M		D	E	L	E	

119

```
C U B E   B M O C   S P O I L
O P E N   R E D O   P E N C E
L O V E B E A D S   R A C E S
A N Y   R A N   T R A C E R S
      F I S T S   E Y E
H A M L E T   P R E S S C A R
A L O O F   B O A S   Y U R I
S L O W   S A R G E   M R E D
T I R E   P E T E   A B A T E
E N E R G I Z E   E R O D E S
      C O E   D E V I L
F O X H O L E   M A E   D U O
E L V I S   W O O D S T O C K
A G I L E   E R T E   O L L A
R A I D S   R E E D   P L A Y
```

120

```
O H B A B Y   M A M A   C U T
T O L D Y A   S P O T   A T O
S P I F F Y   T H U M B S U P
      N E A   I S S U E R S
I N D E X C A R D S   N Y N Y
T O S S   A B U   E A T
E L I   I S O F   L E C H E
M I D D L E O F T H E R O A D
S E E R S   I R I S   M S G
      Y A P   A I L   F E T A
A U D I   R I N G L E A D E R
S T I N K E R     S K Y
P I N K Y L E E   A T E A S E
E L K   R I N D   D E I C E R
R E Y   A M E S   M E T T L E
```

121

```
T A P   D U N C E   S I S A L
I C U   A T A R I   A N I T A
E T S   D I V I N I N G R O D
D I S C   L A M E R   R E N E
      Y O K E L S   O P I N E S
R I F L E     O W N E D
U B O A T   A N I O N   F A N
B I O   T L C   E N S   R O E
S S T   L E M O N   I C O N S
      D E T E R   V A N E S
G A R I S H   I N S E R T
A L A P   A N G I O   D Y E D
M A J O R L E A G U E   A P E
E M I L E   A M E S S   R E M
R O V E D   T I R E S   D E O
```

122

```
B O W L S   D A L E   L E N A
O S H E A   A V O N   I R A S
S T E A L A K I S S   F I S H
C I T   T W A S   C A T C H Y
H A S T I E R   C O D A
      A N D   R U N O F F S
S L A K E   M E R C   I R O N
R O L E   E Y R I E   N E R O
I O T A   C R U E   O G D E N
P O P C O R N   E R E
      O A T H   M A C R A M E
G O A W R Y   L E C H   R C A
A M I D   P O A C H A N E G G
B I D E   E P I C   R A N E E
S T A R   S E R A   D E T E R
```

123

```
P A C E S   S C A M P   A P T
E L O P E   H O R A E   S I R
N O M O N E Y D O W N   S E E
S E A S O N   A S S A Y E R S
      R O U S E   L O E S S
R E G R E S S   S T U N
I D E A S   E S S A Y   O A F
C I T E   D R O L L   E N C L
E T O   A I S L E   U L T R A
      N I L E   E N L I V E N
A G E N A   E S T E S
L E F T B A N K   A T O M I C
B A R   A F T E R R E B A T E
E R E   M A R I O   R O M E O
E S E   A R E N T   S E A R S
```

124

```
A R S O N   E S P   R A D A R
L I T H O   M O O   E D U C E
A D A M B O M B S   A I M E D
R E G A L I A   T O R N A D O
      G E L   T U B E
A N T E   E V E M O N T A N D
B A R   B R E A   E D I T O R
A B A T E   E T A   E M I L E
B O D I E S   I G O R   M A S
A B E L S E A M E N   D E N S
      T A M E   I N E
S A L T I N E   C O O L E S T
A L I E N   C A I N S U G A R
R E T A G   H I T   E X I L E
A X E L S   E R E   D E S E X
```

125

```
M A C E   O M A H A   A S A P
I R O N   S A V E D   D I R E
T I M E   C R O N E   W R I T
Z A P   M A I N S Q U E E Z E
I S A D O R A     U N E
    C O N S   C R A C K P O T
U L T R A   B O O T H   R H O
H I C K   R U S S E   K E N T
U M A   D E R B Y   P E S O S
H O R S E F L Y   D O E S
    T R U   L E O P A R D
A C O R N S Q U A S H   G E E
H O P E   A U S S I   H E L P
E R I E   L I N E R   U N I T
M E E T   S P A R E   E T C H
```

126

```
F A T S   C H A D   S I G M A
U L E E   H A T E   A F T E R
D I E T S A H E F O R F O L K
G O P H E R     M E R C Y
E T E   Z I P   R C A   F L A
D O E R   S I S   A S H L E Y
    E M M E T S   T E A S E
    W H O A R E T H I C K
A H E A D     S M O O C H
B E R B E R   S O U   E D O M
C H E   R E F   P S I   E M O
    S N A R E     E I S N E R
A N D T I R E D O F I T A L L
C A D I Z   S I L L   E L E E
T H E R E   H E D Y   P I T Y
```

127

```
I N G O T   A M O S   L E S T
C O R E R   P A T H   A V E R
O P E R A   T I T O   T I L E
N E E   Y E L L O W B E L L Y
    N A N N Y     C E L
M E T H O D   H E A V Y S E T
O T H E R   G U T S Y   I D O
C H U M   B A S T E   A L G A
H E M   B A L S A   W I V E S
A R B O R D A Y   W I D E S T
    P E T   S A N E R
P U R P L E H E A R T   B A H
O L E O   R E A L   E V A D E
O N E S   M E S A   R I C E R
L A K E   S P E D   S A K E S
```

128

```
J O T S   S T R A P   R A M S
A C R E   A R E N A   I T A L
P A I R O F A C E S   G I V E
E L A I N E     A S H A M E D
S A L E M   T H R E E T E N S
    S E P I A   S L O
A K A   E S S     G N A T S
S I X H I G H S T R A I G H T
K N E A D   L O O   T O Y
    L A C   E N O C H
F U L L H O U S E   L A T T E
E N A M O R S     F E R R E T
A B R A   R O Y A L F L U S H
S A U R   A F I R E   O T T O
T R E K   L A N K A   W H Y S
```

129

```
B O H R   E Y E L I D   G O B
E R I E   D E L A N O   A X E
L E G S D I A M O N D   M B A
T S H I R T S     D A M O N
    G A S   F O R E P A W S
B R E N T   D E S E R T
Y O K E   M U N C I E   C D S
T I E D H A N D A N D F O O T
E L D   E I D E R S   O K R A
    G A Z E R S   C L E A R
S T A N D E E S   E L K
A W F U L     G L U T T O N
L I T   A R M S E M B A R G O
E N E   M A R I N E   L I L T
M E R   P E S T E R   E P E E
```

130

```
D E M O   A L I C E   E D A M
O R E O   D E T A T   L O G E
G R A H A M N A S H   S O O T
M O N   L I T   E N L A R G E
A R T H U R   O D I U M
    E M A I L   C R A T E S
S P A N   L A D D   E X E R T
C A I R O   N C O   S W A L E
A L L Y N   S A D A   E L E M
N O S H E D   R O W E L
    U N I T S   A L L O T S
C H E D D A R   M R S   A R E
R E D S   D A V I D E S S E X
A R G O   E C O L E   R I V E
B R Y N   M E W E D   A S I S
```

The New York Times
Crossword Puzzles
THE #1 NAME IN CROSSWORDS

 St. Martin's Griffin

Available at your local bookstore or online
at nytimes.com/nytstore